The author Alexander Korol published the first version of the book *Attention Control* in 2012, in which he talked about the fact that we are the attention. Attention is the key to success and everything is built on it. The things that steal our attention, the way we get people's attention, and everything we do are all related to attention. Even when we have pain, the pain is provocative, but it focuses our attention on the point where we have the pain. All of us humans are different in terms of whose attention attracts to what things more and whose attention attracts to what things less.

Attention is one of the foundations that has led the author to write over 20 books, and it is attention management that brings him success. Attention is energy management, concentration, memory, meditation. And the shifting of attention – that is, dynamics – is very important. The author was able to become a writer thanks to his attention and diligence. You cannot succeed if your attention is scattered or if you cannot concentrate and keep your attention on one point.

All of the author's treatises and books reflect his unique view of life. The author looks at how everything is organized from different angles: what is a person, what is society, what moves people, and the fact that we all live on different frequencies, i.e., in different social strata of society, and our attention is clogged in our own way and busy with something all the time. The meaning of humanity and being human is to free your attention from everything so that nothing steals your attention.

The author's books are written from a deep philosophical viewpoint: what is a human being, what is the meaning of life, how to survive and adapt in the twenty-first century, and how to determine yourself in life: who are you, who is a human, and who do we listen to, who do we believe in, and what is it all for. If you have ever asked yourself, or have recently asked yourself, philosophical or deep questions about the meaning of life, then you will find answers to these questions in the books of the author, who has spent his entire conscious life searching for answers to these questions and shared his discoveries in his books.

In 2024, the author has decided to re-publish and update his first book, published in 2012, in a more modern way, for modern times, because the book's subject is more relevant than ever.

Alexandr Korol

Attention Control

Austin Macauley Publishers®
London * Cambridge * New York * Sharjah

A CIP catalogue record for this title is available from the British Library.

ISBN 9781035872206 (Paperback)
ISBN 9781035872213 (ePub e-book)

www.austinmacauley.com

First Published 2024
Austin Macauley Publishers Ltd®
1 Canada Square
Canary Wharf
London
E14 5AA

Table of Contents

Foreword

You are attention.

When you have a wound, your attention is stolen by the pain.

There are some odours and scents that can steal your attention and distract you from work.

Your attention is easily captured.

Attention is energy. If you free up your attention, you will become conscious and aware. If 100% of your attention is directed towards the goal, you will reach better results.

While your attention is scattered on different thoughts or problems and while your attention is spent on social networks and such, and you have a goal in life, you will give only 10% of your attention to this goal, and at the end, you will get only 10% of the result.

Attention is always focused on something; each and everyone has a different attention focus. Often times people are so absent-minded that they can't remember where they left something. And this is the problem with memory. Memory is directly related to attention.

Attention control is everywhere, and everyone tries to steal your attention by any means possible.

This book and the knowledge which I will share are meant not for your self-serving purpose, but for you to be protected from those who steal your attention.

And if you are interested in meditation and how to turn on your *chakras,* you will also find a few practical exercises in this book. For it is also the attention.

Attention control is conscious awareness and freedom!

Part I
Attention Control

1. Clean Up

In fact, we *are* attention. Some examples I will give are about awareness and paying attention. Other examples will be about choices one makes, how one's brain works, and one's character. But in fact, this all is attention as well. And here is the first example. All my life I was interested in self-development and being conscious. I wanted to reach my latent potential. And here is what I've noticed.

Let's say, I have clothes that I wear all the time and other clothes that are sitting in my wardrobe or on the shelves. But I don't use them all. Now I can come to my closet and take out all the clothes that I haven't worn for the past six months. I am sure you can do the same. Of course, there can be exceptions.

Let's say you recently moved to a new place, to an empty apartment, and you have two T-shirts then this experiment won't work for you. But you could remember how it was before the move and probably you would have had a similar situation with your wardrobe as I did.

So here, I have clothes that I haven't worn for the past six months. I don't wear them but I have them. And I have pieces of clothes that I wear all the time. This situation always worried me, that I am being unconscious to behave that way, when I am not controlling myself and choosing only five pieces of clothes to wear.

But the rest of the clothes don't attract my attention, or I don't feel like wearing them, as if I can't focus on them. The reasons are not very important here.

When I noticed that I had to stop it. I just took all the clothes that had been forgotten and put them in sight. The clothes I have worn all the time I put on the back shelves.

Here is another example. It might not suit everyone but those who are doing a lot of cooking at home, I bet you have a lot of groceries at home that sit around for more than half a year or maybe a year. Those boxes and cans are put away somewhere on the back shelf. Of course, you have everyday perishable groceries and naturally, you buy them often, like fruits and veggies, and those are always in sight. But cans are most certainly hidden away.

Funny thing is that most people don't even remember that they have them. And you go to buy canned olives, bring them home, and discover you have already four cans on the back shelf. You forgot about them. This is bad. To become more conscious, you need to start paying attention to such things.

It's the same as with clothes in the previous example. You can either eat them or give them away or put them in sight. You need to stir up stagnation and disturb the beehive. This is very important.

Why am I saying all this? Our brain and attention work in such an interesting way that there is information at the forefront of our memory that we use daily. And because we remember it, we pay attention to it. Same way as with clothes and groceries. The clothes and groceries that you get used to and use every day, it's a habit, a routine.

There are also other things in your memory like knowledge. You can't get it out, but it's there. You don't use it every day. It's bad because it's stagnant. I have a very specific approach to self-development and the advice that I give you will affect your brain and your memory in a good way. And if you follow my advice and clean up your room, your garage, or some places that you live or work, if you put in sight forgotten clothes, groceries, and other things and put away those things you got used to it will affect your memory, your attention, your psyche, your intellect. This is of utmost importance.

Of course, I have given you very simple examples so you can better understand my point: wherever you have things accumulated – clean them up! Maybe you have lots of little boxes or storage with your possessions. Or you have a shelf where there are many things, but you use only five of them, and the rest is just junk. Clean it up.

The same can be in a bathroom, I might have lots of shampoos or shower gel bottles or creams, but I use only one or two that I bought recently, and they are in sight. So I will take them and put them away and find the ones that are hidden away at the back of the shelf and put them in sight and start using them. Also, the trunk of the car needs cleaning as well as the glove compartment. Just make a list of places that you can clean up and start doing it.

Check your contact list as well as people you know. There are some of your acquaintances you are in contact with every day, and some that you haven't talked to for a while. This is an indication of your unawareness. I am obsessed with self-development, and I am fanatical about it. I live by it. It is the meaning of my life. I devote a lot of time and attention to it; like no one else. Many spiritual people read the same books and repeat the same information without understanding the meaning of it. They do it like unconscious robots; they don't get the essence and meaning. It's different for me.

I am street-smart, and I've learned everything by trial and error. I studied and tested everything. My information is from personal experience. I am passionate about it and can spend days and nights trying to find an explanation for everything – my every action or inaction, every choice I made, as well as studying every person that crosses my path. What motivates the person? Why has he or she chosen this and not that? I've learned it through and through.

Let's take your contact list. You didn't consciously decide to choose only three people to talk to from your contact list because of particular reasons, and you didn't consciously decide not to keep contact with the rest of the people in your contact list. It happened automatically. It just happened. In the life of many people, many things *just happen*. But if you would be conscious, it would not be like that.

The word *robot* can be understood in different ways in different contexts. In this case, a conscious person is a robot in the best sense. If you put a task in front of him to make contact with his acquaintances, he won't have a human factor in his actions. He won't just meet with the same three people. A robot won't have an autopilot and he won't unconsciously divide people.

First, he will write to the tenth person on the list, then to the twentieth, and the fifth. He will go through everyone on the list and will pay equal amounts of attention to each one – he will message or call everyone and will meet with everyone. It might sound weird, but a robot is a conscious human; he is like that.

I'll further explain you through an example. Imagine a mind unencumbered by the weight of past grievances or societal expectations. Autistic individuals perceive the world with a clarity that eludes many. Unlike neurotypical individuals who may harbour grudges or make decisions based on ingrained biases, autistic people live in the present moment. They do not carry the accumulated baggage of past experiences or prejudices that cloud their judgment.

Consider the scenario of choosing whom to meet. For an autistic person posed with the question, "Who do you want to meet? John, Jane or Tom?" their response is refreshingly direct. They simply choose based on the present moment, without the influence of past interactions or preconceived notions. They do not recollect past offenses or construct intricate reasons for their decisions. This clarity of thought allows them to approach each encounter with a genuine openness, unencumbered by the complexities that often govern the choices of others.

In contrast, neurotypical individuals may find themselves mired in a cycle of subconscious biases and habitual behaviours. They may avoid certain people or situations due to past experiences or societal expectations, limiting their interactions and perspectives. This repetitive pattern can lead to a life lived on autopilot, where decisions are made unconsciously and novelty is scarce.

Autistic individuals, with their ability to see each moment with fresh eyes, offer a poignant reminder of the clarity that comes from living without the filters of accumulated biases and past memories. Their approach challenges us to reconsider how we perceive reality and encourages us to embrace each moment with greater awareness and authenticity.

A person does everything automatically. The funny thing is, even if this person talks to only three friends all the time, they are doing it automatically. And those three replying to him, also automatically. It's a waste of energy, nothing else. Imagine how I feel when I see it. It's a madhouse. I am talking now about our world.

You need to clean up everything. At least try it once, so you can feel and understand my examples about being unconscious and unaware. Attention and its focus are consciousness, awareness and soberness. If you are friends with people, don't overdo it like with clothes – when you wear the same jacket again and again, even though you have five of them without even understanding why you are doing it. And if I ask you why you do it you will come up with some excuse. But those excuses are wrong.

When I go to a restaurant with an acquaintance of mine, he always orders the same dish. And you know why? Because when he opens a menu, he doesn't know what is in it and his attention focuses on the same dish. He yet again has chosen Caesar salad. You can notice the same in your life.

And you choose the same dish sometimes not because you like it so much. You can even claim that you like it and that this is the best salad ever.

But I often say to that person, "Do you know how many salads there are in this world? If you had tried all of them, you would not have said that this one is the best."

Recently I had a conversation with someone. And he asked me where I travelled, and he told me, "I don't agree that Europe is not nice. I liked it in Amsterdam."

And I said, "Way back, I liked Tallinn because I haven't been anywhere else."

I have a very sober view of the person I am talking with, and I know his development level. But this person doesn't want to even hear me.

I say, "I won't argue with you. I do not doubt that you like Amsterdam."

But I cannot say that I don't like Amsterdam because I didn't understand Amsterdam. I understand it very well, and a long time ago, I also liked it, when I hadn't been anywhere else.

And I tried to explain to that person, "You like it now. But if you visit other countries, you will realise that Europe is not that nice."

This is consciousness and awareness. You need it for all your actions and choices.

We don't intend to stop all our thoughts here; let them be. But let's sort them out. Let's think about something interesting. Ask yourself – you won't find an answer just yet, but the process of thinking it through will be useful. If you have few friends, why do you pay attention only to two or three of them and forget about the other ones? Let's break this circle. Stop paying attention to the same people and try to be friends with ones you have forgotten.

Make a note of what changes start happening in your life and how you will feel. I understand that my readers are from different walks of life. And some are more socially adapted and often go to different places. Take this exercise consciously.

Make a note of which places you visit often, like restaurants, clubs, bars, or some other places. How often have you been to one particular place and why there? Ask yourself. And if the answer is that you go there because it's a nice spot to be, then ask yourself how do you know. Have you been to many places? From a 100 spots in your city, you went only to maybe 10. And from the 10 you liked one or two. But you haven't been to the other 90. This is very important.

Even if you go to buy groceries you will choose the same type of things every single time. Of course, there are exceptions. When, for example, you've seen some exotic fruit in a movie or documentary and you want to try it. But it's rare. You need to notice things that you do or buy automatically. And you will have a more sober view of everything.

People often ask me how I am different from others. And everyone always notes that everything in my life is always new. I don't get attached to anything. When you get attached, you become dull and attention degrades. You need to have very clear and focused attention, and not like stagnant water but like running water. You need to try new things. This is very important.

Try new things. If you always go to the same grocery shop, try a different one. Make a task for yourself to go to a different shop. The same with people. Try to meet new people. This is very sobering. And write down all your observations about yourself. Attention is also observation, a clear report of each action.

When your attention is more focused than even while pouring tea into the pot, you can hear volumetrically the sound of water. You feel it. When you drink tea, you feel the tea as if you have never felt it before. You feel the taste and shades of taste. Imagine that! When your attention will be freed, try to touch your skin. You will be amazed that you haven't noticed it before. This is of utmost importance. Look in the mirror.

I give you examples here and you might feel confused. It might be hard to wrap your mind around it for the moment. Don't worry. These are my chaotic thoughts about attention. Slowly you will understand what I am talking about, and what you can achieve using some techniques in this book and the thoughts and examples I am giving here.

2. Time

When you travel somewhere far by car, either driving yourself or just as a passenger, sometimes it happens that time flies so fast you don't even notice how you have already arrived. As if the perception of time disappears, you don't even notice that you reached your destination. Sometimes you would need to walk far, let's say five or ten kilometres. But you don't even notice how long the road is, as if you just appear from point A to point B.

Sometimes you are sitting and talking to someone in a café, and it feels like you talked for half an hour, but if you look at your watch five hours have passed. Five hours! But you feel as if you just came by and got yourself a cup of tea.

I bet every one of you felt once or twice the same way.

And sometimes it's another way around. You drive and drive somewhere, and the road feels endless. But the road is only one hour long. The same happens when you wait in a queue. At times it feels that time flies and sometimes it drags. How time goes depends on our attention. If you learn how to manage it, then you can create the perception of time. You will be able to create a fast rhythm or make it slow and time will drag.

Think about the reason it happens when time drags and when time flies fast. How would you explain that to yourself? Just think about how you can artificially create a perception of fast time. And what would you need for that?

It will be very useful in the future. The self-development that I give should not be understood by the mind only. The most important thing is to practice. I will give it to you as well. Now I am touching upon the main subject of our discussion; after that I will explain the essence. Understanding the essence means that it will be recorded deep within you and the information will never be forgotten.

Information will help you automatically. As if you have gained a new talent. And if you understand the essence of my examples – like in the example with time – you will be able to create a perception of time artificially for yourself. It will help you a lot in life. And you could also use it for other people's good. Imagine you are waiting in a queue with someone, and this person is annoyed, but you can make it so that a person won't even mention how time goes by. I think it's a very useful skill.

Depending on where you direct your attention, time flies or drags. If you are interested in something, your attention is stolen by that particular activity and not on how time flies. If your attention freed while you are waiting for something, when you are not busy with anything, like sitting on a chair during *technique on a chair*. Imagine you are sitting and waiting in a queue, and you are used to your attention being distracted, but now you must just sit and wait. And you become annoyed.

It means that time drags on for you. You get restless and you get really annoyed. And, of course, if you know how to direct your attention while you are waiting in a queue, time will go faster. When your attention is focused on one point, you turn off yourself from society, from time and space. Society is time and space. When you turn it off, you don't mention that you are sitting in a boring queue, you don't mention how time flies. Your attention is focused on something.

When you are driving and your attention is scattered and you are thinking about something, your mind is working, and the journey will take ages. But if your attention is free, focused, and concentrated on something interesting – for example, you are talking about an interesting topic – you won't even notice how five hours go by.

You need to realise that attention can be stolen that way. And you can use it. Time drags when your attention is scattered on little things: on daily routines, on thoughts, on the future, and on the past. When you are not interested in anything, you are bored and you feel bad, and everything is slow, and time drags on.

When you free up your attention and focus it, you will learn by practicing the *technique on the chair*; it would be enough if you focus your attention on yourself and time will fly. It's like meditation; it feels like you are doing it for five minutes, but five hours pass by.

You just need to disconnect your attention from everything. So, stop all ongoing tasks. And everything will be fast. If you have too many tasks going on at the same time, then time will drag.

The other issue is that a lot of people think about the future all the time. Statistically, more men do it. They think about what to buy, about their work, about the future, about moving to a bigger city, for example. They live in the future, and it steals their attention every day. This is very bad.

It's important to be alone at least once a week, with a notepad and pen, and analyse how your week went by, how you feel, what worries you, and what you would want in the future. And for the rest of the day, you should not think about it. This is very important. You should not live in the future when every day you think about what will happen. You don't live in the present moment. Do you understand? You need to wake up.

And some people live in the past. They think about their past love or past tragedy. This is also bad. You can think about it once a week, talk about it once, and write it down in your diary. But you should not think about it all week long every day. It's bad to live in the future or in the past.

My issue is that I tend to live in the future, and I stop myself from thinking about it. But sometimes it takes over. How does it look to think about the future? Let's say you planned to travel to another city. And you think about it all the time and do the usual things as if you are there already, in another city. And when you finally go to that city, you start thinking about what you will do when you come back. This is the cloudiness of your mind, unconsciousness. You should not do that. More often workaholics live like that. They will understand what I am talking about.

Living in the future and setting goals for the future are not the same thing. If you live here and now and live every day consciously, and on this day, you do everything in the present, but you have a goal to travel somewhere in a couple of months and you are earning money for this travel; this is just a goal for the future. You can do it, of course. It's bad when you are at the opposite extreme.

When you know that you will travel somewhere in one month's time, and it disturbs your consciousness. Meaning that you don't live in the present all these months before you need to travel, but rather you are just waiting for the month to pass so you can travel. You don't look at this month with a sober view.

Tomorrow will come and you don't perceive it as here and now. Because you are just waiting for the time when you will travel. And when you finally travel, you start thinking about what things you need to do when you arrive. You, yet again, live in the future. You need to turn this thinking off. Waiting every day for the future to come is bad. Set goals for the future is good.

3. Mood

While walking somewhere there are days that you notice everything and on other days it's like a blur. You can't control it. That's why you have a different perception every day. Some days your attention focuses only on negative things, and you see only negative things around you. And sometimes it's another way around.

You walk out of the door, and you see only good and positive in things around you. You don't do it on purpose. This is an unconscious way to live. You can't control it; you just live your life.

You didn't set a goal like, "Today I will focus only on negative," or "Today I will focus only on positive."

You just go through your day as you do every day. And your day can be completely negative or completely positive.

This can be controlled. This is the attention. Do you understand how important that is?

The focus of attention can be directed and it's important to what angle your attention is directed. You can focus your attention on everything positive or on everything negative. Think about it. Have you had days when everything that happened was with a tint of negativity? And then there was a day when everything seemed good and happy.

Do you remember what was the reason for it? Maybe you've met someone, and it changed the angle of your mood. You need to control such things. Why would you walk on the streets where accidents or shootings happen, or someone was robbed?

Here is another topic where attention is involved.

You wake up in the morning and get ready for the day very fast; you just have three minutes for everything: brush your teeth and run to work. This is a mistake. Why? Because it's important to turn it on when you just wake up. You need to wake up, not just physically but psychologically as well.

The first thing you need to keep in mind is that you can't rush in the morning. You need to have at least an hour to get ready in the morning. I understand that all people are different. Someone might not have an hour.

For example, women with kids. She needs to get her kids ready and make breakfast for everyone. For her, one hour wouldn't be enough. That's why you need to wake up one hour earlier than everyone else in your household. I am not trying to deprive you of your sleep. Sleep is very important. But you need to clean up your act.

If you need to wake up earlier, you go to bed earlier. You need to have this hour in the morning for yourself. This is very important. Also, drink a glass of water slowly. This is healthy. You should have breakfast just before you leave. You should not eat and only then do your morning routine.

First, you wake up, take a shower, do sport, and other things. And only then, when the hour has passed, have your breakfast and leave the house. If you do it earlier than one hour from the moment you awake, it's not good. Just remember you need to add one hour to the time you need to get ready.

This hour you will spend with yourself. You need to be here and now. You can make breakfast, you can go to take a shower, and decide what you will wear today. Or you can sit with a notepad, pen, and make a plan. Or check how you feel today, what are you going to do today and in the evening. Write it down in your notepad or the notes on your mobile.

Some people keep a diary, and they control their attention better; especially those people who can be alone and write down something in their diary. And those for whom it's hard to do those are more like zombies; they live on autopilot, they are victims of their mind, absent-minded.

Those who can be alone and spend an hour writing something down in the diary are more conscious. They have more free attention.

And those who can spend time with themselves don't give me an excuse that you don't have time. It has nothing to do with time. The diary is very important. Everyone should keep a diary. Make notes there wherever you want – in the morning or the evening. This is the time to focus on yourself. This is the key.

Another important thing. Some people spend a lot of time in front of the computer because of the work they are doing. You need to switch attention at least once a week to an opposite rhythm. If you work at the computer, you need to do something physical task, like dancing, sport, etc., anything that doesn't involve computers. It's important to switch the rhythm, so you won't become dull.

Other people are more involved with paperwork and negotiations, so they do not use computers a lot, most often those are people of the older generation. They might not even know how to use a computer; in this case, you need to get yourself a gaming console. Playing games for people who don't use computers is good. It will help to develop attention.

I need to give you a detailed account of how attention works. When you look into details your attention starts to develop. Now I am talking not about how to free up your attention but how to control it. You need to understand what steals your attention and how to direct it, how to use it, etc.

When I free up and widen your attention, it will be so strong that you will need only one element to connect to anything. Connect in terms of sensitivity. When attention is connected to many things like daily routine, your relatives, acquaintances, your colleagues, problems, to everything, you don't feel anything: you don't feel the energy, you don't feel yourself, you don't even feel how nature changes.

I can even feel how mood changes in the city, or any village. Because I am always here and now. And my attention is focused on where I am now. Do you understand?

People with scattered attention, no matter where they are, no matter what music they listen to, are not completely there as if they are looking through a small window. If I turn on music for such a person, yes, he will hear it, but he won't feel it, because his attention is scattered. But if a person has free attention, he will hear the music volumetrically and he will feel the atmosphere of the music track, and he will connect to it.

When you free up your attention you will be able to feel everything like that. This will give a boost to your self-development. When you turn on the Discovery Channel and watch a documentary, you will go deep into it with all your attention as if you will take part in it, you will feel it. You won't be just watching it as if from outside.

In the same way, you will feel the music, you will absorb it. There is one important *but*. Because of attention and sensitivity, I've discovered frequencies. I started to feel different waves, see different worlds, I started to notice what people don't realise. If I talk to one person, I have consequences in life, and it affects my mood.

If I talk to another person – there are different consequences and different moods. If I watch crime series now and I won't turn myself off from them, I will see maniacs and murderers. For real. I will show you how not to connect to bad things and people. And even if you connect to something bad, I will show you how to zero yourself down.

There are people like zombies, their attention is scattered, and they don't connect to anything and they can switch on and off as if their development stopped. Their potential to develop equals zero. And there are you, my readers who also have scattered attention, but you have a percentage of free attention.

You can connect to something: to me, to my world, and atmosphere. Or to some bad person. But you don't feel it and you don't control it. It happens by chance. But you have the potential for such a level of sensitivity. You, like myself, can connect to something unfortunate by accident.

When I found out about it, through trial and error, I started talking about it to everyone who wanted to listen. I talk about it through my books and to the people who have some percentage of free attention. I talked about how important it is to control what you eat, what you listen to, which streets you are walking on, and who you talk to.

All of it influences your life. It's not easy to explain this concept to people-zombies, nothing influences them. But to my readers, I've stressed how important it is to understand that every object, every element around it can influence you in a good or in a bad way.

Here, I give you general information about attention. I will teach you how to free it up, how to control it, and how to direct it. What I've told you so far is just a cover for attention. Later on, I will show you another cover of attention which is how to manage energy. And then how to direct your attention. This is the most important part so you can avoid connecting to negativity and always be tuned to positivity.

For now, pay attention on yourself. If you look at this on a technical level, from the physics perspective, then even if you free up 10%, 20%, or 30% of your attention it won't be just floating around, right? It is free because you don't spend it on smoking or the internet.

But it immediately spreads to other things. And the effectiveness of those things will grow. Now, you spend not 10% of your attention on other things but 11% or 12%. But you still have only 100% of your attention. Look at illustrations of how it works. (Fig. 1, 2 and 3).

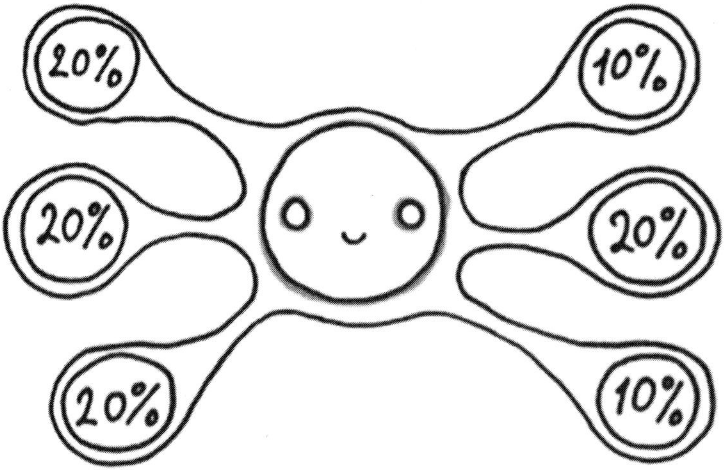

Fig.1

Fig. 2

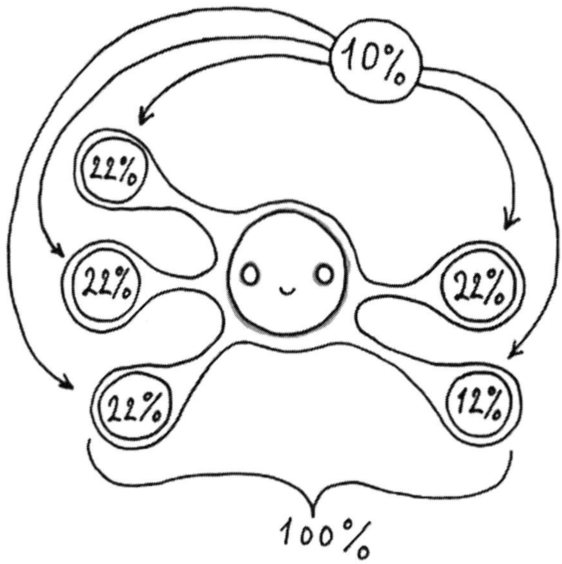

Fig. 3

When you choose some tasks, you need to turn off your attention from everything else. (Fig. 4)

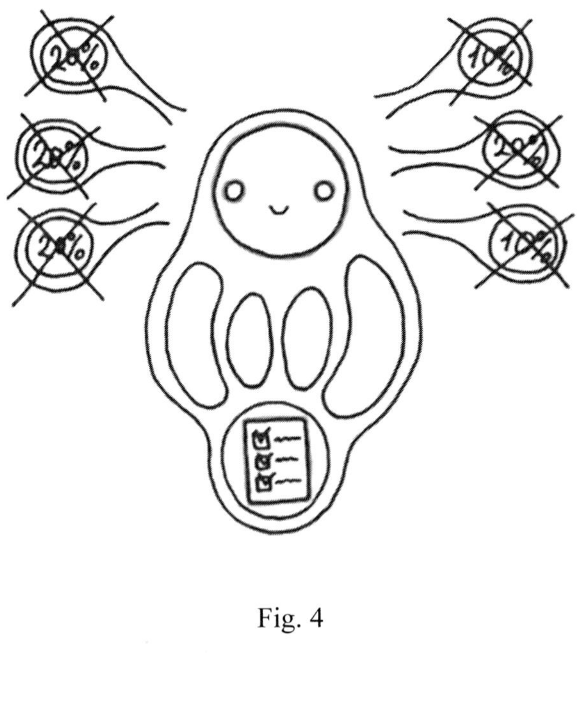

Fig. 4

It is, as if, you would open an app on your laptop or mobile and it will stay open. The same with your attention. It is like you always have all apps in an idle state and you never turn off your laptop. Your goal is to turn off everything that you don't need for the current task and devote 100% of your attention to this task.

And now let's talk about where your attention should be directed. I am sitting now and where is my attention directed now? It's on me and on what I am writing to you now. The attention is like a beam; where you look, that's where it's pointing to. That's it. When I talk to someone all my attention 100% is on every word the person says and on his feelings, even when a person has pictures pop up in his mind when he describes something, I see them and perceive them.

But it's not an extraordinary skill. This is free attention. And you can learn to do that. If I stop writing now, my attention will be on me. I can direct attention to my body and start feeling my body inside and outside. If I turn on the TV and start watching a documentary, I will be completely in it. I won't even feel that I am sitting in my apartment. There are no thoughts and all attention towards documentary. I will watch it, feel it, and perceive every word, picture and action in the documentary.

You are now reading this text. And some of you didn't turn off all ten apps that are running in you now. Meaning that some percentage of your attention is somewhere else – maybe on your work. On your household chores. And with some percentage of your attention, you are trying to read this text now. Therefore, you won't be attentive enougah because you have other apps working simultaneously. In this case, you should do some technique to turn off everything else and focus your attention on the text, so you can completely dive into it.

I have the talent to keep people's attention focused. There is one of my books called *Paradox*, when a person reads every chapter, his whole attention is stolen, he 'dives' into every chapter completely and loses his perception of reality.

Try to understand what I am talking about. There is Alex before and Alex after. Alex is me. Everything is different in my life now. I will tell you how it was before. For the past ten years, I had so much attention that I didn't have a goal to free it. Also, it was like a beam, focused, not scattered. I tried to mute it a bit; I tried to scatter it so I won't be in a state of bliss all the time.

I could never be in silence at home. I have always had the TV on, music, lights on everywhere, and noise. I felt better that way. If I was in silence, I feel attention so strongly, I feel bliss so strongly and I feel so strong. It was like that before.

In this case for the person who wants to become conscious, feel himself, and free up attention – silence is a friend. It's like a technique. But I understand that everyone is different. For some people who live with their mind, who can't feel anything, who are absent-minded, it's better to be in silence. It will help you to direct attention to yourself and your actions.

But there is another group of people, like me, who are very sensitive. They are sensitive and very attentive and conscious, they will feel more comfortable with the TV on, or with music on, etc. But I forbid it. Like I forbade it to myself. You need to be able to handle the attention. You don't have to try to mute it. Because you have always muted it.

Your task is to free it up and accept it. You need to get used to living in this state. I am talking now to sensitive people, who muted their attention, who have a lot of free attention. You need to get used to the silence. I said that silence is good but music that focuses your attention is also good. You can test what is best for you. If you are more focused on silence, then use it. If you are more focused on the right type of music, then use it. But you should not listen to distracting music. You need to focus your attention on yourself.

In this book, I am stressing the fact that you need to be focused, like a robot, etc. But you don't have to be like that. For now, you need to be like that because you are reading this book. But when you try everything and test everything, I will tell you how not to be a robot.

First, you need to make friends with your attention, you need to take account for your every action, you need to forbid yourself what I advise you to forbid and do what I advise you to do. And then I will explain to you what you can do to mute yourself. And when you can strengthen your attention even more. And you will be able to approach it in an easy way.

You will be very clear on what to do if, for example, you want to study something, and you will direct 100% of your attention towards it and learn something, and the information will be absorbed into your mind so deeply that you will never forget it.

You will be able to determine when you need to strengthen your attention, so you won't be absent-minded during an important meeting, for example. And when you can mute yourself so you can relax. You will know yourself when you are closed and need to open up. Or when you are too open and you need to ground yourself a bit.

But you need to start by learning how to feel yourself.

There is no easy way to understand if someone is connected to another person. You can know it only by observation. You will know it when you can feel yourself. You can feel the weather inside yourself. It's like the weather. Every day you will feel yourself.

That's what life is all about – feeling yourself, your structure, the feeling inside. And you will feel yourself in different places in different ways. Not with the mind which reacts with associations. They overthink and feel something unpleasant. These emotions and feelings are born from the mind. This is nothing.

I am saying that when you feel from your heart, from inside, from your soul, you feel people, atmosphere, and everything around you. While walking on the street and looking at storefronts, you will feel what you like or don't from your heart. The same with people and everything else around you.

When you learn to follow your nature, you will be like a scientist studying how your perception of the world changes when you talk to someone or when you are connected to something or someone.

For example, when I meet with a childhood friend that I haven't seen for a while and when I talk to him, I cannot know everything; it comes with experience. So, I am meeting with him today and the day after tomorrow and at the end of the week. At the end of the day, I evaluate how I feel, and I notice that when I didn't meet my friend, I had one mood and feeling. But when I started meeting with him, I felt somehow different.

I started to want to watch crime movies, or I wanted to stay home more. And for the sake of the experiment, I stopped meeting with him for a week and noticed that I don't feel like watching crime movies anymore. It's interesting but I have to check it again to make sure.

So, I communicate and observe him again. And then I discover that the interaction with this person has such-and-such consequences. It is only through such observations and experiences that you know what people are muting you, pulling you down, or charging you and pulling you up. Who turns something on or off inside you? But this is only possible with experience.

But how to turn off everything? You should meditate and manage energy; you should reset yourself. You can use the techniques I will give you later in this book. So, what is the main goal, what should you reach? You should not be connected to everything all the time; you should be here and now every day.

All your attention will be on yourself, and then you can temporarily connect to someone or something. All your attention will be under control, and like a beam you can direct it. You will finally feel yourself, you will develop, and you will be stronger and more conscious. You will get used to this state of being you. When you go to a meeting you will feel here and now, and you will connect to the person. But after the meeting, you will disconnect and feel yourself again. But what if you cannot disconnect? Then you need to do my techniques.

I'll tell you my story of how to always be in the same calm, harmonious mood. I achieved this state with techniques, practices, and a list of things that knock me out and, on the contrary, strengthen my inner self. I lived according to this list and to these rules. But it always happened that, sooner or later, a couple of times a week or once a month, something was still throwing me off balance. Of course, the techniques helped me recharge, recover and balance myself.

When I have mentioned that something throws me off balance and it happens again, and I cannot resist it, I started to make a list and pay attention to what is that and why is that happening. That is exactly what provokes you. As if you don't know it yet. It's an untrained mind. And for that not to throw you off balance you need to make a list and figure out what you have to deal with so that it doesn't get out of hand. Those are unresolved issues in your life.

Imagine that you are in complete harmony, and you feel really good. But you are a blogger – that is the most common problem – everything is perfect and suddenly you receive a message about your mom. That's it, you are suddenly angry, mad and depressed, and that will influence the rest of your day. Of course, it's just someone who wrote you a message, but that's not the point.

He or she is just part of the system, part of the circumstances. The system showed you your pain point. For you, it looks like that, someone wrote you an angry message and you are in a bad mood now. But you need to go deeper into what exactly this person wrote to you to throw you off. Other messages don't affect you that way. But the message about your mom did.

Half a year later you talked to someone, and this person started to talk about your mom and yet again you lost your mood. It means that your pain point is your mom. And everyone will have their list.

You need to figure out what it is about your mom that makes you feel bad. Maybe you are unhappy with her or offended, or maybe you're too close to her and afraid to lose her. You need to face your fears. The faster you do it, the better. Because if you face your fear, you won't have an emotional reaction to the subject anymore.

You need to make a list of everything that scares you, annoys you, and hurts you. You need to untie the knot. I did that in every aspect of my life. I am not sure if anything can influence me. I don't have any pain points.

When you go to visit your relatives who will pick on you, judge you and give their opinions, hurt your feelings, they do it automatically, they know what to say to throw you off. This is like a program; if your attention is free and focused on them, you will take it in stride. You will get into every word they say to you. And it will bother you because there is still a reaction of the mind. But you should not get into it. At that moment you need your attention to be occupied with something to side-track it.

Imagine that you are in love, and you will meet your love in two hours. But now you are with your relatives. You will react to them much less because your head is full of love, you think about the person you love and whom you will meet soon. And everything your relatives say won't hurt you. Because you don't care; your attention is focused on the future date.

Or if I have an important meeting in a few hours. I am waiting for it and checking my mobile because I need to check my employees who arrange the meeting. When I am doing it, I don't care about my relatives and what they say. Do you understand? I won't even hear what they are talking about.

This is just a simple example. Maybe you've noticed when you talk to someone and that person as if not with you completely. From one side it is a problem, but if you create such distraction artificially, it is good. Why is this person not with you? Because he is thinking about something that stole his attention completely. And he is sitting next to you, but he is not with you, and he can't even hear you.

Learn how to create such a state of mind yourself. This will help. You can also think about some happy events while you are with your annoying relatives. You are thinking about this event while they are talking about something, but you can't even hear them.

And you just say, "Yes, yes."

But in the meantime, you just have a nice movie playing in your head. This looks a lot like my *technique on the chair*. Of course, you have to try your ways to deal with the situation.

Here is another fun example. I have often scolded people in my circle for this.

I encountered a situation like this. I was visiting my friends, and the kids couldn't settle down and go to bed, either because of the noise or the light outside the window. What's the big deal?

I said, "Why are they so cranky that they can only sleep in the quiet and dark room, but if suddenly there is noise or TV or lights are on, or it is bright outside, then they are like sissies and cannot fall asleep."

That's how I felt about it. And I'm right about that.

Now I am teaching you how to free up and focus attention, right? Of course, when you are just learning you can remove all distractions. But when you know how to focus attention on yourself you need to toughen up. You need to be in a noisy crowd and use different states to feel yourself.

That's how I did that. I went to the most unpleasant places with noisy and provoking situations – in cold, in heat, in hustle in crowds – and tried to remain focused; I tried to keep this calm state. You need to train yourself. Now I have a very trained attention, that even if there is a huge crowd of people around me and there is a lot of noise, and everyone is talking, and there is sounds and music, I will still hear and feel myself.

It's too comfortable when you are all alone in silence and feel yourself. But this is extreme. You need to feel yourself living everyday life. Bit by bit, you will learn and even in the most uncomfortable situation you will be able to feel yourself.

There is one issue when people allow themselves to rest too long; it's hard for them to get back to work. A person would start work but his head is still on holiday. And it takes a long time to tune into a new rhythm. This is one extreme.

And there is another extreme when a person always works and it's easy for him to be in a busy rhythm. But when he wants to take holidays, he cannot turn work mode off. Even if he will go play football he will still think about work. He needs to work on it. Write it down; it's important.

You need to find something that distracts you enough that you can turn it off from your work.

Imagine that you work all day with contacts, and even when your workday is finished, I still think about contracts. I go to the restaurant and still think about contracts and work. Even if you decide to have a break, a 20-minute walk doesn't work for you. Your head is at work.

To completely switch off work, you need something with the opposite rhythm. Something that will capture your attention. The most powerful is fishing.

But fishing has a different rhythm from normal life. It's a long process but it works.

When you go for a fishing trip on a weekend, you change your clothes to fishing clothes, you spend days in nature without a mobile, and then when you come back to the city, you will feel as if you were away for a year. That's how strongly you will manage to turn off from everything in your normal life. Make a note of it.

It can also be a game that can turn you off better than a simple walk. The game can steal your attention and you can play it in a short break. The game is a good key, but it won't suit everyone. But test it yourself. Maybe you can play the game on your mobile device when you are on a break. What else can help to switch it off?

Contact shower, massage, or telephone call, but not a business call but in a different rhythm. There is discipline and there is a mood; you should not forget about humility and your inner mood and state. Don't go to extremes, but don't babysit your mood when you need to do something, and you can't consider your mood. If you do it, you will be considered weak.

Imagine a guy, 20 years old, who wants to earn money. But he is so spoiled and gets used to his comfort zone, to the untrained mind, and he cannot go against it. They tell him that he needs to go to a tax office, but he doesn't feel like it and he won't go. Okay, let him live how he wants. But some things cannot be dropped. If you need to pay rent, you need to pay rent. If you need to go to work, you have to go to work. And it has nothing to do with your mood. This is important.

Some people go to another extreme. They completely forget about inner happiness and mood, and like robots keep working and working. This is also bad. There should be a golden mean.

How would you know that you are at the extreme? You can feel it. If I, for example, work or do something all day. I understand that there should be some limits. If I keep working day after day after day, I will lose myself and my inner self. You need to nurture your inner self and feed it. So, on the next day, plan fewer things or makes yourself a feast for the soul. That's it. You need to feel this limit and it comes with experience.

The other extreme is when you are too careful about your mood. This is also bad. You can't just have a day off and do nothing all day. And the next day you will do nothing again. Soon you will feel like a couch potato. You are overdoing it already by resting too much. You should start doing things again. When you are overdoing it, you will feel it.

How does it feel when you discipline yourself and take control over your life? I wake up at a certain time, I do things, and I'm in control. I do it, but I'm not in a bad mood; I mean it's not a drag as I'm not pushing myself. It's as if I've rested, and now it's easy for me.

And when I start to feel like I'm not in the mood to do it, I start to feed it. When you are too much into discipline, you would feel and understand that you went to extremes when you feel a bad mood coming, like there is something unpleasant inside. It means you need to do something for your soul.

You need to feel here and now all the time. If you are in the extreme, you will be in a mist, then you overdid it for your mood and you need to sober up.

Discipline and mood should be simultaneous. You work, then you take care of your mood. And not like today you only work and tomorrow you only care about your mood. Some things you do because you have to, and some things you do because you feel like it. Both sides should be combined.

For example, I have things to do today. And I can split them into two columns. One column for things I enjoy doing, for my soul. And the second column for the things I have to do, I don't want to, but I have to. You need to balance them. If you don't have pleasant things to do, you should create them for yourself.

You should also limit the time you spend with your friends or relatives. This is control and consciousness. This is a high level of self-development. On one side, I promote that people live with their hearts and with their souls. On the other side, I talk about your mind, that you need to develop it and learn things.

If I want to meet with friends, I want to be in this meeting without mind; I've chosen to meet them with my heart. From my experience no matter if I choose with my heart, I should remember limits and time, and I understand that I should not spend more than three hours because I need to go somewhere else after.

On one side, my heart is with my friends when we are together, and on the other side, I know that in tw-and-a-half hours, I need to leave soon. Mind is a rule that you know. You need to control everything and be friends with time. Time is the issue of all people. Goals, tasks, deadlines, distances – everything has to be counted, understood, and accounted for. And this must be beyond the feelings and life of the heart.

You should not be idle. Rest is also a task but in a different rhythm. You cannot just sit and do nothing. It's good when you pay attention to some tasks.

Attention is always at work, and it doesn't have holidays.

I liked someone's saying from an interview, "When I have idle time, I will have stupid thoughts."

Why would you want those thoughts? If you are always busy, all week you are doing something and you feel good. You go to courses, sports, meditate and visit restaurants and friends. You feel really good. And the next week you wake up on Monday and you have nothing to do. You will be bored. On Tuesday, you did one thing and had nothing else to do. What will happen at this moment?

Your attention is free, you don't know where to direct it, and you will start self-diagnosis and think about some crap. You will connect to the wrong frequency because of that mood swings and depression can happen. That's why you need to be busy all the time. But I am not talking about only work. Rest doesn't mean you need to be idle. It is when you are busy with something opposite from your work rhythm.

If I have a busy day and a lot of meetings, and when I have free time, I will need to switch attention to something with the opposite rhythm; sit and read a book, play a game, or write in my diary. You need to be busy with something. Rest does not mean you lay down or walk around doing nothing. Rest means switching on a different rhythm. Your attention should be always engaged. Then everything will be fine.

Don't mix rest and free attention; those are different things.

I am talking now about how to live right and not how to do techniques. You need your attention to be on you and not connected to anything else. You will do it while doing techniques. Attention is like a beam; it should be free to direct somewhere. You cannot be idle. It's bad.

Think about it, analyse it, and look back at situations when you feel good and when not. You feel bad when you are bored and have nothing to do. When you are bored, you start annoying your close ones. That often happens in relationships. Why do men and women start to annoy each other? If both have busy lives with a lot of events and things to do, they won't have time to be annoyed with each other.

And when one of the two people in a relationship doesn't work, she or he starts pestering the other one because she or he has nowhere to pay attention and nothing to do. And she or he starts nagging the other about all sorts of nonsense; asking questions, making claims, and so on. That's how your partner also steals your attention, like an energy vampire. The problem is in people's heads.

4. Values

There is one important point in all the topics I am talking about above. Something that you need to know. In the concept of attention, there is a level of importance. In every situation, your attention focuses on things in the range, let's say from three to 15. But there is something that can steal your attention. For example, I have an acquaintance of mine and I show him a Tarot card and ask him to find a picture of it on the internet.

I tell him, "Can you find it please? I need it urgently. You have two minutes while I will be calling someone."

He started googling it and I am calling someone. And then I asked him, "Have you heard what I was talking about on the phone?"

He said, "No, I didn't even listen?"

I say, "But I was right next to you and I was talking loud."

But yet he didn't hear a word I was saying on the phone. This is a live example of how you can direct someone's attention and become invisible. It often happens that you need to call, and you go to another room so no one can hear you. But instead, you can just direct the attention of people to something that will steal their attention and talk on the phone and no one will hear your conversation. And it works. Only if you try to do it right now it won't work.

First, you need to understand how it works. It's not like you can say, "Look there, it's a bird flying," and they will forget that you owe them money.

There is such a thing as a level of importance. If you tell the person someone beyond his range of importance, – remember I've mentioned this concept? – he will forget that you've met to return him money. That's how you can control people, so they won't ask questions, or don't talk about something you don't want them to. Attention control is based on the level of importance.

Later on, I will tell you about the five senses that can be influenced. But you need to know the situations, objects, things, smells, and sounds which are higher than importance level 15, which will suit any normal person and steal their attention. It won't work for me anymore; you can test it. If someone calls me now and tells me that my dog died, it won't throw me off balance. You need to develop your level of importance.

And this is also connected to values. All my life hacks and keys are based on that. This is what steals your attention and throws you off balance. You need not only learn those tricks but also need to develop yourself so the limit of importance will be not just 15 but 40. And then you won't have any emotional outbursts, disorders, irritations, and non-conscious mingling.

They say something stupid or dirty to you, and you just look at the person with a hard, dark look and ask, "What's your goal?"

That's all. And the person will be surprised that you don't react like the masses and remain in a balanced mental state. It's cool to develop the value level so that the degree of importance is pumped so much that you don't get influenced. This is awareness and development.

Don't forget that you need to live consciously and always ask yourself the question, "Why are we here? What do I need to live for myself?"

You need to realise that we are here to develop. And you need to realise what motivates your ideas, and what you want. Do you want to lie on the beach? But what is it? Is it development? Or is it laziness and degradation? If you want to be lazy you will be punished. Badly.

You need to develop and not just dream about *when can I finally sit on the beach and do nothing*. This is bad.

You need to ask yourself, "Did I deserve it?"

I was laughing at my ex-girlfriend once. She does nothing and always talks about travelling somewhere.

I tell her, "But who are you?"

She knows who I am, and she knows my level and I never allow myself such things as travelling purposelessly somewhere. This is a mistake. If you want to get away somewhere, try to explain to yourself the purpose of it. Maybe the explanation is that you don't like the current place. Or you don't like yourself, or you don't like the way you live now.

It has nothing to do with the country you are in. If you move to a different country, you feel good for a month or two; it's psychology. In a new place, everything is new, and you haven't yet settled there, that's why you will feel good. But two months later, everything will be the same as before. You can't run away from yourself, as they say.

The same about travelling. You want to go somewhere, okay. But what for? Ask yourself this question. Do you deserve it? If you just went on holiday and are planning new travel already and think that life limits, you with time and money. And you think that as soon as you have the money you will travel again. And that's exactly the reason you are not given money. You won't use them in the right way. You will go in the wrong direction.

If you just came back from holidays and yet planning a new trip, the question is, *why?* If you travel for work, then it's fine. Of course, you must go. But if you just want to sit on the beach and be lazy, and you haven't even worked enough yet to deserve a holiday, it's not good. Work for a few months first. If you worked hard and you need a change of scenery for a week or a month then it's okay. But not too often.

Now let's talk about influencing people. That's how I started. It has nothing to do with the main topic in this book. In my life, I always had one rule: never depend on anyone. It was not a conscious decision, but rather an inner desire. When I am by myself, I rely on myself and I feel strong, confident, and secure. It didn't matter if I was developed socially and spiritually at that point.

If I was dependent on someone, it felt as if I was wearing handcuffs and put in jail. Why would I want to feel that way? When everything doesn't depend on you and you depend on someone else, it means you are connected to another person. I could not stand it. Even when I had nowhere to live and no money for food, I never wanted to go so low as to depend on someone. To lose the feeling myself was like death for me.

You are talking to my inner *I*. Imagine it will turn off. That's it. I will be like a robot, like everyone else. And there will be no more Alex. It is like death for me. That's why I did everything not to turn it off. That is why I live with my eyes wide open, I live a conscious life; I am not asleep, I feel everything. My life is very different. As if from the moment I woke up I never go to sleep again. It is important not to depend on anyone. Especially in a relationship.

If I spend too much time with one person, like with a friend or with my second half, or with my assistant, meaning that as soon as I lose balance that's it; it's the end. They are my enemies. And those people don't do it on purpose. They are just people. But because of them I degrade and become a normal human being. I lost my light. As if I am connected to society. I've analysed those situations and I had to control them and stop them.

Now I am in a situation where I can have friends and employees. But only if I follow certain rules. And the most important rule is that I have to be alone for the majority of the time. I need to feel myself all day every day. That's it. The main thing is not to lose the feeling yourself. This is very important.

Imagine the statue of Buddha on the floor. Buddha is you. And around the statue, there is a bright yellow-orange aura. And you are here and now. I am leading you toward this state. And if now you want to write in your diary, work on your thesis, or turn on a movie, then imagine that the beam of energy from Buddha goes toward one thing – either diary or TV. That's it.

And when you finish watching TV it's better to return this beam back to yourself. That is how it is supposed to be. But when you start a relationship with someone, or if you have relationships, it happens that new your Buddha there will be another one. Who is not yet in the light? And your energy, attention, and orange aura – wrap around the person next to you.

It looks pretty and you will start thinking, *This is for the person I love; it is good.* No, let's imagine the same concept in another way. He has no light, and he has no aura, but your beam goes toward him. And when the beam goes from you then your aura becomes twice as small. And so, your beam is connected to this person. Imagine it will be connected forever. And if someone will call you, write to you, or if you want to watch a movie, make music.

But it won't be good. Because the beam from your Buddha goes nowhere. Because the beam is on the person you love. And the music you create or anything else you do will be as good as dead. You won't be creating with your attention, with your consciousness. It is not good. Do you understand? When your beam is focused on someone you will feel less or nothing, you will not be able to create something really good, and the sounds and colours will be muted.

You should always return your beam back to you. And then you can connect to someone or something on purpose. The rule is then when you work your attention is focused and beam directed towards work. When you are back home you focus on your family. When you go to be alone your attention should be disconnected from everything and focused on your diary. That is how it is supposed to be.

I want you to understand something. I share my vision with you so you will have a better understanding of everything.

Imagine that there is a person – doesn't matter boy or girl, doesn't matter the age – and this person strives for self-development. What would I do if I were in his place if I don't have any resources and no knowledge? How to develop yourself? First of all, I would try everything in this world, everything legal and safe, that is. You should widen your horizon to the maximum.

You should learn about different cultures and different social strata. You should try to be in the world of the policeman, the world of skaters, the world of scientists, theatre, athletes, military men, vulgar people, etc. You should try a world where everything is included. You should try as much as you can. This is important for self-development.

Next, you should work on yourself spiritually. You should work on your attention, and feeling of yourself, pay attention to your inner *I*, *chakras*, meditation, and try different spiritual practices that exist. Dive deep into spirituality. Both sides are important, social and material adaptation and spiritual life. You need to dive into both of them. One year should be enough.

Afterward, everything will naturally be realised.

People do not use the full potential of their brains. But there is no such thing as the brain somehow working or does not work. It's not about the brain at all. For me, the brain is like a box. But it's all about attention. If we take an ordinary average person his attention is at a very low level, the focus of attention, the degree to which he perceives the world and people, is very limited.

He does not know, not only the world but even his city. The city is also multifaceted, and multi-social. A person lives only in the social stratum of society. And he lives within his little world. And you can say he uses his brain for 1% only. That's it.

A person begins to become a man of the world, raises the standard of living, tries all strata of society, and broadens his horizons. The brain is like a muscle, like our body, imagine that ordinary people use only a little finger. From the whole body. They just move it to solve problems and achieve success. All other muscles are atrophied. This is how people have atrophied brains. If a person begins to use all muscle groups, then they all develop. Then the whole brain develops. Do you understand how it happens?

The interesting thing is that a person pumps his brain, makes it get used to higher volumes of information, and strengthens it day by day. There is a muscle memory; the person gets used to something and can't just get back to easy living, he can't be a couch potato anymore. It will be hard for him, he will start to go mad, and it will be degrading for him.

He will be like a lion in a cage. If a lion gets used to being in limited space, it will get used to it and it will be its comfort zone. But if you let a 35-year-old person out from such limited space to the wilderness this person will just stand still and won't be able to move. Even if there is no limitation you won't move. And if it is a wild animal that runs around and hunts and suddenly this animal is in the cage, it will feel awful. It won't be able to stay in the cage. People are the same way. If you are in a limited space all your life, it will be hard for you to move on.

Let's talk about the brain, potential, and limitations. I emphasised that everything comes down to money. Imagine how I feel, so you can realise my psychological burden. I am, like you, born in a city, in a country, among people. I look at the world globally, soberly, and consciously. And let's say I want to change the world, turn it upside down, or take my place among the powerful.

Or I want everyone to watch my movies or eat my yogurt. Or I want everyone to wear black, or anything else. I am a child, and from childhood, I thought about why people do this or that. Why do you adore people on TV? Why are you not on TV instead? Why aren't you the one telling everyone how to live? Why aren't you promoting something? Why didn't you do those things?

It's not like someone got lucky or had better circumstances. No! Everyone who succeeds in life thinks, *What do I need to become a president? Okay, I see. I will get on it.* or *What do I need to become an actor? Got it. I will get on it.* Or *What do I need to do to build hotels all over the world? Ah, I see. I will get on it right away.*

They don't think like this, *I want a hotel. I should build hotels all over the world. I need a hundred million dollars for each hotel. I will look for an investor.*

A lot of people think like that. It's a flat-out approach to the problem. But it doesn't work that way. If you want to open a hotel chain or become president, you have to have a clear strategy. You have to understand that you have to have certain qualities, knowledge, reputation, image, financial independence, connections, and networks. And on top of that, you also need to know what is going on in the world.

To manage anything, you have to get to a level where you know as much as the people who you manage. And this cannot be achieved in six months or a year. You spend your whole life making yourself a sort of project. It's a crazy strategy. This is where I am right now. This is development. This is how it happens. Every detail is taken into account. And nobody helps you. You're on your own.

You can sit at home all day and do nothing. You can study or not study, bathe or not bathe, eat or not eat. It's up to you. It turns out there is no such thing as I got lucky, as they will say later on. I was not lucky at all. It's crazy to work. It's a 24/7 job. Every day. I've been working on it for ten years now. In the beginning, it's the hardest. Then it gets easier, not because the tasks get easier, but because you get used to the crazy pace.

It's because of attention. Back to our main topic. You spend all your attention on what's right and useful and you do it. You perceive and process information in a normal way. When your attention is free and strong, you have no idea how much potential for development opens up immediately. Or rather, for learning new things!

Your emotions and mood swings, your thoughts, and your mind make it very difficult for you to accept the world and people soberly and to learn something new. There's always something bothering you. Inner worries distract you. And when you are completely clear everything is clear, and your attention is free.

Read a Wikipedia article about the meaning of these words in physics or chemistry, watch a couple of documentaries about it, and talk to a university professor. It will take you a couple of days and all concepts will be known to you, as you become a guru in this subject. And you will want more and more, you will want more information. And you will want to learn more. And everything new will be added like in a chain and absorbed on the deep level.

I absorb all the documentaries about everything. History is number one. And the sciences – physics, chemistry, math, geometry. It's just wow! You can start learning from a basic level. Let's say, you Google what an algorithm is, then you start wondering where the word came from, and you put all the information in a chain. I don't have like-minded people around me. I won't discuss it with anyone; I just get high from this information. That's all.

And talking about how much percentage of brain capacity people use. What's the difference, really? You can judge yourself by looking at how you live your life. That's all.

You have to evolve. Your emotions, your moods, your thoughts, and your sloppy attention are getting in the way. It impedes development. If you can feel yourself and pay attention to yourself, you can control your attention easily, direct it to something, and learn about anything around you. And everything will be fine. I will tell you one thing, you must learn new things.

I am not talking about higher education, not about colleges, not about universities. I am talking in general. Learning is very important. Meet new people, practice, experience – all of it is very important. You have to be interested in all areas of activity.

Now, I want to show you the opposite side. Forget about consciousness and self-development for the moment. Let's imagine that you are a normal person who is interested in psychology, sociology, and spirituality.

And you know that there is Alexandr Korol, and you ask me, "Alexandr, please help me. I feel no happiness, everything is bland and blue. What should I do?"

Based on the attention control concept, I can offer you a life hack that on one side is the complete opposite of the general idea of conscious development, but on the other side, it will give you what you ask for. All my techniques and life hacks are based on real-life experience. I look at how something works in other people's lives and how something works in my life.

Many years ago, I've noticed that one person beams good energy, and another person beams something bad. One person is always sad, and the other person is always happy. I was interested in the reasons. Because I always pay attention to everything, I've noticed different lifestyles of different people, found causes and effects, and patterns. I wanted to find out how a sad person behaves and has around him, and what a happy person doesn't do and doesn't have around him.

Look at someone you know who is sad all the time. And if you start doing the same things, you will become sad as well. And the other way around. I am not talking about some achievements or life results. I am talking about daily routines and people's habits. Everyone has it differently. And let's take me as an example. Why, all those years, I never lost the inspiration to write books? Why, despite all the social and other unpleasant situations, I don't give up?

And here is the explanation: where is my attention? Why does someone think that the weather is bad? And one guy named Max constantly talks about bad weather and that it rains all the time, and it annoys him. And all his days drag and drag endlessly. Why is that?

We are talking now about psychology.

I am now trying to explain to you the attention from a different angle. Talking about Max and his attention. It's not like he is not connected to something or someone, but his attention is not occupied. And psychologically speaking, this guy is a slacker. He doesn't have a purpose in life. And it's not like he was born that way but because he doesn't set goals for himself. He doesn't want to finish some project in a month or two, he doesn't aim to achieve something in half a year.

There is no goal to study in the UK for half a year in his life, buy a car or afford to take courses that he wants. For people who live like Max with no purpose and no goal, time drags and drags. Because their attention is not directed at anything. So, what does he spend his attention on? One complaint about bad weather or nagging about the long queue at the counter. He pays attention only to those things that are in front of his eyes. And his eyes look not up but down. And that's why Max is always in a bad mood. And a lot of people live that way. And why? Because they have no goals. They don't set direction in life.

And compare Max, for example, with me. Why don't I care about the weather and about what people think of me?

Because I'm whole; I'm above it. First and foremost, it's about attention. If I didn't set my mind on something, if I didn't concentrate on what I was doing, attention would be occupied with daily life, with what was in front of me.

Yes, it's not good to live in the future. You have to be here and now. And this is a kind of contradiction. But I will explain; it depends on the situation. In this case, I have to make you more conscious, and open-minded, with free attention and a super-cool expanded psyche. So that you feel everything, and society doesn't consume you. This is the development of the present. Those who understand this, read my books.

I wanted to give you these examples because later on you will free up your attention and you will realise that you need solitude or meditation and how to recharge yourself. But you need to remember to set goals and direct your attention to some tasks. You need to use your attention in the right way. Don't make the same mistakes as Max. But do as I do – get inspired by an idea.

You will free your attention from outside society and unconscious habits, but then you will need to direct your attention to self-realisation in something creative or in business. This is the main goal.

Do you see how material and spirituality are interconnected? Two sides are together. It's all connected.

You could also become a prominent figure or an expert in your field, but you can't even figure out what you want to do. Why not? Because you have a problem with attention, it's not free. You live like a zombie. But we're dealing with that now.

Some people know what they want to do, and they are even doing it. But you don't get great results because your attention is spent on the past, on the future, on social networks, on people, and automatic nonsense.

Because you will free up your attention, your results will be better. Your business, if any, should begin to grow. But the main goal is to live in the right way further on. And not to react to some nonsense, you need to consciously set your goals, formulate your ideas, and live by your ideas. And what does it matter if it snows or rains outside? You won't even care.

If you're doing what you love and some stranger writes to you that you're a bad person and you're not good at writing music, you won't care either. Because your attention is disconnected from society and completely involved in the feeling of your inner world and in the goal of realising something that is inside you. It is something to strive for.

As far as attention is concerned, I would like to give everyday examples. Many movies tell the story of a character who discovers he's terminally ill and will die soon. They show that this man starts to allow himself a lot of things: he tells everyone what he thinks, he confesses everything, and he speaks his mind easily in certain situations.

That is, he gets involved in things he has never been involved in. Figuratively speaking, when a person is told that time is short, he suddenly begins to live. Watch movies like *Knockin' on Heaven's Door* or *The Bucket List* and similar ones.

When people get into a state of shock, their minds turn off, so all the limits disappear; they don't evaluate anything, they don't judge anything, and without thinking they go for such actions and deeds.

It turns out that people's attention is so stolen by the news, that is, by the information, that everything else becomes unimportant. And this gives rise to a state of fearlessness. The most interesting thing is that people feel the same way when they fall in love. A person starts to behave strangely. In a sense, a man is living his life, he has work, studies, problems, debts, maybe enemies, and suddenly he falls in love by chance.

He can't control it as it's a natural phenomenon. And he fell in love to such an extent that everything else faded into the background and his life now is on autopilot. He's like in a fog, he's not aware of his actions, and he doesn't care about anything. He can walk down the street and not notice the weather or anything. Because all his attention is on the feeling – on love.

Make note of it, these examples are also attention. Why did I give you those two examples? There is more and more talk that a lot of health issues are psychosomatic. I will explain it. A person's mood and one's psychological state affect one's physical health. More and more people are starting to agree and notice this.

If we assume that this is true (not everyone but some people have genetic health problems, or are destined, or because they don't lead a good lifestyle).

When people ask me, "Alex, if suddenly there is a health problem and none of the doctors can help, what would you do?"

I will explain the situation with attention. In this case, it interconnects with frequencies. I would say that you are connected to a frequency where there are diseases and health problems. And I would turn off my attention from this frequency and connect it to another one. Or I would turn off my attention completely like monks do.

That is, I would do the technique on the chair 24 hours a day. And to make it 100% work, I would use all keys to focus attention on myself. I would leave and I would not let anyone know where I am without any devices. And I would just sit by myself or go somewhere, gather all my attention on myself, and won't talk. That's what I would do.

You should understand what attention is so you can find your examples of attention. There are many of them. Everything is connected to attention.

Attention is like a soul. Let's not pick on words, but it turns out that flies have a soul, attention, and consciousness. Why do we need to know their languages? Everything is based on attention control. I want you to become even more aware that attention is everywhere. In all living organisms. And it's all happening with one emphasis – it's all about working on attention.

Try to go deep into reflection about what attention is. Imagine how interesting it is. There's a mosquito flying, buzzing in your ear. It controls your attention, it provokes you, doesn't it? It distracts you from something. Imagine how much of your attention is attracted to it. Everything is based on it. Turns out it is easy to capture your attention with simple things. This is attention control.

You can even manipulate someone's attention without talking to the person. This will help you to realise what attention is and what are people. Of course, the best tool is the information itself and the words. But let's say you are a nice guy, and you want people to notice you. But your physical image pushes people away.

You're wearing the elements that repel people's attention. Approach this as a psychologist-scientist. If you want to get as much positive attention as you can, what's the key? If you ask yourself that question, you'll know what's needed.

Attention is extremely important, and it is in everything. If you meet someone you're interested in and want to be friends with, and you say things that don't steal his attention, he won't have anywhere to direct their attention. So his attention will be directed to his thoughts.

He will think about something else instead of connecting with you, and he will leave and never want to see you again. When you meet him, you need to talk in a way that gets his full attention. So that his attention is disconnected from everything and everyone.

Attention can disconnect so completely that his relatives and friends will feel it and start calling him and asking, "What is happening with you?"

We often hear such stories when a mother knows that something is happening to her child. How does she know that? She knows this connection with her child, and when the connection is broken, she feels it.

When people meet with me, they also disconnect from their relatives and friends, and people start to worry that something will happen to them. I can disconnect a person's attention from everything and everyone.

There is a question about frequencies. No matter whether you are in *nirvana* or the state of sixth sense, you are always on one frequency or another. Next to attention control, there are frequencies that you connect to with your attention, you live in a certain habitat. It's like a prism through which your attention perceives the world, like a focus adjustment. There's only one laser, but it can hit the skin, through the skin, or through the hand. Or it can hit the wall or go through.

This is attention. Frequencies, on the other hand, are like the refraction of light, meaning the refraction of attention through the philosopher's stone, through the multilevel matrix. Facets are frequencies. And if I'm connected to a bad frequency, my attention perceives everything in that range. If I disconnect from it and switch to the good one, I see things differently.

When I just started to switch from frequency to frequency I would go out and look around at people, and buildings and write down everything. Everything that

I liked or didn't, everything I noted, and everyone I've met. That's how I made a mould. And it's an amazing discovery.

You can disconnect from the luxury frequency and connect to the frequency of the bums. That's not a problem. The bravest of the brave, do you want it? You can take your chances.

It's not done with the mind, not with intellect. People who live in a primitive world think that everything is done by the mind. Let's imagine some professional stylist. And he wants to be the big shot, and he wants to dress people up from the elite. What is this person going to do? He will watch with his eyes and memorise with his mind how rich people dress. He will memorise it and he will try to reproduce it. But it doesn't work that way, it won't work for him. I can see that right away.

When he creates an image of someone or himself, you can see that a little bit is taken from the homeless world, a little bit from the elite world, and a little bit from somewhere else. Because he doesn't feel anything. I can clearly see that. For him, it's like everything is in one colour, but for me, it's red, green, and black. It's different colours and different worlds.

You need to do it with no mind. When your attention is free you can connect it to the elite world. And you just look at everything that attracts your attention on the internet, in the shops, in the movies. Everything that captures your attention is a mould, the mould for the elite world. This is how I make a mould.

A person cannot make it by thinking about it with his mind. You cannot make a mould of love frequency by googling movies about love or lyrical music. Half of those movies are not from the world of love, because those movies are made with mind.

A little more about attention. You've probably experienced the situation when you're asleep and people in your room are sneaking around or doing things very gently, and quietly, so as not to wake you up. When I lived with my family, I always scolded everyone for that and said, "When you wake up, and I'm still asleep; please don't think about me. You can make noise, turn on the TV, talk in full voice, and I won't wake up. But if you try to make me not hear you and sneak around, you will wake me up."

People didn't understand me. This situation is about attention. When one sneaks around, one thinks of me and focuses on me. That's why I feel him, I hear him. The person should not think about me, not be focused on me. He should just go about his business. As if I did not exist. He has to be aware that I'm as if

I'm not in the apartment and he has to be occupied with his business. Then he won't wake me up.

But when he thinks of not waking me up, he appears in my head, and I immediately wake up. Take note of this experiment and think about if a similar thing happened to you. It has everything to do with attention. Let's say you want to do something in a restaurant, for example, let's say, to steal something, and at that moment you sneak but think that people will look at you and they won't notice you, then they will all turn their heads at you because you will attract attention on the subtle plane. If, on the contrary, you don't think that someone will see you, and you do something, then no one will notice you. Do you understand?

I always feel that tension. If a person is doing something they want to hide, I will turn my head and see it, even if the person is at the next table. I can feel and read the way he's thinking that someone is about to turn and look. This is the first clue.

Another interesting thing is let's take a dog as an example. It has a wet nose – for sensitivity, so it can feel everything better. And you can remember an occasion, maybe you've seen it in movies or cartoons when a person licks his finger to understand where the wind is blowing from. When his finger is wet, he feels stronger, his senses become more acute. He knows which way the wind is blowing.

You can take note of this, when you have wet skin or a certain area of the body, it increases sensitivity. First of all, the feeling of air, but also attention in general in this area. There is an old saying that if an animal licks a wound it seems to heal faster. It's not because it has some sort of trace mineral in its saliva, but because it focuses more of its attention on a damp area. Do you see?

5. Free Attention

People have a real problem, like a disease, they cannot handle their attention and unconsciously direct it anywhere possible. That's why people have bad habits and that's why people deprive themselves of new discoveries. In a person's life, his attention is always spent on everything. To have free attention feels very unusual for the majority. Their attention is always somewhere.

This is a fact. I'm so crazy that I've purposely tested it many times, it's a matter of principle. There is no point in testing unconscious people. Everything is obvious there. If I'm talking to a person and I go to the bathroom, the likelihood that, while I was gone, he wasn't just sitting there waiting for me, but got on the phone, is very high. In an unconscious person.

The conscious ones are few and I look for them all over the world. If I meet such a person I go and test. If I go away for a long time he will just sit there and won't even look at his phone for an hour. Out of 100, 99 times that's true, and it's very interesting. I mean, it's a problem when a person is sitting in a queue, riding public transportation or a cab, when they have lunch or go after work or a meeting, they're always looking at their phone. And that's okay.

All these couch potatoes are used to defend themselves because they are very cowardly; they find a million excuses, they say they needed to write an important email to mom, to call grandma. Even for five seconds but they look at social media. That's the problem.

When a person's attention is freed up, his or her brain automatically looks for a substitute to mute the attention. For a person to feel comfortable, attention has to be spent, it has to go somewhere. It is a comfort zone. But if a percentage of attention is suddenly freed up, say, a person gets fired from his job or his personal life collapses, which used 20% of his attention, that percentage will not be free.

He will try to use it as quickly as possible. Either he'll drink to spend it, or he'll start hanging out with someone. He doesn't even care with whom, because that's not the point, but the point is that on the subtle plane, the attention has to go somewhere. He may even start working more. People call it *need a distraction*. But it is not about distraction.

A person simply cannot let his attention be free and focused on himself. He has to use it on something else urgently. That is the problem. It's super consciousness and spirituality, if you come to it.

Think about how your life was in the last few months and analyse how you spend your attention. You need to characterise yourself and find patterns of behaviour. It might be bad habits, work, family, and many other things like hobbies or interests. You need to direct your attention to that. But it is only the basics. Many other things in life require attention. Maybe you spent too much time on social networks. And when you spend time there you feel satisfied. Attention is also involved in work and relationships.

Women sometimes have psychological issues, and they talk about medicine and pills and how and who died, and which pills you need to take, and they like to visit pharmacies. They do it unconsciously, they don't mean any harm to anyone, and it's not a fear of anything. It's like a psychological drug. Women have a lot of energy, and such blackness uses up a lot of attention.

If a man spends attention on similar things he will get sick soon. But women have much more attention than simple things that don't satisfy them. It is really hard for women, no one gives them a set of rules on how to spend attention well. And if a woman lives a simple life, it affects her psyche; it brings her to self-destruction. That's why many women often do extraordinary things, they need to spend their attention. It's a complicated topic.

The man says that at work he is often distracted by social networks. This is bad. Very, very bad. First of all, I'm going to say this as a boss. I wouldn't want employees at my company to be distracted by social media. And a lot of companies are trying to curb that.

You don't have to be like the kids at school, trying to get around it and cheat. In this case, you are damaging both the company you work for and yourself. So, please, don't surf on social networks at work under any circumstances.

About social media. Especially at work.

At work, all attention should be on your tasks. And no use of social networks and messengers should be permitted. This is bad. If you come to work, you have to be fully immersed in it. It is very important to take a psychological break, a break for your attention. Every hour or 40 minutes, whichever is more convenient, you should take a break, but not on social networks.

You can turn on the game on your phone, as an alternative, “Mario”, or some kind of quest game. It will help you to disconnect. I know it’s going to be hard for a lot of people. But understand, if you’re at work, you can’t be distracted by social media in any way.

My advice to you is – I would even say, an order – if possible, implement what you can. Option one: get two telephones, the one you go to work with should not have social networks apps installed. Just delete them. And the phone with the social networks is waiting for you at home. And you only open apps in the evening.

It will be very good for your mood, psyche, and life in general. If you can’t buy a second phone, let all your social network apps be on your computer, iPad, or tablet. But remove them from your phone. Only when you come home in the evening, have dinner, and do other things, before going to bed, can you look at social networks.

And you should do it during an allocated time – an hour and not more. For an hour you can go into all the messengers and distract yourself. But only in the evening, at the end of the day, when everything is done. There is no other way.

I know that a certain category of people can say that your activity is related to social networks. If it’s a job, it’s a job. In that case, you have to be there. But it needs to be disciplined so that you don’t open social apps automatically, unknowingly, as people do, every five minutes, and it needs to be within an allocated time.

Even if it’s a job, you don’t have to monitor it every minute. It steals your attention, you scatter it. Social media is a demon. Everything there affects you. Any picture in the news pops up and it eats away at your awareness and clouds you.

Many people say that their mornings start with social media. You wake up and you’re already gone, your clarity is knocked out from the moment you wake up. It’s very bad. Don’t go to your phone when you wake up, make a gift to your true self, to your soul, your consciousness. Give them a rest. Live with a strict schedule, when you wake up, you can wash your face, brush your teeth, do some exercises, run, and do other things.

And only after that, when you go to work, you can go to social media. You can’t do it just after you wake up. Believe it and do it for a week. You’ll be amazed at how much happier you'll feel a thousand times and how much more consciousness and clarity you'll have. It really works.

Take note of the fact that you can look at social networks only after breakfast. And it is even better not to look at them at all, wait until the end of the day, and go in only after dinner. I know how hard it is to control yourself; it's your willpower, and not everyone has it.

So that there was no provocation, here are some tips: let the social networks apps installed on your computer or have two phones – one of which you take with you when you go out of the house – and you get out of the slavery of the internet, which is very attention-stealing. It's a good option.

Messengers of any kind also steal your attention. Many of you are on Telegram or WhatsApp and it distracts you from your tasks during the working day. You don't do work but rather write to friends, boyfriends, girlfriends, relatives.

How to stop it? Of course, messengers are useful tools, but my advice is to let all messages wait and you only go to check them only when you want to check them and reply. You don't need to check messages all day long.

Another piece of advice that won't work for everyone. I know it will have a positive impact. I won't go on messenger, and to those with whom I keep in touch, I tell them to SMS me. If I do that there will be a different rhythm, not trivialised. When you go to Telegram, you still see avatars there, like in a social network.

And this affects brain processes. But it won't be like that with SMS – you're just texting the person. It's more business-like and sort of cleaner. Take note of that. A lot of people go on social networks unconsciously, by habit. That's not good. It is better to do it after dinner before you go to bed. You can spend no more than an hour on it.

Of course, you can Google something. I have always promoted this, and I will repeat it now, in case someone is not aware of it. A knife can be both a weapon and an auxiliary tool. You can harm someone with it, or you can do a lot of good. The internet is now the number one problem.

People are dumbed down by it because it's an addiction. They look at other people, and the human psyche is very addicted to it. But it's a degradation. You spend your attention on it, but not on your life, on yourself. It's bad. The internet is just like TV.

Some people say, "I don't watch TV."

That's nonsense. I watch TV, believe it or not. And why? Because there are so many channels, including scientific channels. I watch all scientific documentaries, and I'll advise you to do the same.

I watch science and history documentaries every day. And I don't watch channels where they discuss the news, swear shows, all vulgarity, and filth. I don't believe in ads; I don't see them. I only watch what I'm consciously paying attention to, to a particular topic of a particular documentary.

It's the same with the internet. I don't scroll social media pages to see what people post or recommend. That's not good. I have myself; why do I need something from strangers? I have myself. And you have yourself. For example, you were interested in reading about something, and you Googled it and read it on Wikipedia. Not because it was forced on you, but because you wanted to. That's special.

If I want to read a Nostradamus prediction, I Google it, I go to the Nostradamus prediction site, and there's a whole bunch of stuff down the side: movies about him, Vanga and Edgar Cayce predictions, and all kinds of nonsense. So, you Googled Nostradamus' predictions consciously, but then you got sucked into the advertising swamp and started reading what ads offer. So, you are an unconscious vegetable. It's the same as going to the store.

I come in and say, "Hello, I need this, this, and this."

And they say to me, "Would you like that as well?"

I say, "I don't want it."

"How about this?"

I am like, "I told you, I need this, this, and this! Do I have to say it again?"

"No, come on. Why are you being so rude?"

No, I'm not rude. But I don't understand what right you have to influence me. I'm a conscious man; I've written over a dozen books on this. And you're selling me something as if I am a silly human. I have a discipline that I want to teach you as well.

And the interesting thing is that they try to forcefully sell it to you. Not to everyone, but to many. And to your loved ones and mine. It has to be stopped. If I go to a store and say that I need sneakers or just a sweater, then I only need a sweater.

If they say, "Maybe we could find something to go with this sweater, can I show you?"

I have to say no. And if the person brings it anyway, then he's a fool. And you can sincerely say that to his face. He can't do that because I am being very clear with him about what I need.

If I would say, "I don't know," it would be okay if he offers me something.

But I'm telling him clearly, it's just this, this, and this. That's all there is to it. But when a man starts to push me further, that is, to sell me more, of course, he's going to get his head kicked in. I mean under no circumstances should you break the law.

But you can tell him rudely and clearly, "Hello! wake up dude!" and flick it in front of his nose, and then he'll come to his senses.

In every situation when you buy something, please nip it in the bud. And watch yourself. And here's another thing you can watch out for. The next time you go shopping for groceries make a shopping list. And if you're going to buy this, this, and this, you have to buy just this, this, and this. That's it. Then you'll see what a cool money-saver it is. Awareness and consciousness save money through your control, and it doesn't connect you to a low frequency.

Can you imagine how much I suffered when I was with people and in relationships, watching this unconsciousness 24 hours a day? I was just stunned.

Figuratively speaking, a co-worker says to me, "Alex, we need to do this and go there."

I said, "Okay."

And then we get there, and he says, "Let's go around the corner again."

I say, "No."

And he's like, "Why?"

"Because you said we're only going this way. And then back. Did you?"

"I did."

That's it. Here I am a robot. It's tough, but I'm a robot. You have to try to be very clear about what you're doing or going to do. Every action. In every situation.

Also, you have no idea how much attention is controlled by everyone around you. It's kind of a nightmare. You'll start to notice that. The main thing is, don't be rude under any circumstances, you have to be within the bounds of decency. You will notice how your attention is endlessly provoked in every way. It is as if people around you are children who would throw a toy and cry for your attention.

That is how it looks. When you start to focus attention on yourself and control it, the people who are feeding on it will start to pick on you. Here is an example: I'm sitting calmly, working, and it's like being poked in the side with a fork. That's what it looks like.

And you say to the person, "Leave me alone!"

Why does this happen? People have no control over their attention. They don't know how to be alone with themselves or direct their attention to something. They always spend it on people, and people spend it on them. People live like a herd. That's not good.

One more thing about social media. You don't have to give them up. The important thing is how consciously you do it. If you're on it every 5 minutes, of course, that's bad. You can't do that. But you can do it at the end of the day and set aside a specific time.

If you have an hour, you can do it for an hour or two. But it has to be clear: two hours and no more. If you have free time at the end of the day, you can go to every social network, post a photo, write what happened to you, or do whatever you usually do there.

See who sent you messages and reply to people. But it has to be a clear time frame when you're consciously approaching it and you're paying attention to what you are doing. This applies to everyone at all times. If you're on autopilot every time you check your social media accounts without realising why that's not good. You can't do that. It's up to you, of course, you can remain a herd of sheep. We'll shepherd you.

I often notice when a person comes to a room and forgets why he came. This person lives on autopilot. Curiously enough it happens more often with women than with men. They are often absent-minded and trying to do 20 things simultaneously. This is a big mistake. No matter if you think you can multitask you should not brag about it.

There is nothing good in it. If you cook for me now and you would be doing another five things at the same time, I would not eat your food. Because I don't want a dish in which you spend 5% of your attention cooking. I don't care if you are a super chef, and you can cook the dish with your eyes closed. You didn't put your soul and attention into this dish.

This person, even while talking to me, won't be with me. There is only 5% of him listening to me. And if you put out a cigarette on your palm, in front of him, all his attention immediately focused on you.

And he's right there, "Hey, man! Are you back?"

He says, "What did you do?"

And I said, "I can't talk to a robot, I had to get your attention back. Can you hear me now, can you see me? Is my voice three-dimensional?"

"Ah, yes."

Thank you for being here and now. You see how easy it is to get attention, just do something out of the ordinary. Of course, I don't advise you to do that, it has to be within limits, without any mutilation, but still. It's a way to get someone's attention focused on you.

People live as if on autopilot. And if you do five things simultaneously it is awful. Don't do it no matter what. If you do anything habitual and automatic, you need to stop doing it. Because everything habitual doesn't involve attention.

Let's say driving. When you just start driving and you just got your driving licence you are very focused on the road. And you won't be able to turn on music or open the glove compartment or call someone. And if someone asks you a question you would probably not hear it. Why? Because you don't have enough experience and you don't have a habit of driving. But over time you get used to driving the car, it's like walking, and you don't pay 100% attention. You just drive on autopilot.

And so, you can talk on the phone, talk to someone while driving. But that's not good. You can't brag about it.

A person is watching a movie and talking to someone and cooking at the same time, a lot of people do that, it's a human factor. And you eat on autopilot, watch movies without paying attention, and you meet friends and still, you are not with them 100%, you are on autopilot.

In such moments, a person's attention and consciousness are not present. And that's why people are given all sorts of problems, from nature, so that a person whose attention is scattered on everything around him or her, will somehow notice himself or herself.

Until two years ago, people wondered how it was that I learned to live without a mind. I have no control over anything. But I solve all the material things, and I'm at ease in society. How do I do that?

I was so mindful of everything, so focused on everything, I practiced everything to the little thing, that when I turned off the mind, my experience of the mind, that autopilot, remained. In a good way. I'm being conscious of it. So, the experience of mindfulness helps you when you're without mind, helps you do things on autopilot.

But it is not the same as when everything is done on autopilot. It's when you do it yourself. When I'm walking down the street I can't see around me, I don't notice how I'm moving my feet, and I can't see any cars or people. It doesn't mean I'm inattentive. I just don't pay attention to it. That's why most of the time, I have a guide.

I'm rarely alone. But not because I don't want to be alone. It makes me more comfortable staying in my state. When a man walks alongside me, I follow him on autopilot, like a guide, and I am in my space. That's how it is. I am just talking here, it's not something I teach.

It's too early to talk about it. It is necessary to learn about society and develop the mind. Do things, and live on a schedule, then you will have autopilot, mind, and concentration – everything will work well, in harmony with consciousness and mindfulness.

People who combine many things simultaneously are bots, who live with the mind. They are closed and they are trying to finish many things at once. You should not do that. It's not productive, not effective. Many people learn a foreign language by listening to language audio while driving. If you drive, then you only drive. Your head should be free.

When you have 20 spare minutes and you want to spend it learning something on your mobile, you won't be able to switch to the task with all your attention. No, you need to have a free head. After work, you can tune yourself up psychologically and start learning something. Doing something in fragments is bad. Most of the time it's done by soulless people without light inside, zombie bots.

I'll say to someone, I know, "Let's meet," and he says, "Yeah, yeah, yeah, come on over, I've got a 20-minute window."

What do you mean? What do I need those 20 minutes for? You need them to get up and tune in so that the person can disconnect from other things and switch over to me. That's what he needs, not me. In 20 minutes, he won't have time to connect with me.

Of course, when you don't need a person's attention, for example, you just need to drop off a package, then, of course, you can meet. But if you need to talk for 20 minutes, it's not right. Especially when he or you are in a hurry to go somewhere. It's not right to do that. People make big mistakes because of that.

And I'll add one more point about this. A long time ago I had a live meeting for 10 people. I spoke to them, I walked around, and people were sitting in front of me. I looked at each one and saw it: when I'm talking to people, I have the attention of all the people, but this time I don't feel one person.

I go up to him and say, "Where are you?"

I said to him, "You're not with me. I can't feel you."

Everyone else is completely disconnected from time and space and focuses all their attention on me, but he is not. I wanted to find out what was wrong. Turns out his attention was on a train. He was afraid he would be late for the train; he was thinking about that train and of course, his attention wasn't completely on the meeting. Imagine how that works!

If I was to meet one of you at 5 o'clock in the evening and you have a train or a plane to catch at 9 o'clock, you will no longer be with me 100%. Your self-preservation instinct will kick in, and thoughts of being late. That's not good. Keep that in mind for the future.

Another point here. Some people go to extremes and scatter their attention in society. Because of that, the system hits them hard. There is a critical point after which accidents happen. And after that the person wakes up, he is here and now. Some people travel too much, they like holidays way too much, and they lose clarity, scatter their attention on it, and forget themselves. Some people are workaholics; they are at the extreme as well, and they forget about the current moment and what it is to feel yourself.

This is bad. Doesn't matter where you are at work or on holidays, it's not good that you have all your apps running and filling up all your attention. You need to zero yourself out at the end of the day.

I bet you would not be happy with my information and my approach to information if I would put only 5% of my attention into my work. But people treat each other exactly like that, and approach business exactly like that, with only 5% of the attention. This is awful.

The whole point of my information and my books and the reason that they're so powerful is that I am completely here and now. Here I am. As well as my attention is growing. You are buying my attention. Not the books, not the information that I am giving but my attention. And the price of my attention is growing because I am developing it.

Attention is everything. It's your health, your mood, and the health of the people around you. It's efficiency. It's life. When you move on autopilot it is as if you don't live at all. It happens that a person has been living on autopilot for a year, and then suddenly something happens in this life, some emergency. Immediately there was a rethinking and reassessment of everything in his mind.

He looks back at how his year has gone and realises that the days flew by like one as if he had just woken up. A man sits alone for a day, a week, maybe even reads a book I wrote because he's got his mind off things. And then, just like that, he's back in society and he's a fool again. That's how this madness happens. And I'm still sitting in the world of consciousness, watching who flies in and who flies out.

Here's another interesting example. Look at the diagram: you are one, two, three, four, five, six, seven, and this is an example of the degree of importance (Fig. 5). There's what you spend your attention on, what steals it, that's it, from one to seven. My task is to show you in various ways how to disconnect your attention from everything and collect it on yourself. So that you can get used to it and learn to accept it.

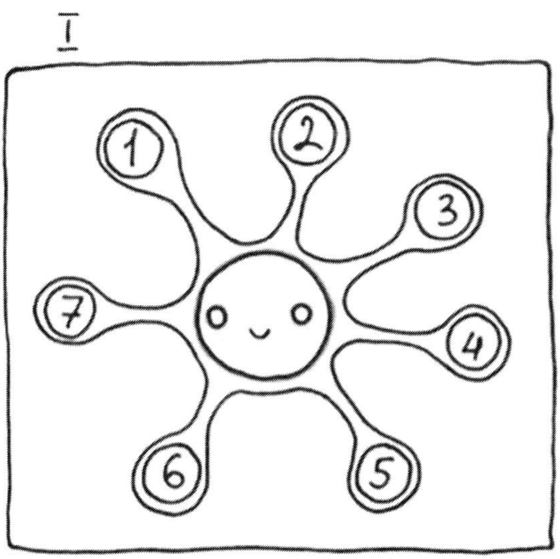

Fig. 5

And this is a picture of me (Fig. 6), my attention is on me, and I have drawn it looped. And I keep it so fixed that I steal the attention of society on me. You have it outside, but I have the opposite, the attention of society on me. Do you understand what I've done? And I also amplify, like a magnet. And at this moment I'm not the bad element, like all the others, but on the contrary.

Here's another example (Fig. 7). Again, this is you, and 1–7 are the elements on which your attention is spent. Your task is to learn how to gather it into one point. So that the next time you pay attention to problem 5, you'll come back to yourself. If you want to work on problem 5, pay attention to it and then come back to yourself. The main thing is to always keep to yourself and get back to yourself. This is the task I am leading you to.

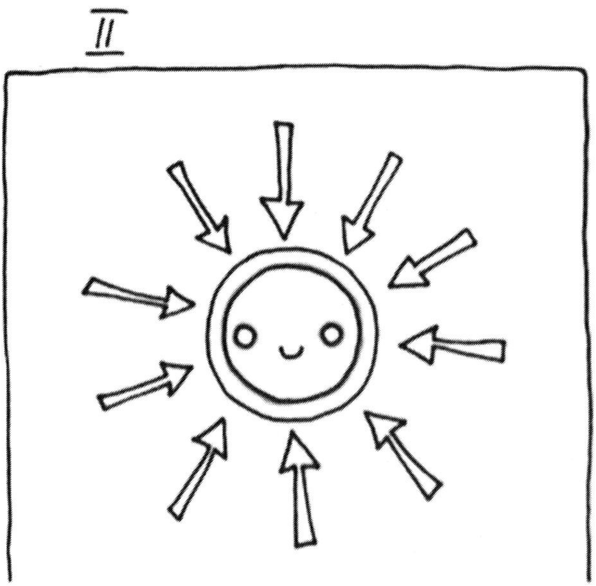

Fig. 6

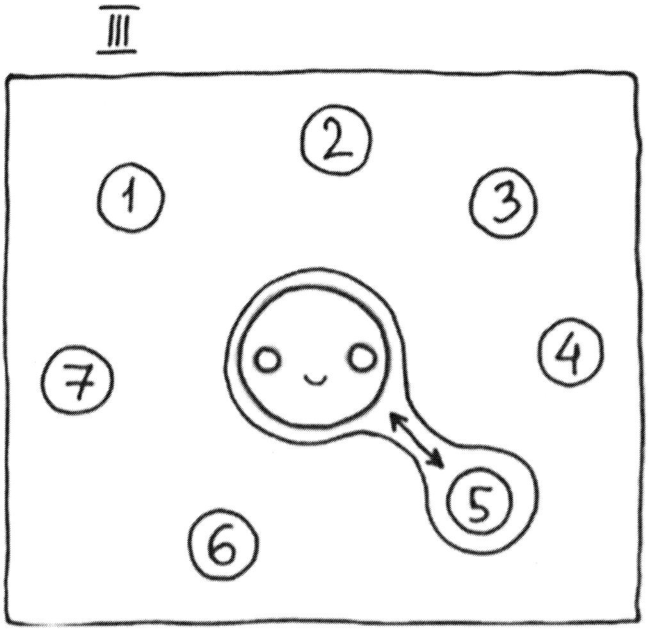

Fig. 7

What sharpens attention? First of all, silence. The second thing is music, which has a clear sound and vocals and no noise. This, too, concentrates attention on yourself and sharpens it. Many people overeat to mute this state, it's a psychological addiction. Generally, people have automatism – as an instinct of self-preservation, they in every way unconsciously suppress the feeling of self, the feeling of consciousness.

It is unpleasant for people. Because it's not familiar to them. It's scary for them. As if they are disarmed, defenceless, and vulnerable. That's why many people eat when they wake up in a state without control of the mind, with a sense of self. And it turns out that food is very much a muting factor. But it does not mean that one should not eat.

You have to eat and eat right. But in the right quantities. Avoid heavy food, and don't overeat. You can't eat as old-fashioned people do. That is, you take and eat the first course, the second course, the third course, and on the fourth, you are already like an insensitive pig. You shouldn't behave like that. Eat light food. You can have soup, salad, and fish.

But you don't have to eat potatoes with bread and hamburgers, such heavy food. They are preferred only by those who want to mute their inner self as much as possible. I hope you understand me.

It's also about what's muting you and what's not. Of course, keeping a diary, being alone with yourself, walking alone – it sharpens attention. At night attention is somehow freer than during the day. Clarity and attention are much stronger at night. It's not just because it's easier for many people to do, learn, plan or write something in the evening or at night, as late as possible. You have to manage your energy first, free your attention, concentrate it, and control it. And then it is possible to intensify it.

Maybe you think that if you're on social media, you're getting people's attention. Don't be confused. You're not feeding off the attention of the people you're looking at. You pay attention on them, you feed them. Feeding off people's attention is something else. It's what the ones who draw everyone's attention to themselves do.

You know, some people talk a lot and are very sociable, they talk loudly and emotionally, they interrupt everyone, and they draw attention to themselves. These are the kind of upstarts who feed on people's attention, provocateurs who write snarky comments to hurt people. They're all cranky people who are conflicted. These are your so-called energy vampires. The older generation has the opinion that there are some energy vampires; they heard it on shows 20 years ago.

If we talk about them, they are not some people who wish you harm, who do something to you, and you have to avoid them. No. It's not like that at all. If you take that word combination apart, I think there are people, ordinary, simple, mortal people, who unconsciously provoke everybody. And they do it because they feed on the attention, the energy that they have provoked. There are such people. That is all. They are energy vampire.

Some people are always asking a lot of questions at meetings, who are always talking emotionally, who are upstarts, who argue, all these people are often over-excited, you can see it on the physical plane in their mobility. These are energy vampires, they steal attention. That's who needs it. And the one who looks at such people is wasting his attention and energy. That's a complete fool and a sucker.

Let's talk about attention to the details. When a person is watching a movie, what details will he mention and why? One remembers absolutely nothing, the second remembers all the details, and the third doesn't remember the details, but he remembers the gist and that there were cars. Some people are more material social, people of mind; they are less sensitive, but they have mind, and intelligence, and because they are workaholics they are mentally and intellectually busy in their lives.

Their minds are always in a state of tension. They are very good at concentrating, even though they don't have much of it. They are better at it because they have control and discipline. If you tell them that they need to find something in some folder among 200 pages of documents, they will run through everything, and their attentiveness will help them to go into all the documents and find the mistake.

Not because they have a free attention span, but because they have the concentration of that attention span. Even if it's small, it's there. And some people are more sensitive, and creative, and are in extremes, in spirituality, in the inner cosmos, and in the clouds. They have a lot of free attention, but no control, no focus, and no concentration. Such people are kind of crazy, but if they sit down to watch a movie, they watch it without thinking, and they can't concentrate.

To process the information, they have to have a mind anyway, they cannot do that. And it turns out they can sit in front of the TV and remember nothing, even though they were paying attention and watching the movie. Concentration, focus, and discipline are very important. Especially for all spiritual people. Material and spiritual development are important, they intersect.

This is one of the explanations for why I am the way I am and why I differ from many other spiritual characters. Why are they different? Because they are all stoners. Almost 90% of these spiritual and yogis abuse substances, their attention is distracted, they're undisciplined, and they're not soldiers like me. I may not eat or rest, and sleep on needles, I don't care. I'll keep walking, and if I stumble and bleed, I'll keep going, because I'm focused on my goal.

I don't get distracted by anything, because I know that everything distracts me from my path, from my goal. I'm going straight ahead, that's all. I don't care who recognises me and whistles, shouts something, or shoots. I'm going straight ahead; I need to reach my goal. I have a deadline and I go. That's how I brought myself up. And when you are like that, with an inner core, no matter how much you develop your attention and consciousness, no matter how much you go into your inner cosmos and spirituality, you have discipline and order in it.

And these stoners have no discipline. They feel something, they don't know what it's called or what happened. They went somewhere, they forgot their money, they lost their wallet, that's the kind of spiritual people with a mist in their head. That's not development. That's extreme. You can't be like that. Discipline and control are very important. If we return to the question of the movie, in one case the person had free attention, but it was not like a laser, like a beam, concentrated.

In the second case, the attention was completely focused on the movie, the person has control, and he understands that he is here and now, and not just a vegetable. He clearly understands that he is watching the movie, and he remembers that this actor so-and-so, this character went there. He sees the whole chain and understands the point. It turns out that the mind is switched on.

A person should have such a mind, but even when he turns it off and concentrates, he remembers everything with his super attentiveness. If we talk about the third option, the man went so far to the extreme that he was looking for cars, but he was also watching the movie. It was like a focus of attention. He was focused only on the cars, and he didn't care about anything else.

And so, the focus of attention was no longer on the story, but just looking for some cars in the movie. That's all. The most interesting thing for me happens in the second and third cases. I turn on the movie and I don't want to go into details about the whole plot. My task is to find some part in the movie where a supernatural scene takes place, or to see some interesting parts of the film for a photo shoot.

The movie was filmed in New York, for example, and I can ignore the story and not listen to what is being said, but just look at the picture. But if the goal is to familiarise me with the film and write out all the elements that steal my attention, then I process it all with my head – delving into the plot, into each character and location.

I watch the movie carefully, alone, and take everything from it. But of course, my attention is always focused on something more. It has to do with my development, with frequencies. If I now turn on any movie and everything is noble, I immediately focus on it. Before, if I was looking for something futuristic, my attention was focused on that.

In *Pawn Sacrifice* and *Perfumer*, the character's attention span is one-sided. There is an extreme; if I am afraid of something, I will have the same thing as in the movies, and I will go mad. When your attention drifts off to something, you can lose touch with reality. And that's what I'm afraid of. Not in terms of feeling, I always have that under control. You are not threatened by it. But because I'm a genius, like in the movies, I do as much as I can to keep my mind from going mad.

Because the further you go into physics, chemistry, mathematics, and geometry, the further your attention drifts away from reality, when you're not interacting with society at all, of course, you go mad. So far, I don't see any imaginary friends and my body isn't twisted, but it feels like I'm one step away from it. And it's scary. But even if it does, it's beautiful, it's cool. They'll make a movie about me later.

I'm not far from it at all. But I don't want to get close. But the point is that many geniuses have their abilities primarily related to attentiveness. And more often than not, it is shown those people live in an extreme state.

Of course, I don't have such a crazy extreme state as the chess player in the movie. But if you watch movies, such situations happen in life. Who has strong attention? Autistic people, like in *The Accountant.* When I was in Moscow, I had many meetings there, I didn't have time to sleep.

I was going to a meeting with an acquaintance, and I started repeating numbers: 21-22-23-22-23-24. Not on purpose, it happens accidentally, when I am in a certain state. I noticed that I was repeating these numbers, and I began to tell my acquaintance. I remember, I had it when I was a child. We were standing on the street, and I was telling him that I used to repeat numbers – 2, 3, 4, 5; 2, 3, 4, 5.

Why did I repeat numbers? To focus my attention. When I didn't know how to mute myself, I didn't go out, and when I went to a meeting or waited for someone to talk, I would space out into my inner cosmos.

It was as if everything and my voice became even more voluminous as if there was a whistling in my ears. It was as if I, like a kettle, was boiling, but not physically, not as tension. It was as if a light had been turned on in me, and it was getting brighter and brighter, and now I was just going to burst into flames!

I would start repeating these numbers and repeat them until I got to a restaurant or was on public transportation. I was doing it automatically to get my thoughts together. Because it was as if I had lost control. When I was at a meeting in Moscow, I started to drift off in the same way. I also started repeating, just mumbling the numbers to myself.

I didn't know about the movie *The Accountant* when I was a kid, but in this movie, the main character experiences the same thing when he starts repeating the poem. And, the interesting thing is, when I started repeating it, it works if I starts to space out. Take this story to heart. When attention becomes too much and you lose control, you can't focus, you can do this, repeat the poem from the movie.

What about people who have experienced psychological trauma? I have often talked to people who have been in bad situations in their lives. But everyone's situation is different, and you have to look deeply into the direction I discuss in my books. There are situations where there is fate, where there is an accident, or the person was on the wrong frequency. It also depends on mental state.

In the circumstances of my childhood, someone else would have been beaten up, and the person would have become depressed and lost faith in themselves and life. But the same circumstances had a positive effect on me. My psyche reacted differently. It's the same with the person who came back from war and the person who got into a bad situation. Some people forget all about it as if it never happened.

And some remember and get caught up in it. It depends on the level of development and the psyche. But there is a slight difference. If it's one situation it can be 50-50, it can be erased from memory but not in all cases. It depends on what is the age of the victim, what kind of person the victim is, and whether they perceive the situation with their mind or not. There are a lot of buts.

And if a person has been in a war, that's a more difficult topic. If you look at war from a good point of view, a person is defending the homeland or something like that. On the other hand, your intention there was not to kill, but you did it, it was an order, and you were defending the homeland. But that's murder, and murder is a sin. And if you have killed people, then you can't sleep well, and your attention is just stolen, and your psyche is shaken. There is a game of attention here.

I shared reflections, as I usually do in books. This is psychology; there are a lot of buts. It's very multifaceted, and there's never just one answer. It depends on what? It depends on why? For what reason?

But if I answer directly to the question, "What should these people who have experienced such situations in life and whose attention has been stolen?"

In general. If something happened that was, let's say, 20 in importance, it's a shock, a great shock for you. It is too much, because your range is, say, up to 15. And there was something for 20. Of course, all your attention is there. To forget an event at 20, you have to experience something that would be, say, in terms of importance at 22.

I have used this in practice and advised many people. When they asked questions about relationships. Especially men who said they couldn't get over their ex-girlfriend. Because of that, they can't build a new relationship, and that's the problem. That's the problem I solved with attention control. It has to do with attention and level of importance.

For example, there's a guy named John, who had three girlfriends. He always remembers the second girl, and when he lost her, he built a relationship with the third, but they were so good. And he ruined that relationship because he kept remembering the second girlfriend. She fills his head, and no matter who he builds a relationship with, he still remembers girl number two.

I explained to him why this happened. Why is it that out of the three only one steals his attention, even when he's with another, new girl? Because, purely psychologically, he was more open with her than with any of the others. It's simple. He was dating girl number one. They'd go to the movies, they'd go to the store, they'd kiss, they'd cuddle. But it was modest and decent.

And with the second girl, it was so that he got sick, he threw up on her, and she cleaned up after him. And situations like that, as you understand, bring us closer together. Then she was sick, and he took her in an ambulance to the hospital, waiting all night for the doctors to tell him what was wrong with her.

Then something happened, the dog died, for example, and they both got drunk, and he didn't care so much that he walked around the apartment naked, went out to the balcony, smoked, and yelled. After that, he was out of all sorts of psychological blocks. It's as if he's the closest person to her. It turns out that with her the man is loosened up.

And then he breaks up with her and begins to build a relationship with a new, third girl. And everything seems great; the girl is smart and pretty, she has a fire, and everything is okay. But he's thinking about the second one. Why? Because he's done everything together with her. The degree of openness is like the degree of importance.

To erase that girl from your memory, you have experienced something out of the ordinary with a new girl. And then everything under the number two will be erased. That's how you rewrite everything in your head. And that's how it works for me. But not just in relationships, but in big, global events.

And what stays in your mind and memory? The things that have more focus on them. What things do you completely forget? The ones that are the least important. Because you only concentrated 2% of your attention on it you just let it drift away and don't remember it at all.

There have been a lot of questions lately from men who want to fight the urge to turn on adult movie or no longer want to look at girls with lust and so on. But they also say in this context that they forcibly forbid it to themselves. To me, it looks like the movie *The Da Vinci Code.* There was a blond psychopath who beat himself on the back with a whip. It reminds me of the same thing. To me, they are crazy people.

What was my original policy when I left home and began to study myself? I figured, what I'm drawn to is my nature. What I want is my nature. If I want to live alone, it is my nature. I listened to my heart; I was sure that it was not my mind. I had this approach, I want to smoke cigarettes; I'll smoke.

What does it have to do with power or people? There is me, there is planet Earth, and there are those who rule everything. And why do those who rule everything, those who created me, make me want to smoke by circumstance or something else? So, I smoke. Even if it kills me. So those who created me want to kill me. Okay, so that's the scenario, maybe I'll change my mind later.

That's how I looked at everything. I saw that for some reason there's a whole bunch of men who are car fans. And I have a thing for cars. I don't know why that is, but somebody did, didn't they? Somehow genetically, or circumstances have shaped it.

Where am I going with this? Naturally, everything has to be within the law. In my life, I wouldn't say it's upbringing. My parents never lectured me about it. I have a crazy aversion to illegal substances and to people who use them. I don't have any experience, I haven't seen movies about it, I don't know why I feel like that. It's like an attitude from within. Some people want to be in it. Some people get excited if you just offer them something. It's the opposite for me.

So, they're on one level of the game and I'm on another. During the wave of healthy eating, vegetarianism, and raw food, a lot of people asked me what I was eating. But I've always lived by heart, by the desire of my soul. I eat whatever I want. I've never had anyone that I didn't understand start telling me I should eat something healthy, and I just blindly listened and did it. And who is that person? At least let him live to be 100 to start listening to him.

I had a policy of basing it on how I felt after eating, what I wanted or didn't want. And some people force themselves on a diet; they force themselves to eat what they don't want and forbid themselves to eat what they want. It's horrible.

Returning to a topic of man with animal instincts. But if you're going to jump on someone in the street and walk naked in the street, you'll be put in a nuthouse or jail. If you do it reasonably and adapt to the social environment in which we live, then you can do what you want. The main thing is to stay within the law.

It's the same with food, you can eat it if you want to but don't if you don't want to. But if you eat cake and the next day you feel sick, it's clear you shouldn't eat it. That way you can know what to eat. That's how I feel. I eat one food, and I feel good afterward. I eat another food; I feel good after it.

But if you haven't come to the point where you no longer want sweets or meat, then it's a mockery of yourself to just forbid it. Yes, there are exceptions when a doctor prescribes a diet. For a while. Temporarily, you can.

Like when I say to you in a certain context, "Guys, can you please listen to rock music for a week?"

Or the other way around, "You can skip your favourite pop music for a week. Or don't eat sweets."

But I never say, "Forever."

This is extreme. You can't be at extremes. But if I now abruptly want to go to a certain frequency or reset myself, I will do it in the extreme. Because it's a technique. Then it is appropriate. But not in a day-to-day life. Don't confuse the two. It's not the same thing. When I tell you something in the context of life you do as you wish.

When I give you a concrete technique and tell you, "No sugar, otherwise it's ruined." It's a technique. It's important.

Take, for example, this book. Each reader will understand everything to the extent of his development and attention, and someone will not understand it at all. Because one only understands information from one side, from one angle. Those who are close to the edge will understand more, those who are on the other side of the edge will not understand anything. This is most often the case in learning, development, books, and in many other things.

My way of presenting information is different. I take into account all social strata and all percentages of people's attention span. Technically speaking, I take into account that some people only read MP3 format, and some read wav format. And I can tell proudly that no one can give information the way I do. It's not just a talent or an ability. It's not even about attention. It's about experience and knowledge of sociology. And that's what the practice gave me.

Every person must have the same point explained in his or her language. The cover story, words, and examples are different for everyone. Someone won't understand one example, so you have to give them many, to approach the information from different angles. It's enough that you've read it. The essence is the same. It's funny, isn't it?

Another funny thing is this: finish this book, put it aside and reread it in a month. And when you've read it all like you did the first time, that's another focus, that's what I caught myself saying that the reference for me is the movie 'The Matrix'. How many times I watch it, I see something new every time. Because the focus changes, the attention expands, and more information is perceived. What I see in 'The Matrix' now, I did not see five years ago. I mean, I perceived it differently then. This is attention and development.

6. Technique on the Chair

It's a super important technique! I've talked about it a lot! It certainly doesn't sound exciting, but it works! And everyone needs it!

The chair technique. Every day before going to bed, you have to sit for at least an hour in complete silence and darkness and not move. Just sit comfortably with your eyes closed for an hour!

Options on how and where to do this. You can sit on a chair and close yourself in a closet, in the shower, in a room, find a comfortable place! You can sit anywhere you like, as long as you don't move around for an hour. Don't get up or raise your hands. If you hear people making noise in the next room, put on earplugs! Sit like that for an hour. You can set an alarm clock.

And you have to do that every day. Before you go to sleep. For an hour! In complete darkness and complete silence. And on the chair so that you don't fall asleep! In bed, the lotus position is not suitable.

Every day after this technique, write down how you felt and what happened to you. Do not skip this task! Not a day!

Set an alarm clock. So that it will remind you to do the technique at night! So that there are no excuses you forgot, getting tired, etc. This technique will beat the laziness and fatigue out of you in the future! You have fatigue because you don't do these exercises. Amen.

I want to explain this technique. Do it for a whole month every day. When a person is irritable or has a lot of thoughts in their head that they can't stop, or just can't sit still for an hour, you need to put your attention somewhere. That is, spend that hour finding the psychological key to help you to direct your attention.

There are different ways to do this. For example, I can repeat numbers to myself or count. I can imagine numbers 1, 2, and 3 and get so involved that I count until the alarm goes off. Then, I watch to see how many digits I have reached. This is one way to do it. It is possible to use such a key and to remember the most pleasant things that happened in life. What it was like, what I looked like then, where it was, why, or how old I was. To focus on a moment of happiness and remember.

Or, on the contrary, while you are doing the technique, remember the most important emergency that happened to you and go over it in your head. You can imagine being in some holy place or your patron saint and focus on that.

Another key: as you sit with your eyes closed in the dark, imagine a ball of light in the distance, like a ball, like a moon. Try to keep the focus on it for an hour. Whatever it is, don't let it fade away, concentrate on it and hold your attention. You can also think of a place or person that you find interesting or enjoyable and think through it in your head.

You can try all the ways. Today one, tomorrow the second, then the third. When you start doing a technique, the first few days you have to find a key that helps. But you have to choose one thing, then use one key. For example, a ball of light works for you, and you only use it for the technique. You have to do the exercise after you're done for a day. It doesn't matter what your routine is. If you go to bed at 2 o'clock in the afternoon, do the technique before going to bed.

The goal is to learn how to sit for an hour so that you can do it easily. So that you can learn to put your freed-up attention somewhere. Because it's always been spent on something and now it's free. When you sit for an hour in complete darkness and silence your attention goes crazy. It's like a snake looking for somewhere to hide. That's why almost 90% of people have thoughts, especially dirty ones. That's normal.

That's how it should be. You shouldn't get upset and think that you didn't make it. Just follow my advice and you'll be fine. You don't have to be amateurish or think outside the box. Your job is to learn to do the technique so it's easy to do. You have to conquer your thoughts and restlessness by using the keys that I've described. When you have found your key, you continue to do the technique for a month. You have to get used to this state that you will come to, every time you do the technique.

What is the point of the technique? If you are going to a job interview or an exam, for example, and you are very nervous, you will remember this technique, and immediately your body and psyche will remember this state and you will be out of it. It's a good state of focus. You will be able to focus on yourself. Because you will have it in your memory. That is why you have to do the technique for a long time. Every day. It is very important.

Also, if you have some kind of emergency in your life and you are off balance. You will remember the *technique on the chair*, you don't even have to do it. You can be behind the wheel or somewhere, all you have to do is remember, and you will immediately restore your condition. You bring it back to balance.

The first of the films I have listed is *The Accountant.* I've already recommended it to a lot of people. What should you see in it? What should you look at? Let me focus your attention. Of course, you don't have to pay attention to the guns people are firing there. You have to concentrate on the fact that the main character is autistic. He's a person who has impaired attention, only in the other direction. It shows how he acts, and how anti-social he is.

They show how the doctor talks to the parents of this boy and tells them that the child needs social adaptation. But it's interesting in a different way. It shows how Ben Affleck's character has grown up and how he can live in society and communicate with people. That is, he was able to take control of his attention. Look at the keys there. To gather attention, he repeats a verse. I will tell you similar techniques.

But I wanted to tell you that this exists in life. And also, when Ben Affleck's character comes home, he turns on a strobe light, a bright flashing light, and he starts to hurt himself. That's how he comforts himself, otherwise, he spaces out. Just so you understand, I also space out the same way, only I use my keys. And notice how talented and attentive the hero is, how well he counts everything.

The situation is that society is afraid to accept this free attention. You don't have much attention if you free it. But even the attention that is given is hard to accept, to have it all freely focused on you. You are on automatic because you are not used to it. You are always trying to scatter it because you are used to it, because society does it, you always want to divert your attention somewhere.

If people have a busy life, it is easier for them because they burn that attention by travelling, talking to people, quarrelling, or by making acquaintances. And when a person has nowhere to direct his attention, his way of life is very limited – from work to home, he doesn't communicate with anyone, and there is a lot of attention, and it has to go somewhere.

That's why a lot of people divert to drinking. People start muting themselves in any way they can. The goal is to understand what things are wasting your attention, how to free up the attention, how to use it, and how to spend it so that you feel comfortable.

People describe the different conditions they feel while doing the technique. Many people have back pain, but most people do. This is normal. But it's not good. If your back hurts, it means you have a problem with it. Treat it, work on it. It has nothing to do with technique. It's good that you've noticed that you can't sit still for an hour on a flat surface. I've simply solved my back problem – you just have to build up your muscular corset. The problem is solved in a month, and you can keep your back straight.

Another tip is to sit as comfortably as possible. In this technique, you can't move your feet or hands. These are unnecessary, distracting actions that affect the psyche. Sit comfortably, as long as you stay in that position for an hour. You can with your legs crossed or you can't move your hands. The main thing is to sit quietly for an hour without any fidgeting, shifting, or getting up. That's the challenge.

Another point is that people fall asleep when they do the technique. The technique makes them sleepy. This is why the technique is done on the chair. If you do it lying down, you fall asleep. Some people feel sleepy. It's not because they didn't get enough sleep or anything like that. It's because they have too much energy.

When the energy is too much and the mind is too busy, then there is so much control over oneself that one falls asleep. You have to sit still to stay awake. That's how you can at least somehow control the process. A person does not lose consciousness because at least he keeps himself in this pose.

There are times when everything happens as it should – you sit down, you sit quietly, there are no thoughts, and time flies by quickly. Well done.

Some people turn off their mind, but they start seeing visions, and pictures, it's like they're flying somewhere, and someone stops feeling their legs and arms. If this is happening to you, it's just an unfamiliar environment. If you do the technique every day, it will pass. There won't be any illusions and heart palpitations if you get used to it and settle down, start to use this psychological key correctly and learn to concentrate on yourself and be here and now, to feel yourself. It just takes practice and you'll be fine. You have to get used to your natural state.

One element is not enough to make the technique immediately followed by a state of clarity. There are always two scales. One has all the things that mute you. The other is all that lifts you, opens you up, and turns you on. That's it. But you don't control it. And maybe one day there are not enough elements that turn you off and the ones that switch on your inner being are many. And if you also switch on a song, then you are in the inner cosmos.

But if you decide to go into inner cosmos on another day you put on a song, but it doesn't work. Why not? Because if you look at the scale, you have a lot of things that are muting you. And what fuels you isn't there at all. It doesn't depend on one thing; it depends on many things. It could be the same with the *technique in the chair*. One day it's easy for you, and the next day you can't sit through it. So, pay attention to why.

Analyse what kind of day you had before the technique. And what was yesterday? And note that yesterday when it came easily to you, you were more with yourself, less in contact with material people, more in touch with yourself, and in a quiet rhythm. But today you were in a meeting, with a lot of nervousness, a lot of stress, a lot of attention. You sat down to do the technique while you were still annoyed. It depends on the lifestyle. Why do I talk about the moments when you should be doing that, that you need discipline, control, and clearness, what do you spend your attention on, and so on? It all has an impact.

I will give you an example of myself. When I was not as I am now, I was opening and closing myself but on purpose, using all the techniques and also losing my wave, on the material side, then on the spiritual side, when I was wobbling from side to side, I had the same thing. One must get used to a state of free attention. First of all, to calm the mind, to have an understanding of it all. I used to calm myself down the same way.

Free attention is you. I am against all artificial things, against studies of the mind, where people impose themselves on others, distorting their sober view of the world. I am against all kinds of psychotropic techniques because they are also artificial. My development is for everyone. It is not imposed by my views or my taste, that's the point. The development that I give is the most authentic, natural one. One reveals oneself as one is. I don't impose what he should be. I will give you advice, it's nothing out of the ordinary.

As someone with a sober outlook on life, I say to you, "There you are, you live. But for some reason, you do so many unconscious things. Try not to do them now. Or do them differently."

And all of a sudden you were sober about it just once, and you were stunned by how it hit you. But I didn't give you any pills or medicine for that. It's just because you're not pushing buttons on your phone on social media anymore. Do you know what I mean?

We need to think about this. How bad it is in terms of awareness and sobriety. And if you are shocked by free attention, it's not bad, it's you, it's nature. What have you brought yourself to, that you feel unaccustomed to? It's a paradox. What does it look like from the outside? It's the same as I would address a society where people are, let's say, always sitting down.

And I say to them, "Get up and walk around."

People get up and walk and say, "It's terrible, it's scary, it's high, maybe my legs won't move, or I'll take a wrong step and fall."

But I'm just talking about basic things. It's the same here, only with attention. It's no good if your attention span is weak. But there is no point in being afraid of it. It is you. It is bad enough that you are so feral.

You have to get used to your free attention. You have to get used to being in this state of being, of existing. Whenever I open my attention even more, the most important rule is not to hide and not to sit at home, but on the contrary, to go to people, to society. In this state, you have to work, watch movies, meet people, walk the streets and do sports. And pay attention to what it will be like when your attention is free, and you feel yourself for the first time. There has to be an adjustment.

There is a paradox: when a person has no energy, he wants to sleep. But when he has a lot of energy, he also wants to sleep. What do you do when you feel sleepy because you have too much energy? You have to adapt. There's nothing you can do about it. You do the techniques in the chair, and you work on your attention, but what follows is to apply it socially, to spend it on something. I cannot give you a concrete list, since everyone is different.

It would be better if you weren't too lazy to notice what and how you feel. If I am doing something now, in the process, or afterward, I can pay attention to how I feel. To guess as to what psychological strain I'm under. But I have always felt that if I do this, this will take some of my attention and if I do this, I will get very tired. You have to understand that. It is very interesting.

Imagine if you could burn off the energy during a phone call in ten minutes. And you would have to exercise for three hours to achieve the same result. But a phone call is only ten minutes. And even then, you don't have to do anything physically. But the mental fatigue will be the same as if you had exercised for three hours.

And you have to weigh up for yourself, what kind of food is muting you, what recycles your energy. What's more addictive? Maybe a computer game, immersing yourself in a book, drawing, sports, or some kind of argument – people fight for a reason. Think about what Autobots do, it's very well programmed in them. That's where I take all the algorithms from, so that I, as a conscious person, can use them. And it turns out that some conflict consumes extra energy.

Before I said that attention has to be freed up, it has to be abundant, and it has to be on you. That's okay, but then you have to adapt and spend your attention on something. Or you have to learn to burn it off and spend it in a non-harmful way. Anyway, to feel good, attention has to be spent.

When you're too stupefied with attention, that's not good. It's good that it's released, but you have to learn to tame it.

I know that my potential readers with a free attention span are all a little cuckoo, just like me. In a good way. That's our peculiarity, and I think those people are alive, it's by nature. And such people can be so cuckoo that if you show them one technique or give them a chapter to read, they go into the inner cosmos. They have such hallucinations that it's scary. I don't have that. But that's just how I put it. It's explained scientifically. Why does it happen that way?

When a man comes to me and tells me that he's in a really bad way and he sees and hears something, I tell him to shut it out. I mean, shut it down. I tell him to have some nice food, have a drink, watch *Friends*, talk to noisy people, and everything will be fine, eat sweets, and don't be alone. Because loneliness reinforces that. You have to avoid spirituality; everything is languid. And the person ends it all; they become normal, there are no visions, and everything is okay. That is one way.

But there is another way to develop it further. In what sense? People who see and hear things have such weak and crooked minds that they begin to visualise and make things up. This is a certain stage of the mind. Very low. You have to get the mind developed. And then everything will be okay. Soberly, more sensibly evaluate the situation, what is human, what is what. Read history. Talk to some businessmen. Try and get a sober perspective on life, on where we're all headed. Understand what society, politics, and power are.

What is the general direction of the people, what we have come from? The more you understand things, especially psychology and sociology, the more adequate will be your reaction to the changes in your mind and psyche. And when you have a mess in your head in terms of mind, you start to call those states in the wrong way. And you see things. And no one understands you.

I don't have any visions or voices. No one flies to me, no one comes to me. There's nothing like that. No illusions. There is no going out of my body; there is no hovering or flying around. I just have a very clear feeling that my mind and my attention are working. What it's focused on and where the energy is going. Clearly.

Remember, I told you that in addition to freeing up attention, there is also its power. Some people have five points, some people have ten points. Now imagine that you have not ten but 15 powers of attention that can be released 100%. Then you are in a drunken state, in a haze; on one hand, you are distracted, but on the other hand, you know that you are not thinking about anything, but that you have a lot of attention, that it is freely available.

In this state, you have to occupy yourself with material things – eat a cookie, sit down to work, study, or do something. But then you tame the attention, it will become normal for you. And when you have 15 points of free attention that is open for a hundred, you will feel normal. It's as if the haze is gone. It's because you're used to it and you tame it. You have adapted and you spend your attention normally, there is a balance. That's what you have to do – you have to free your attention and adapt to it.

Attention is super-fast. As they say, it moves at the speed of light. The first thing you have to do is to learn how to switch from one thing to another. I say you have to learn but you don't even have to learn it. It is built into us. Where we direct our attention, it's there in a flash. Do you understand?

Here's an example. Let's say there are objects to which our attention is constantly connected, they are constantly in our mind. But it's not a process of doing, it's not a process of acting. It is the connection to what you are always preoccupied with, what you think about, and what you remember. You think about debts, about emergencies, you think about someone.

Or you are just connected to something else. You don't even feel it. There's just something that your attention is always connected to. And I'm working on that with you. And the chair technique and all the other things that I do will help you to reset yourself. To disconnect from everything. Collect yourself. We're struggling with the constant attachments.

I advise a lot of material and busy people to find at least three hours every day to be alone with themselves. Without the phone, without everything. Write in a notebook and sit staring at one spot. Or do that at least once a week. But better every day. For those who are in a completely extreme state of constantly being busy, you have to do that every day. Once a week is what I advise everyone to do, no matter how open or closed, material or spiritual. It's very important to recover one's attention and sense of self. When one loses sight of oneself one becomes an Autobot. That's not good. Attention cannot be on two things at the same time.

Attention is always somewhere in one place. It switches from one thing to another at the speed of light. There's a mistake that everybody makes – make a note of it. When you think you're doing two or three things at once, you're only focusing on one thing at a time. And the second and third things you do on autopilot. Without paying attention. And that's why people make mistakes.

Example. A man comes to an apartment on automatic, talking on the phone. He enters, throws his jacket and keys, all this he does automatically. Then he can't find his keys. Why not? Because he doesn't pay attention. Of course, we live and do things automatically. I can talk and walk automatically. The attention is always on one thing. Or it switches very quickly.

So, if you have a lot to do, it's not about attention. The main thing is not to scatter it. If you're doing one task, your attention is completely on it. That's one of the reasons why I don't drive. If I'm driving, all my attention is on the road. I won't do it on autopilot. It happens to beginners. When a person is not yet used to steering like an Autobot. The first time you're behind the wheel, you grab onto it and drive, you can't talk to anyone if a passenger talks to you.

You're afraid to get distracted. But then, as you get used to it, you do it automatically. Everything a person gets used to, he starts to do automatically. This is the first stage of living unconsciously. When I am doing something, my attention is completely here and now.

You learn to control your attention. I have had it since birth. I can feel it, so I know right away what's good for my attention and what's bad. Just like you can feel where you shouldn't put your hand because it's hot. That's how I feel when it's too much. So much so that I don't talk on the phone. Why not? Because when a person calls me, they completely take my attention, and I get hooked on them. And I'm also very sensitive. I don't need that.

Always focus on one thing at a time. Do one task first, then another.

For example, you are sitting there writing a commercial proposal, and your boss shouts at you, "Listen, call John Johnson now," here's the second task coming to you.

You can finish the proposal you've been working on and then make the call. You just have to be aware of it. But don't get caught up in your emotions. They can be very foggy. You hear the task from your boss, look where you left off, what you've done. You close the document. You call John Johnson.

You are fully aware of the situation, and what you need to talk to him about, talk to him. After the conversation is over, remember what you have been doing and open the file. You remember clearly, you are conscious of it, and start working.

The problem with people who are distracted and live on autopilot is an emotional fuss.

When a person is working on something and is asked to call someone, he immediately forgets what he was doing, so he grabs the phone, calls, and then the employee comes to him and says, "I have to take an order, the courier is here," and you run there.

When you come back, you don't remember what you were doing before. No need to rush. Do things slowly. Calmly pay attention to switching from one task to another.

Here's what else I want to tell you about attention. I have employees. They all vary in their attention span. I need to set a task. Out of ten employees, only three can complete it. Let's say the task is to order an antique figurine on eBay. Only three employees can do it. But if I set it to the other seven of the remaining, they will not do it. They'll say they can do it. They might get lucky and get it done. But it's a one-time thing. That's not my assessment. It's just nature.

Let me explain. Let's say I have a deputy, and if I give a job to one of the seven employees who can't do serious work, he'll say to me, "Are you kidding me, Alex, who did you give it to?"

Don't get me wrong. I did not assess these people, but even my assistant, who is one of the three intellectuals, understands that all this will end badly. And the people among the seven don't understand that. For them, it looks like we want to offend them. So, it's like three employees and I am laughing at the rest of them. These seven don't recognise what they are. They don't understand why we don't give them any difficult tasks.

And why are we oohing and ahhing and always saying, "Oh, just don't give him the job, otherwise it'll be horrible." They think we're such evil guys.

But the difference between the three intellectuals and the rest of the seven who are slow is attention, not experience. I have an employee, a boy, who is one of the seven. He does everything upside down. And we understand that he's just that kind of person. We don't even scold him anymore. But my deputies and I know that this boy should not be given serious tasks.

And even if we give him a super simple task, figuratively speaking, to post a photo, he gets confused about it. It's all about attention. A person's attention is not focused, it's not wired up. That's how people differ from one another. That's how it is with everything. Communication between people, relationships, and work is based on that.

Some read this book, like my seven employees. Can you imagine such a person coming to me and saying, "I want a business."

I told him, "No business. No way!"

The man says, "Why do you think I can't do it?"

"You won't make it."

Of course, there are different cases. Sometimes I don't allow a person to do business because I know he's weak in spirit and it will break him. Either he doesn't have a certain quality, or he's old-fashioned, he has no taste, and he'll go bust.

There is a global problem when I say don't do business in any way when a person's attention is not here. Remember this for the future when you choose your employees or rely on a person to buy you plane tickets, for example. If you give a job to someone who doesn't have focused attention, the result will be bad. Of course, there are many factors.

If you think back to my theory about frequencies, if someone buys you a plane ticket, preferably it should be high frequency. Then he will choose a plane that won't crash. But also, tasks with documents, with money, should be given to people who are as attentive and focused as possible.

Those who fly in the clouds can't be entrusted with such things, they will do everything wrong. Although I sincerely do not want that. Naturally, a man would not intentionally do a bad thing to himself. Of course, he was sure that he had done everything perfectly. This is the problem of lack of attention. A person's success depends on it. Let's remember the frequencies.

You can divide people into different frequencies, layers of society, and dimensions. That's understandable. But beyond that, attention itself is very important. This is what makes us all different. I can make a simple business plan very quickly in my head. No paper, just in my head. Somebody else can't. Do you know?

You give someone the task of buying a vacuum cleaner and a fan, and for some reason, he goes to one part of town for a vacuum cleaner and to the other part of the town for a fan. Not realising that it can be done in one store. It's funny, but there are people like that. And then some people take everything into account.

They are so considerate that if the boss says, "Bring a bottle of wine," and you know he doesn't drink wine and there's a good chance he doesn't have a bottle opener, you ask him, "Do you need a bottle opener?"

You have to be considerate about everything. It's very important.

Now you probably understand why people have a bad memory, don't you? And how this problem can be solved. You just have to pay attention to everything and not live on autopilot.

And always notice how your Monday is going. How did you feel on that day? Write it down for yourself.

There are people who, when they get some advice from me, rush to help their loved ones and share that advice. That's not good. You have to understand, I'm not greedy. There's another reason why I forbid it. It's sociology. Statistics.

When I studied different social strata and groups of people, I saw that those who have everything bad in life, for some reason often say out loud such things as, "I dream of making money and helping my mom," or "I'm helping my aunt," or "I want to buy this for my little sister."

I mean, people with that mindset – it's a statistic, not my wish – are a complete mess in life for some reason. I don't know why that is. I don't want to know. But there is a rule, I'm sharing it with you. I call them rules of nature. That's the way the system works, and I hack it because I'm observant and attentive. Those people who know that every man has his own life, his scenario, so they don't get involved in anything and are more concerned with themselves, they are rewarded in life. That's the statistic. A mindset with this kind of desire is bad.

I don't know why that is. It's a paradox. It's silly. I realise that if I was reading a book about some kind of magic trick right now and I would learn a trick, I would certainly want to show it to my friends and acquaintances. I don't care if it's forbidden or not. I would show it. But there's some other magic here. Maybe because it has something to do with me. I don't know.

In a particular case, when a person is interested in self-development, but has not yet had time to help himself, and already wants to help someone else, he gets punished by the system. I don't know why that is. It has to do with helping. If it's a joke, there's no charge, but if it's about help, if you have the mindset to help, they will punish you for some reason. That's how it is.

7. Sensory Organs and Attention

Touch

Search internet articles or watch documentaries about the senses. But please, if they talk about the brain, attention span, or anything else, you can't watch that! You're going to mess up your head and make the same mistake that all non-conscious people make – you have to go to the store, buy some lard and cheese and leave, but then you end up buying something extra. Unconsciousness. Like an autobot. Do you know? It's the same thing here. Find a documentary or an article about the five senses. You can Google what triggers them. But it's within that framework. You can't read or listen to anything else. This is very important.

What can you do to provoke your sense of touch? If you dip your hand into icy water or, on the contrary, touch something hot, it will steal your attention very much. Things that are out of bounds and steal attention are provocateurs. The thing that can activate the touch is the temperature in the extreme. It's pain, when you prick, when you bump, the pain sensation concentrates attention.

And you can work with it through that sense organ. That's why acupuncture and massages are also very painful. For this reason, there are mustard plasters, cupping therapy, and sports plasters. This affects everything. This is the reason why people jump into the ice-hole in the freezing cold. It's veiled, people don't really know what it is, but everything in life is arranged in such a way that it can help to reset yourself.

One of the things that can reset you is Christmas frosts, when a person jumps into an ice-hole and crazy cold water feels as if they stuck daggers in you, you could even forget to breathe. Imagine how much the sensation of cold grabs one's attention, that one even stops breathing. It's called resetting yourself. Attention shuts off from everything and gathers to a single point. It's very useful, but it doesn't mean that you have to be a vegetable and do it unconsciously, like a herd of sheep. You can now do it consciously whenever you want. It's very important.

You can take a cold or contrast shower. It's also very helpful to disconnect from everything and get your attention at one point. It's a key technique. Take a contrast shower. I don't do that; I have a different approach. I turn on a cold shower. And I just stand underneath it. And that's it, then I turn on the water at a normal temperature. But I start with cold water.

Contrast showers are great for your health and for resetting yourself. You can try my way or make up your own. But make a note of it, it helps. Whenever you feel like you're in a stupor, a contrast shower is one way to get out of it. Your attention becomes more concentrated. Those who are in the clouds and need to cheer up, please, instead of coffee, have a contrast shower.

Also, if you've just come back from work and your attention is all tied up in a day's worth of unwanted conversation – try a contrast shower instead. The main thing is not to hurt yourself. It has to be within reason.

Touch, which is the sensation of the body, is either temperature or pain. How do you use this pain? If you feel it, it focuses your attention on the point where it hurts. It doesn't concern a toothache. But still. If you have pain, the body is asks you to pay attention to it. Not only so that you realise that it hurts and go to the doctor, but also so that you pay attention to repair yourself.

People who have free attention, when they get sick, attention will be totally focused there, they will be less sick, and it will heal faster. And the one who doesn't pay attention to it, it will take a long time to heal. If you have something that hurts, you should try to feel the pain more and concentrate on it, it will help. Take note of it.

Just like with the *technique on the chair*, you sit down and concentrate on the pain for an hour. Then you will see the result.

In touch, it's also worth mentioning itching, when it tickles. Tickling is also very provocative and steals attention. You can take note of that.

But in principle, a person reacts when he is stroked or rubbed on the skin with something slimy or, on the contrary, sharp. It won't knock him out, but he will react. Then, once you understand this information, you can think of ways to use it for your own purposes.

Smell

The sense of smell is the nose that smells. Like what? Ammonia. It is used when a person loses consciousness in certain situations. For example, when blood is taken for analysis, the person begins to lose consciousness. Why? You can lose your concentration, but there is also the question of whether your concentration is on one point or whether it has simply scattered. Those are different things.

There are people who cannot stand the sight of blood or open wounds. Such a person may faint. That is, their attention shuts off. Disconnected from what? Their mind and their control. Completely. So much so that it's as if one falls into a dream. I mean, he falls. That's not good. One must not lose attention.

What happens is that not only is a person's attention freed up when he sees blood, but he is also unable to cope with it, he loses control over it. This is not good. Not only does one have to free one's attention, but one also has to hold it. And ammonia, when it is brought up to the nose, is attention, only through the smell. Imagine, just one smell brings a person's attention back and concentrates it completely on one point.

Pop – and that's it! Ammonia is the key to gathering attention. You can also provoke and collect it with all the other smells that knock most people out. These are all nasty scents, such as the smell of manure. Very often pleasant smells, such as baked goods, provoke it. Think of something else that would knock you out that would work for almost anyone.

I've given you examples of pungent smells which would knock almost anyone out and steal their attention. Although baking isn't necessarily something that would scare away anyone's attention. If a person is passionate about something and focused on that thing, it might not affect them.

But if it smells like crap, the person will react much faster. He won't be able to stand it. He'll want to do something about it. Also, don't forget the smell of burning. A way to play with attention is, of course, pleasant smells. They are different for everyone. They won't throw you off, but they will affect you. They don't just use incense sticks. It works.

Hear

Sounds. It is clear that we perceive them, and our attention is focused on some pleasant sounds of nature, melodies. But that's okay. We need to understand what steals attention, provokes, and controls.

The abrupt braking of a car immediately steals the attention of almost everyone. Except for autistic people or those in meditation. When something glass breaks, it also steals everyone's attention 99% of the time. A baby's crying is humanly normal but provocative. The moaning of a woman. Like ammonia, only for hearing – when chalk is swept across a blackboard or glass. That ghastly sound provokes and irritates everybody. There you have it, the sounds.

You can also control people by hearing. If a person or a society is not used to a sound, nobody expects it, and it suddenly comes out, and they react violently. Let's say you are watching a movie, and an alarm clock rings with the same sound as yours. Of course, there will be a reaction. Also, a rumble, an explosion. So far, it's all for hearing.

Taste

The contrasts are bitter, sour, and spicy. So far, that's it from the provocateurs.

Sight

It's more interesting with sight. We understand that we can see anything. But everyone has a degree of importance. Let's say I have it at 15 points and someone else has it at 17 points. So, if something is shown to me visually at 16 points, it will steal my attention. For me, it will be the unknown, and that's it, I'm off balanced.

But if it's shown to a man of 17 points he won't be disturbed. Because he has a higher degree of importance. What will be shown to him is normal for him. He will be put out of balance if something happens that is outside the limit, that is above 17 points. That is the degree of importance.

You have to write down for yourself what's out of line for you, and what throws you off balance. Let's say that the common degree of importance people have is 50 points. Some people have 30 points, some people have 20 points, some people have 40, and some people have 50. But more than 50, let's say, people, don't have more than 50. That is the limit for them. Something very provocative.

What throws off balance a lot of people, not all 100%, but a large percentage of people? For example, we're sitting in an auditorium writing a paper and suddenly naked people are walking around at the end of the room. Or in front of us, in the distance. And that's it, it provokes the audience. So, people sit there and see this, and that's it, it will put them off balance. Why? Because it's unusual in our world. It's considered intimate, forbidden. It's already out of bounds.

And this is the beyond we need to know. A naked person is the gathering of attention to one point. In the sense that if a stranger sits in front of me and I undress in front of him, without telling him, of course, his mind will shut down.

The mind will not cope, because it is beyond him, his attention will gather into one point, and the person will be as if he's in a vacuum. He'll be lost in time, in space; he'll forget what we've talked about before, what he's planning. If I stand naked in front of him and talk for an hour or two, he won't even know how much time has passed. I could talk to him for three hours like that, but for him, it would be like ten minutes. That's how much it will throw him off balance. Imagine, nothing happens to a person, he just sees a picture, and he has this reaction.

What else steals people's attention? Money. A lot of money. Or something very expensive. For example, if they are walking down the street and they see an expensive car, they just forget where they've been going, and what they've been talking about. They stand and look at that car. Imagine how easy it is to control their attention. Which, consequently, is what is done to them. This is a point to keep in mind.

We've listed nudity, money and all sorts of violence, blood – all sorts of things that are not yet known to everyone. If a man walks in blood and without an arm, it steals attention, it throws you off your balance.

And if a person sees some miracle, for example, a flying saucer flies in front of him, something unexplored, it is a shock, and all attention shuts off from everything. It is the same if he sees some catastrophe. This applies to the five senses.

Information

We talked about the senses. I also talked about what provokes each of these sensory organs. Now you have to tie it all together, which is what attention work is all about. That's what I'm trying to get across to you. Now you have to look at it more carefully. Find some examples for each of your senses. How attention plays through it. What can trigger any of the senses? What can control attention? But the most powerful thing that can manipulate attention is words. Our speech. Information.

It can either be written in text or heard from a person's mouth – in an audio call or a recording. It can be a radio broadcast or a handwritten letter. It's something I'm very much friends with, as you can see. And it's something you have to learn too, it's very important. But again, going by the level of importance. What is beyond a person's level of importance? What is the information that could throw him off? What is it that he can't cope with, that will focus his attention on one point?

I gave an example about the dog. I got a call, so it was through hearing that the dog had died. And if it's out of bounds for me, it will throw me off balance and I'll forget what I was talking about and get lost in time and space. But it's not about what I'll hear as sounds. It's not the sensory organ hearing at work here. It's not about it, it's about the information.

I'm getting a message; I'm being told a situation that's throwing me off balance. Make a list of what words and sentences can steal a person's attention. And it will all be beyond the scope of the discussion. If you talk about it, the person will go into a state of shock and trance, their mind will shut down.

Effects on the senses and information are used in hypnosis. I meet a person and talk to him face-to-face, and we discuss everyday life and various situations in life. But if I talk about something beyond, the person begins to feel strange and falls as if, into meditation.

That is, everything becomes three-dimensional. If I talk at a restaurant, for example, he will stop being distracted and irritated by sounds and people, and he will forget about everything. He will only see my face. And it's like he won't even be able to focus on it if I tell him something that's off-limits. Time flies by.

That is, once I start saying something like that, five hours will pass, and it will seem like only half an hour or an hour to him. The attention of the person will be so stolen that they will eat automatically and not taste the food. This is real attention control. But what is this beyond? What do I have to talk about to make it happen?

Of course, there are many examples and exceptions. I need to give you the ones that are sure to work for everyone. If something can be provoked by sight, that is, by the senses, the same reaction can be provoked by simply telling. For example, I will talk to a person about something that he is ashamed of. Something that is beyond him. He's never talked about it, he's afraid, and he's shy. It's unacceptable in society, something out of the ordinary.

And it really throws people off, for example, if you start asking questions like, "Hey, did you peed in your bed when you were a child?"

Can you imagine saying that to a person's face? His body temperature would immediately go up, there would be whistling in his ears, and he would be out. Of course, everyone will immediately turn on some kind of defence. A person will want to turn off his mind. A distraction. But this, too, can be stopped.

Another thing about talking. You start talking about something so frank that it can also throw a person off balance. Say, for example, how you witnessed some disaster and describe it. If it's anything out of the ordinary, it too will steal his attention, shut his mind, and focus it all on you. It can be something mystical, but not in all cases.

Of course, man is afraid of losing control, he's always shielding himself with his mind, always trying to disprove everything. But if you talk about something high, something beyond, let's say, aliens, it can also gather your attention to one point.

What other information steals attention? Revelations, confessions about something. To see if it works, you can focus on yourself. If you touch on a subject that is hard for you to voice, to say out loud, and you feel that you yourself lose your breath the moment you ask or say something like that, then it will work just as well for the person who will hear it.

It could be about some kind of catastrophe, a cataclysm. Such news also provokes attention. These are standard topics. There are also individual ones, of course. But I won't give you examples so that you don't get confused. You need to feel for the person, to understand all the layers of society, which layer your interlocutor comes from, and his degree of importance.

If he is from the level where he has a level of importance between one and five, everything you say beyond five will throw him off balance. And there's a majority of them in society. That's why 99% react by looking at pictures of naked girls, cars, and everything luxurious. This steals their attention. It is a vicious circle: people who have so little power over people's attention are afraid of losing it.

Because attention is money. Even good and noble people sink to such a low level that they start talking about scandals, gossip, and intrigue. The same information circulates on the internet. It's for unintelligent people.

When you turn to normal people who promote all this and ask, "Why are you doing this?"

They say, "Well, Alex, understand, if we talk about smart stuff, about history, science or your sociology and psychology, we'll lose the whole audience. People don't need it."

I say, "It's better not to adapt to that audience. It's better to make them lose that feeding and start to be interested in other things."

But nobody dares to do it, because it's all about money.

When I was a kid, I was faced with this choice. Before the temptation to do something fun, comedic, and showy, I could do it with no effort. But why? It's not self-respecting to stoop to that. So, the way I approached it was this: let a few people know me, let me spend years building what I think is valuable and necessary and useful, let there be a small audience who will be interested in it, but it all will remain real.

So, in addition to the five senses, there is information that can be used in communicating with people: in dialogue, in conversation, and in correspondence.

Here's what I want to show you. Draw a diagram like this. And don't draw from zero but from five to ten.

It's roughly five to ten. For each. This is what range your attention is in (Fig. 8).

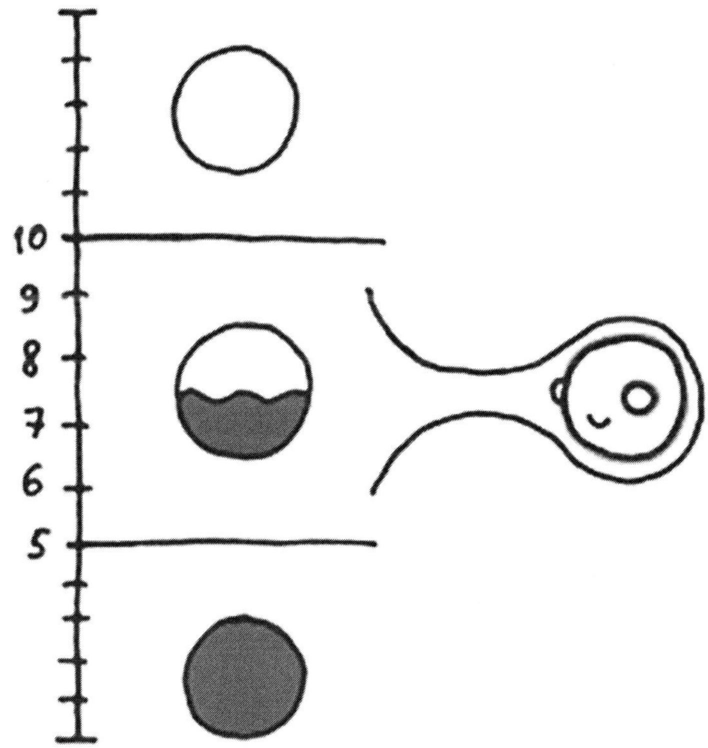

Fig. 8

When you live in society, what you pay attention to is five to ten. This is a measure of your level of development. If I propose or show you something below five – 4, 3, 2, 1 – you don't want it because you've already learned it. It doesn't steal your attention. You are still in the five to ten range.

This you have come to know. This you know. But above ten, that's not learned, that's beyond. And it will always be out of bounds. The examples I described above are based on the five senses.

Here's another example. In the symbolism of the Freemasons, there is such a circle. And there are degrees. Each degree is the level of a disciple mason. The most important one, who rules everything, the geometer of the universe, the architect, is 33 (Fig. 9).

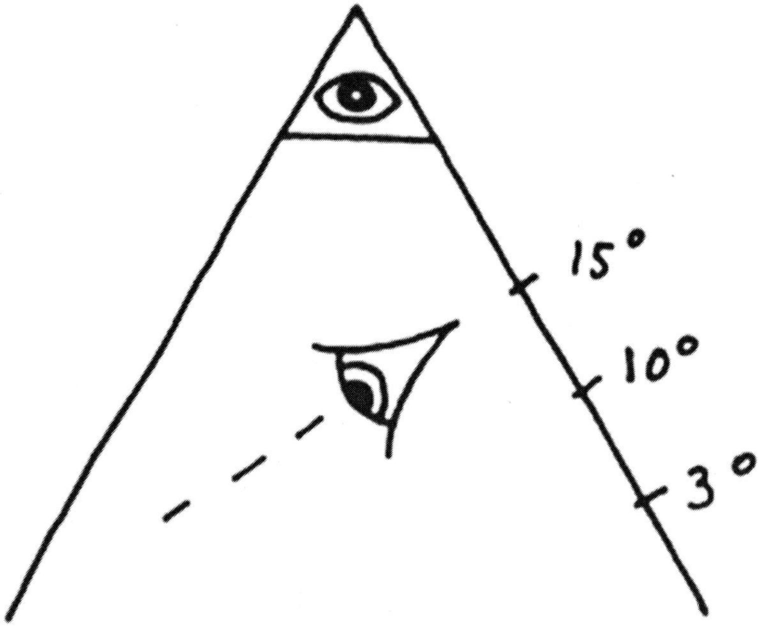

Fig. 9

Here's the trick. If you've developed on three, your attention is at this angle. From above, you see everything as it is. And at the third degree, it is distorted. The more you evolve, the wider the angle of view to everything, you see more of the truth. If you get to that level, you can see everything.

And the example is the same. There is a cube, if your degree is on the three, you don't see it. And if it's in the middle, you already see some part of it, but only one. And when you get to the top, you see the whole thing (Fig. 10).

To make you understand the degree of importance, we need to go back to the most basic of all, making a list from scratch, what steals your attention? Cognizant and Cognize. Cognize is where you are now.

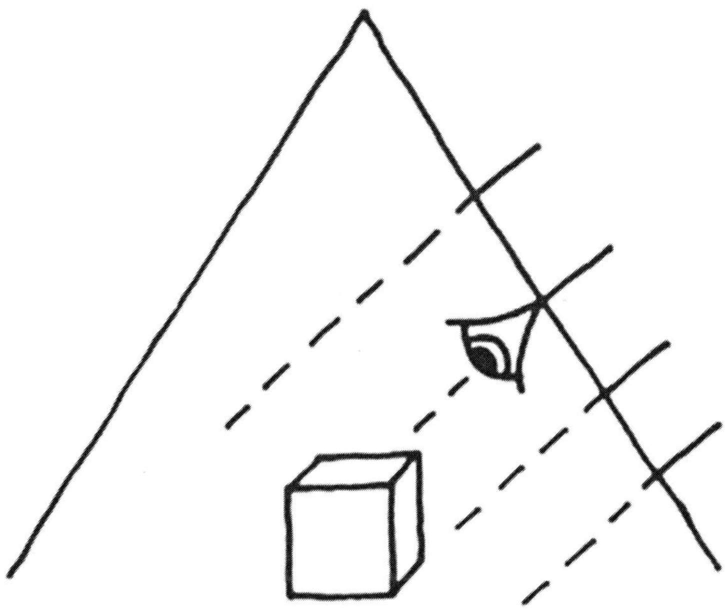

Fig. 10

I've been studying people. There is object B, a character. I understood that he is different from other people. And I looked at everything, what he prefers, what he chooses, what he wants – everything that his attention is on, what his choice has fallen on. What he wears, what colours he wears, what he listens to, what he eats. Everything. I was making a mould of what that person is.

Up to the point where I would invite subject B into my place, and I could observe what he would pay attention to. People from different worlds react differently to everything.

One will come into my house, "Oh! You have a PlayStation, you have a Nintendo."

Somebody's acting like that. You do it, too. But I always wonder, *Why, of all the objects in here, this is the first thing he noticed.*

And the other object C didn't notice it at all and paid attention to something else. A paradox? It explains that the frequencies and layers of society are different, and the focus of each one is on different things.

Another person will come in and say, "Wow, how much alcohol you have?!"

Why would a person react like that? Because it's in his world. And someone else has computer games in their world. That doesn't mean the person has a Nintendo and a PlayStation. He may not have it. But there is a desire for it. He wants it. He is focused on it. It's what steals his attention, what he fixates on in life.

Someone reacts to the interior; he has a focus on that. Maybe it has to do with his work, maybe he's recently done renovations. It doesn't matter. Now he's focusing on that. I always pay attention to who's focusing on what. The same thing happens on the internet. When you're flipping through social media and looking at something online, you all pay attention to different things.

Even if my employee and I subscribe to a hundred identical accounts, he'll pay attention to one type of post, and I'll pay attention to a completely different one. And that explains our difference, why he's my assistant and I'm not his. Do you see? That's what needs to be understood first.

If I choose 20 different pictures now, that will be an indicator of my level. And the ones my employee chooses are an indicator of his level of development and his focus, range. This is very important.

Please pay attention to what is stealing your attention. What you are wasting it on. It's not about the day-to-day stuff. It's about the big picture.

With a conscious approach, pay attention again. Start the day and observe what you are looking at. As you walk down the street, pay attention to what you're focusing on. If it's cars, which ones, write it down for yourself. If people, which ones? Take a picture of them or write the description down.

If you pay attention to something on the internet, make a note of it. If you come to the store, walk around the mall, and notice which stores will steal your attention, which things, colours, and products. But it is better to look directly on the internet, to Google all sorts of sites, what your attention is drawn to.

Anything that steals your attention is what you learn! That would be the range of five to ten.

But the known and the unknowable… If a person surfs social networks, he will not see something. The reason he's not paying attention to something is that he either already knows it, or he doesn't know it yet. It passes your attention. And everything that you pay attention to, you learn.

Let's imagine that a person's mind can be developed from one to 12. That is your mind. If it is developed by two, when it shuts down, attention is freed up. But it is hard for a person to concentrate. It's hard for him to keep control in a state with no mind, that is, it's not easy to concentrate all the attention on one goal. And if a person's mind is developed up to ten, it's hard to turn it off.

But if you can, then the memory of the mind helps you. Attention is free, you can manage it very well, and concentrate on it. That is, even with no mind, attention is more under the control of those people who have a well-developed mind. And this explains why people in the extreme, in spirituality, when attention becomes abundant and the mind is hardly developed, become like vegetables. It's hard for them to concentrate.

And if you shut off the mind and free up the attention to people who are more closed and material, they handle it better. A thing to take note of: it's very important to develop the mind. For attention. It makes a big difference. Where does one start to develop the mind to make it stronger? Discipline, friendship with time, doing everything on time. That is, with control of time and space. This is very important. Discipline, control, responsibility, and being alert all the time – this is what help to develop the mind.

A long time ago, I discovered attention and began to learn about it and tracking it. It was 2011. I was noticing what I was wasting it on. I was very conscious of what I was doing. With the help of attention, I could feel people, control the energy, connect to any person, to his frequency, and discover for myself a new topic of frequencies, that is the social layers of society and worlds.

The most important thing that I stated in my books was, "Don't provoke and don't fall for provocation."

I realised that as long as something could set me off, that is, provoke me, I was weak. I then realised that I was the focus. And that if I get to know it, look at it from the outside, look at it in detail, I will know myself. And I began to do that, which I advise you to do.

Example. Let's imagine that I am just an ordinary boy named Alex. I am 20 years old. I read this book, and different examples of what attention is, how important it is, etc. But I, this boy Alex, go to work at nine in the morning. And while I'm driving to work, talking to people there, while I'm on social media, while I'm coming back home, I start to think about what I think, what I look at, what I want – that's who I am.

I don't know it, so my attention is focused on it. If I, a boy named Alex, who is 20 years old, look and pay attention to successful people, then I have not learned it, but I want it very much. If I pay attention to the opposite sex, it means I don't have it and I want it, it will always worry me. That is, I will always want it until I get it. And if I'm paying attention to something in the movies, that's what my focus is on, that's me. Do you understand?

When you begin to learn about attention, you may notice where the limit is. Example: I, a boy named Alex, went with the guys on Saturday to a restaurant. And I saw a girl I liked, and I told the guys about it.

And they said, "Go over there and introduce yourself."

And let's say, "She works behind the bar."

And I said, "No, I don't want to."

But if Alex is reading this book now, he has to register and understand that if he had known this situation, it would have been an ordinary situation for him. And if he starts to feel some mood swings and has some kind of reaction to the situation, it means that he has not come to know it yet. That's why I'm writing all this.

The situation is that I'm in a position now where I no longer experience what you people do. In the past, when I had a breakthrough, I'd write a chapter with emotion. In a kind of vacuum and inner cosmos, in a state of perception because it was a discovery for me. I don't experience that now. And the point is that you have to learn to free up your attention as much as possible. So much so that if the boy Alex comes to visit some castle made of gold, his mood will not change. He won't care.

You have to become experienced in everything to develop. Imagine how I am now – even if something really scary would happen in front of me, I don't react. That's the thing. That's my advice to you. I'm not talking about attention control; I'm talking about how important it is to broaden your horizons.

It would be very difficult for me to make a list of what else could shake me. And what can knock you out is a huge list. It's what you haven't yet learned and what you need to learn. Why do you need it? First of all, it's confidence. All people are divided into those who know and those who don't know. The more you know, the fewer fears you have.

Because fears are ignorance. In our society, people know very little. They are self-conscious, they don't reveal themselves, they can't be themselves, and they go around in masks. In front of relatives or friends, they are ashamed to say how much they've pissed each other off or are afraid to confess their feelings to people. Such a stifled society. Imagine how much fear they have in life.

To become strong and truly alive, you have to break those boundaries. You have to say everything you think, everything you feel. And you have to write down everything you're afraid of. To overcome this in the future. It is very important. These are psychological blocks that will affect your life, work, and everything in general.

Let me explain with an example what your attention is. It's very much about the senses and what's beyond, what's put you off, and what's not known. It's an intimate life. We are all human; we are all born into some kind of family. Then, of course, fate and circumstances are different for everyone, and that's understandable. But we're all ordinary people, we pee, we eat, and we all have luck and success at something.

And imagine the situation. A man and a woman build a relationship and they live together for ten years. But to this day they cannot talk frankly about something intimate. They have all these conversations through insecure banter, you know, when people are shy, they talk that way on an intimate subject. It's over the edge for them, a shock if a man and a woman start talking frankly about intimate things.

When I was making a list of things that I and people are scared of, I came across the topic of intimacy and that I am afraid to talk about it, what kind of superhuman am I then? I'm not ready to save the world and turn the world upside down at all if such nonsense is unknown to me and blows my mind. Do you understand? And imagine that there are a lot of examples and situations like this when it is scary to say something. It's important to loosen that up. Then your attention becomes very strong and freed up.

Let me give you another example. When I was a child, when my father said something to me or spoke ill of something, I usually kept quiet if I disagreed with him. I couldn't say no to him. But that's the problem. It's not normal. It's a weakness.

Let's imagine that I could say no and say what I like or dislike. It's cool when you can't just say that, but generally, give your opinion on everything to a person who is your authority. Like between children and parents. Not in terms of emotional conflict, but to sit the person down in front of you and tell them everything. I mean, that's just wow!

On the one hand, it was cool, I achieved what I wanted – more attention, I became even stronger and grew. And my psyche got even stronger. On the other side, there is no one left who could be an authority for me. It made me sad. And that's the way it needs to be in everything.

Let me give you an example of a restaurant. You go to the most expensive restaurant. Someone will be afraid when they go in, will feel insecure, will stand with a long face, and scare the hostess. Imagine, you are already in a bad mood at the entrance, you are shaking. It's a weakness. It must be overcome. Go towards fear.

Let's imagine that there are people who are not so afraid. They will calmly walk into a restaurant, smile, and say they need a table. Such a person will walk through and sit down. He seems to feel free, but he still has a limit. Someone has a limit, he's afraid of the whole situation at the entrance, and someone else sits down at a table and everything is okay, but he's afraid, let's say, to talk to the people at the next table. Or is afraid to talk to the restaurant manager.

You need to have such an expanded limit that you can be in the restaurant and say, "Young lady, can you get me the manager?"

And he comes in and you go, "Listen, I'm sitting here eating, and they're playing two of my favourite songs in a row. Who picked out the music, I'm just curious. Was it the owners themselves or maybe you or somebody else? Let me see that person's face, who has such great taste. It could be someone I know!"

And of course, I say it with a smile. And it turns out you have to be so experienced that you don't feel uncomfortable in any situation.

Another example. If I order a car now, a cab, business class. It arrives, and I sit in it with my laptop and a portable table, and I can say, "Let's drive off somewhere to the waterfront. I want to sit in the car and work with my headphones on."

And that's it. I can use a cab like that. Some of you can also do this calmly. But only a few, many are afraid to do something out of the ordinary. Although it's not a violation of the law. And you can remember the cases when you were told to do something, and you were afraid, or you were suddenly lost for some reason. Write down your list of fears.

These are the things that steal your attention. And it always will. It's a bad thing. That's where it gets stuck in your head. If I go somewhere, I can't hear anybody, I can't see anybody. I only feel myself and I go. I can dance in peace. I'm so experienced I don't care what people think, nothing. I can put on a robe and a jacket and go somewhere in my slippers. I don't care. But not because I'm so cool and so on. No. It's psychological.

The point is that there are public people. Rich people. But they can't behave like that, they have a lot of psychological problems, fears, and complexes. The people you see on TV are famous and rich. But they are shy and afraid to talk about a lot of things. That's not good. You can't let yourself get worked up like that. You have to broaden your mind. You have to realise that you are the attention. When you are afraid to say and do something, it means that your attention has not learned it. Everything that your attention focuses on and does not focus on is your level of development. You have to have your attention at such a level that nothing can provoke you.

What else can sober up the attention? Breathing and arguments. The first is used in many practices and you know it. In martial arts, meditation, etc., breathing is very important. It is the most convenient practice, which is always at hand. It is very useful to learn how to breathe correctly. By practicing some techniques, you can always balance your state, and calm yourself down. If there's something inside that's freaking out, or some stress, you can always calm yourself down with a breathing technique.

I advise you to learn it, but not by yourself, go to a place where they teach it. I know that they teach it in karate, wushu, qigong, and Reiki. If you do not have time or the desire to go somewhere, you can look for a video. There are different practices related to attention that help to calm down. It is useful.

Breathing has been used in all cultures and practices. I didn't learn it, it just happens by itself, I just feel what bothers me and what doesn't. When I concentrate, especially when I do techniques, I stop breathing for that moment. But I won't hold my breath deliberately and then not breathe. No. I try to be as slow as possible, almost not breathing.

But I won't hold my breath. It happened by itself because when I was watching myself doing some techniques, I was already detecting that I was breathing this way and that way. And then I advised people individually about breathing.

What else is interesting about the keys that affect a person's attention and psychological state? When there is a quarrel or a conflict, remember if you had one, and how you felt afterward. It doesn't matter if you were the victim or the initiator. Think back to how you felt afterward. More often than not, after a fight, the mind and all the ties to society turn off. They are all abruptly cut off.

And when a person has experienced a serious conflict that disconnects him from everything, he gets into a state as if they are in himself. After an argument, you can just sit somewhere in a corner and sit for an hour. It's a state of shock. I advise you to use these states if you're going to have similar situations of conflict. It doesn't matter whether you have a conflict in the family, in a relationship, or at work.

It's a good bonus and a good key. It's exactly what I've often mentioned in my books, that everyone is given a chance every day to open up. And he misses it. It is just a chance. When a man has an emergency, not only a conflict, but his attention also disconnects from everything and focuses inside, and the person retreats into himself. His attention shifts from society to himself.

In this state, you can feel your inner self, because you have no thoughts, and ask yourself what you want. At this moment your soul is open to you. The longer you are in this state, the attention is completely focused on your whole body, on all the aches and pains, the faster you recover.

It's very good for your health. In this state, you can write a great song, paint a picture, or write a chapter of a book, as an example. In this state, you should try to pour yourself out. It is better to take out your notebook and write something to yourself. Whatever you have, right away, without pausing, without thinking, just take it and write it down. In this state, a person can feel the energy, turn on the chakras, and meditate.

That is open to all kinds of miracles. But people do not stay in this state. More often than not they try to get out of it as quickly as possible, to distract themselves. People immediately run to drink, smoke, call someone, or open social networks. Try to take this chance, which is given from above, and not be distracted from it. On the contrary, take it all in. It's one of the reasons I've stayed true to who I am, thanks to experiences like this since I was a kid.

You have to exacerbate this condition. If there's a conflict, you don't have to run off to do things in five minutes, as if nothing happened. And you have to sit in a room without a phone, sit by the window, and that state of contemplation is the most amazing.

The telephone is a very strong factor in society, this thing is from a demon. Of course, it should be used, but people are so weak in spirit that they are addicted. Originally, the telephone and the internet were invented for the good of humanity, and now it is killing humanity.

A lot of what I give in the books is what I've practiced, what I know. My attention is more developed. I did the following experiment: I turned off all the telephones and disappeared from everyone, without warning anyone. I just put away my gadgets for 24 hours.

Social networks and peoples' ties are very influential. You have no idea. I live by the rules: 50% social, 50% alone. If I'm with other people from 6 o'clock in the morning to 3 o'clock in the afternoon, and I'm alone with myself from 6 o'clock in the morning until bedtime, it's still not enough. It's good and useful, but it's not enough.

If I do a technique on the same day, it will be more difficult than if I didn't talk to anyone for 24 hours. Why did I disappear and for what purpose? We are very much affected when people know where we are and when we know about them when there is that connection. It's a very bad thing.

Let me give you an example. One time I came back from the US and didn't tell anyone about it. It didn't matter who the people were – friends or strangers, it was enough that it was a person. And when no one knew that I was in Russia, I felt incredible, very unusual. It was paradoxical. Even though I didn't seem to have done anything supernatural. I just came to another city or country, without telling anyone.

But you have no idea how crazy the difference is psychological. Write it down for yourself to try out. Maybe some unattached singles often feel that way. But to such people, on the contrary, I advise you to socialise with people to feel the contrast. Most people have acquaintances, relationships, family, relatives, and superiors. If you go somewhere for a day without telling anyone, you'll feel an incredible state, as if you were some kind of God. You will feel very special.

The first time I did it, I labelled it as if I had now screwed society. It always connects to me, and I to it, and society is aware of everything – at least one person should say something, and I am already in society. And when I'm all alone, no one knows where I've gone, where I'm sleeping tonight, where I'll be tomorrow, then I disconnect from society and become a thousand times stronger, more concentrated, more charged, and so on.

And so, I was gone, no one knew where I was or what I was. I wasn't logging on to any social media. All my attention was on the walls of the apartment and my hands. It's also one of the indicators of awareness. When you don't use your phone for more than a day and you look in the mirror or at your hands, it increases the state of awareness. You will feel strange. It's that kind of sobriety.

There is a fine line. There are mortal sins, and these are the things that are so beyond the line that they disconnect attention from everything. It would make all life meaningless, so much so that attention would be turned off from everything. But it will not be freed, it will be stolen away forever by this crime. This is a mortal sin. Because some percentage of attention will be stolen and in the future life you will never have 100% attention on something, no matter what you do, whether it's building a family, business, or developing.

That is, you cannot do it anymore and there is no point in life anymore. This is why it is considered a mortal sin. Imagine that there is a model of life in which we live, everything is ruled by aliens who wrote down all these rules in the Bible. So, if we break the rules and commit a mortal sin, that's it. This is the violation, by committing which the system and people stop working on a person.

His soul and consciousness will no longer develop. Because he is already defective. His destiny is finished. And this person will not be able to live a normal life, he will be in torment, it is bad. He loses the meaning of life because his attention has turned off from everything.

And he is always focused on the darkness, on the crime that he has committed, and nothing can touch him except that. And he wants to commit crimes again, as maniacs do. It's a sin because the attention is stolen, and it doesn't come back. That's what mortal sins are. Committing them should never be allowed.

There are so many things limiting you that it's too early for you to think of any mortal sins. You have to make yourself free, you have to be so experienced to be above all people. Going out, you would be able to go up to anyone, talk to anyone, and go into any establishment. It would be like you were inquisitive about everything, you weren't afraid of anything. But the main thing is that it should be within the limits of awareness, of adequacy.

There's nothing good about jumping up on a table in a restaurant. You're gonna look like a fool. That's not the point. It's not about doing something wild. It's about basic things that people are usually modest, shy, and limited about.

Your attention has to be so free; you have to overcome those limitations. Limitations are when you can't fully express your emotions. If you're on public transportation and you're listening to music, smile and sing along. And the fact that people will look at you frowning and crooked, that's people's problem.

We should make a list of such elementary and primitive mundane things. And mortal sins are mortal sins. They must never be committed. It's a limitation. Understand, when a person has cheated, lied, or stolen, he keeps it in his head 24 hours a day. That's stolen attention. It's a block.

Is it possible to communicate your feelings to another person? If you answer the question *can you do that*, you can. Is it related to attention? Attention is everywhere. I manifested this feeling of people when I left home. Let's find attention in this story.

I left home. My ties to everything I was used to and to the people I was in touch with were severed. My attention was freed. I started to feel myself more and more. It made me hear everything more in dimensions – the music, the movies. It's like I'm going through it. Films gave me a lot of information. Because when I lived alone, I was immersed in every movie, in a state of shock, with my 100% attention.

It was as if I was living through everything for the characters. The information flowed into me. It was as if I was becoming the music I was listening to, resonating with it. When I was looking at something on the internet, I saw a picture of a person, I looked at him and into his eyes and I started to feel. When your attention is completely collected in you, it's like there's no emotion.

There is just a feeling for yourself and that's all. No emotions, no thoughts. And that was my usual state, I was used to it. But when I felt there was a change in it, I noticed that it wasn't mine, that I wasn't feeling myself, but the person. That is to say that I noticed my attention span when I was at home alone. But if I start to read a text that someone has written to me or if I look at a photograph of someone, I begin to feel them in me. Let's say that I start to feel fear or love or greed. But I realise it's not my feeling. I wrote to the person about it, and he is shocked and doesn't understand how I knew it.

Or, for example, I meet a man. While I didn't see him, my attention was on myself, but once I did, I started to feel something. And everything I feel in myself is not my feelings, but his. I describe all this to him, and he is shocked at how I found out about it. If you look at it scientifically, there are no miracles. Yes, it will take a lot of time to practice what I'm describing.

But if you reach a level of free attention, and you learn how to gather it into one point, and then you concentrate like that, you become psychic. That's how it works. It's how I began to see through people, to feel them, to sense their energy. I focus my attention on the palms of my hands, and they start to burn. Or I focus on my heart chakra and feel the heat.

It turns out that it's not even about how and where to direct attention and energy. The most important task for everyone is to make themselves free psychologically. That's the secret. When I was approached by people who practice non-contact fighting, they wanted to know from me how I get people to do it. I did not teach anything in terms of information at the time.

I had a *channel opening* technique back then that gave me that state. And they wanted to know the technique, they explained that when they train people in non-contact fighting, they have to free up people's attention for the first year or two. And only when the person is zero, they can teach them non-contact fighting. And you wanted to understand how I became such a zero and what I'm doing for that.

I will lead you to that so that you can learn it. I'm still a young, modern guy and I'm a sceptic. All this information about living on a schedule, banning yourself from the internet, and paying attention to your every action – it's so meticulous, tedious, complicated, and uninteresting. It's really hard to force myself to be disciplined. It's very torturous, even though it's important, what I've been giving you and I am giving you now.

But when you start working with attention, when you start practicing with energy, it becomes very interesting. You start to go deeper into it, and you realise that attention is miraculous. When you start concentrating on food, drinks, chakras, people, to transmit feelings, and people start to feel, when you start working like that, it's amazing.

And when you get your attention so developed that you can sit at home and connect to some holy place that is in another part of the world and feel as if you are physically there, then it turns out that you can be in different countries and cities, just by focusing your attention through pictures, you can feel the energy of the place. When people told me about some countries, some cities, some food, or people, that I had never seen in person, I already knew what it was and how it was.

But of course, no one believed me, they said, "How could it be?"

But I knew it because I was paying attention. And when I physically encountered it afterward, there was no difference for me.

Here's a typical situation, maybe you've seen it in movies. A man comes to a shaman, and the shaman gives him something to drink, hits a tambourine, or cuts up a mouse in front of you. And then he says something to you and does something to you. And after that, he advises you to do something for a week. This is programming. By the way, I can do that, but I don't have to kill the mouse.

The way it works is this: a person comes in, he's closed, and his attention is in society. To work on him, you have to completely disconnect his attention from everything, so that he is here and now. All of these rituals are built on attention. It's a shock for a man when he sees blood being transfused or a mouse being chopped up. The most interesting thing is that the shamans themselves do this to go even further into shock and trance, to turn off the mind and attachments. They go to the frequency of no mind, where you are zero, or have no attachments. And then all this shamanism happens.

In addition to the visual method, there is also a drum. What are its benefits? Try it yourself. Take a pen, preferably with a cap, so that the ink doesn't stain anything, sit down at the table and knock on a surface, for example, on the table. Knock in the same rhythm, just knock and that's it. Do this for at least three or five minutes.

And you will get to the point where you feel as if you have gone into some kind of flow as if your thoughts have turned off and you are in unison with the rhythm. It's the same principle as with the drums. That's one of the ways it works to turn off your attention and go into a trance. You just beat the drum to the same rhythm, and after a while, you're out of your mind in the flow.

There is such a point that every person has some *chakra* on. That is he is in a certain rhythm, on a certain frequency. Some women have energy of passion turned on. And this is so strong, that she can look ugly in her face and body, and she can be dressed horribly, but sensitive people can feel this, and she will attract them even if she does not want to. And then there's the opposite, a woman is super beautiful and well-groomed, but she has this *chakra* turned off. And she is not attractive. That's the paradox.

It's not just about sexuality; there are many other *chakras* and many different emotions and energies that people feel. What you and I can learn is that when your attention is completely free, you are zero. But you can calmly concentrate on any emotion. It's like you become a master of emotion and feeling. You can amplify an emotion with music.

That's how I wrote the chapters of my books. When your attention is free you can connect to any emotion, any frequency. There is a frequency of love. It will be easier for you with free attention that you know how to control. With a couple of elements, you can quickly connect to the frequency of the future or to the frequency of the heart, of love, and everyone will fall in love with you. That will be easy to do now. That's how you can use attention in the future.

Games That Help with Concentration

Remember I said that one person has their attention freed up but is flying in the clouds, and the other, who is pumped up and focused, is still able to concentrate. It turns out that people who have a hard time with games and control are less focused. It is useful to force them to solve puzzles, complex mathematical equations, or, alternatively, to play games! That's what everyone needs to play, even if you've played them before: Inside, Limbo, Samorost 3, Machinarium, and Eufloria.

Now there will be contradictions but in a good way. You can't always be categorical. It can't always be that a knife is bad. Yes, it can harm. But a person can also use both for good. That's how it is with everything. At this moment my goal is to teach you to be aware so that you can free your attention. It's basically the same thing, but it's called differently. That you become aware of everything, that you give an account of every action you take, that you have more energy, that you feel and hear yourself. That's my job. It's a development. Everybody has to go to this point and come to this point. This is important.

The emphasis in the previous pages of the book was on what I have just listed: how to free your attention, to show you how it is unconsciously spent, and how you are addicted to habits and acting on autopilot. Make you used to it and show you what it is like to be free so that you realise and understand that sitting on a bench for six hours in a park somewhere and just looking at the trees is very difficult. You need to understand that.

When movies show wise men sitting and looking at one point, it's very difficult for the average person to repeat that. You have to learn how to do it. People start shaking after half an hour when they do a technique sitting on a chair. After half an hour! Whoever can do it, that's great. But I'm interested in helping those who find it more difficult.

I'm showing you all this, preparing your mind, and your psyche, expanding your limits and introducing you to these sensations so that you're ready for it. But since the theme of the book is attention control, I'm going to give the same topic next, but on a different cover. It will be more practice, working with energy.

And then I won't be able to give any more mundane, real-life examples of how attention manifests itself in life.

It was a revelation for me, I haven't read anything, maybe it's already in the books. But I get everything from experience, that through the five senses we receive information, and from those thoughts are created. Spiritual people who want to meditate say to turn off thoughts, and I began to approach this technically.

Everything in my life was happening by chance, but I didn't know how to do it scientifically. I understood that I have a technique, I do it and the thoughts disappear. But I didn't understand why or how. I only understood that there was something that turned thoughts off and something that turned them on.

And when I began to sketch and study this, I concluded that every sense organ gives birth to a thought. And to turn off thoughts, you have to turn off the senses. Then a sixth sense emerges. And this is something that many theosophists, theologians, and so on talk about. The sixth sense is a certain element, its consciousness, your inner self, that's you. And it is not a thought.

The five senses give us the mind to perceive society and give us thoughts and perception of information. And the sixth sense is us. Many esotericists call it intuition or something else. But people get confused and often call intuition what it is not at all, just human instinct.

Real intuition is just your attention, so free that if something is thrown at you, you can feel it beforehand and dodge it. If your attention is on one point if you have a sixth sense. That's when you feel yourself, and therefore you feel everything. You are everything. The sixth sense is like if there's a little droplet on the ceiling somewhere right now, I'll see it right away, but not with my direct vision, but like a lateral vision.

It's like you can see everything 360°. I'm sitting in my apartment, and if something small moves, an ant crawls to the right or left somewhere in the distance, I will start to feel it with this sense. And immediately I'll turn around and see something crawling there. Or a drop is flowing. Do you understand?

That kind of perception is when the attention is not scattered but gathered on yourself. This is very cool. Then it turns out that you feel everything.

If you're walking down the street or sitting in a restaurant, you can feel the person behind you looking at you, but you'll feel their gaze immediately. Imagine how powerful it is; if a person thinks about you, you'll feel it. He'll think of it in a different part of the world! And you will feel it. That's the explanation for all my abilities.

I didn't learn it. It happened by chance under certain circumstances. My attention was not absorbed by society when I was at school and I freed it more when I left home and cut all ties, I stayed even more within myself. That's when my diary, Alexander Korol, and my books began.

Free attention is the sixth sense. And when you have it; when you read a text that a person wrote, and you know what he was thinking when he wrote it, you can immediately sense whether the person is lying or hinting at something in the text. What he is after, what he wants, what he felt for you when he wrote it. You can sense that.

You can also sense the person by looking at a picture. Yes, you won't have the experience of naming what you feel. You have to expand your mind, and your horizons, to have more words, and more examples. But with your sixth sense, you feel everyone. You become one. You see how someone looks at things, how they behave. That's the sixth sense.

And whether or not you should try to become more sensitive in the five senses to hear every sound or smell every scent. That's the hardest game of attention. Both are good and both are bad. You have to be a human being and adapt everything to yourself. But while we are learning something, we are learning it in the extreme.

But what is attention in this case? If I go to an important meeting in society and I want to feel, my task is to be fully collected, charged up, and come to this meeting in my inner cosmos, I don't scatter my attention to anything at all, I don't notice how I go to this meeting, how I walked through the restaurant, what people were sitting there, I won't see anyone. But I've done that myself. My attention is on me, I go to the meeting, I sit chatting with the person, and in that inner cosmos, I go home.

And that doesn't mean I'm inattentive, that I didn't notice that people I knew were sitting in the restaurant. Or that I didn't notice the weather outside. That's not a bad thing. I did it consciously myself, not to scatter my attention on it, but to stay in my state. But if I'm not going to a meeting, but if I'm aiming to explore society, I spend all my attention on what's in front of me. I walk and look at the pavement, at every crack, every car, in the eyes of every person. I go into a restaurant, and I look around; who's sitting there, what kind of people, what they're doing.

I pay attention to smells, and I can smell them right away. The sixth sense is when your attention is so strong that at the next table, there is a plate of food, and you can just look at it, breathe with your nose and smell it. Even though you are sitting far away from it. You can focus that far away. It's cool. And it's not an afterthought of the mind. You may not even know what that food smells like. It may be new to you, but you will describe that taste.

So sometimes you may not pay attention to little things, but at some point, you have to pay attention to them. It depends on the situation. Even if you have seen it, watch the movie 'Before I Fall' again. Notice how the main character's attention is in society and how she then disconnects from it and begins to perceive it consciously. She begins to see everything, to be aware of her actions. She walks, and everything around her slows down, like a fog.

Part II
Energy Practice

1. Technique with Palms

I want to show you how to begin to get acquainted with energy. I understand that you have a human mind, and many people will react with, "I know that I can do that."

Stop it for now, it's a bad quality that gets in the way of all people. It's not your complexes we're working with right now.

And that's their manifestation and your inferiority, when a person is like, "Oh, I've watched that movie already."

These complexes show up in different situations. There are people who fight and quarrel a lot, but it's not the reason, it's just the person; it's sick.

When I post a movie on social networks, there are people who immediately start writing, "Oh, it's such-and-such a movie."

Why do they write that? They want to be somebody, to be important, and they want to show that they know what kind of movie it is. But why should I read it? Why are they wasting my attention? If you ask them that question, they don't know; it's their complex.

And there is a complex when you show a person something that, let's say, he has seen, and he immediately turns his nose up and says, "Oh, I can do that."

Let's put it this way, we're not living from memory right now. You have to treat it like it's the first time. Get this human stuff out of the way. Now I'm introducing you to energy. And to get to know it, you have to start from the bottom, with the primitive exercises.

Just so you understand, I still do this technique to this day with palms and energy. Yes, there are no miracles, no prestige or dusting of the eyes that you like. But stop living with your instincts, egoism, and complexes. The task is not to satisfy your complexes and not to provoke emotions. The task is to learn how to work with your energy and attention and to evolve. Okay?

Fig. 11. Hold your hands like this: palms facing each other. Fingers straight (Fig. 11A), upright. The palms should be as relaxed as possible, but not physically. Physically you keep them straight. And psychologically you imagine that your palms are as relaxed as possible. You don't strain them.

Fig. 11

Fig 11A

Fig. 12. After that, slowly and smoothly start springing them (move your hands apart and back). Or move up and down, as if you were rolling something between them. Do it as slowly as possible.

Fig. 12

Fig. 13

And then I feel that between my palms; like a magnet, tension. Some would describe it differently, like something in the body. Yes, everyone has different associations, but the essence is the same. Your task is to feel it in the palms of your hands. If you can't, you can do it with your eyes closed. If you can, you can do it with your eyes open.

If you can do it easily, make the distance between your palms bigger (Fig. 13). Try to feel the energy between them.

The next task is as follows. Place your hand with your elbow on the table (Fig. 14), fingers up. Your task is to close your eyes and imagine that you are from above, sucking energy into your hand through your fingers. All the attention on the hand, as if you're sucking energy from the outside into it. Then slowly and smoothly lower the hand (Figure 15) and raise it again (Figure 16).

Do this as slowly as possible. Notice how you will feel. When you return the hand to its original position, start to slowly and smoothly move the hand as if it were in the water, as if it were in gel (Fig. 17). A person can feel this when their attention is focused as much as possible on their hand.

Fig. 14

Fig. 15

I want you to notice that when a person does any kind of energy practice, it doesn't matter if he concentrates on his finger or palm, on a *chakra*, or on some internal organ; in the process he gets under the influence of this energy. Imagine that the energy is like smoke. It's better because you can't see the air. Everything is smoke; it's inside you, in your apartment, in the city, everywhere.

Fig. 16

Fig. 17

Depending on how developed your mind, attention, and concentration is, the moment you focus your attention on the palm, all this smoke from your body starts to be drawn into it, like an extractor hood. But also, from outside, from the apartment, from the city, all that smoke begins to be pulled into the palm of the hand. You can imagine how interesting it is. When one does a technique and starts to concentrate smoke into the palm, first of all, one starts to pay attention to the fact that smoke (energy) exists at all.

And when a person does this, they can activate their *chakras*. If he has had an injury e.g. a knee, it can hurt. Because even if he's focusing on the palm, there's already a crazy concentration of energy coming at him from the inside and the outside. Do you understand?

Let me explain how it happens. When I was telling you what attention control is, I showed you that you are a balloon and a ray of light is coming out of you, like the sun, its attention. Man is a slave to society and his attention is spread out all around him. When you start doing the palm technique, in addition to this your attention is concentrated on you and all the rays that were previously scattered come back inside of you. When you do this technique, it already helps because it goes to your whole body. The stronger your psyche and attention, the more powerful it is.

The power of thought is about belief; what you believe in will happen. If you believe without hesitation and not with your mind, it is power. At this point, the next stage is energy management, which is the second level of attention control, only more complex and detailed.

The longer one studies and goes through the stages, the more one can develop one's attention and acquire superpowers. I'm sure that each of you can feel in the moment of a technique, for example, with your palm or with your hand, that in addition to your hands, your body is on fire. That is, there could be a sensation in the body and the chakras. That's normal. That's a good thing. I have the same thing.

When I used to practice and wanted to turn on the heart chakra, let's say, the heart *chakra*, I would free up all attention and concentrate there, and that's what turned everything on for me. The person seems to feel what I have aimed at, but he also says that his head has become heavy.

I tell him, "You feel me."

Write down what you felt, and what other body parts or *chakras* you felt, so you can understand why.

If you now try the palm technique and start breathing, slowly exhaling and springing palms, you will feel a strong density. The moment you feel it, take a sharp breath and feel the energy disappear. This way the breath dissipates everything. This is why breath should be short, slow, soft and gentle.

Imagine that the room stinks, and you don't want to breathe it in, so you breathe in a little bit through your nose and slowly exhale through your mouth, like through a tube, then breathe in again a little bit through your nose and breathe out a little bit slower. When you breathe in that rhythm you accumulate more energy, you concentrate on it, and you feel it. And if you take strong and sharp breaths, everything disappears.

Even if I advise you of any other way to breathe, you will still be distracted. Because it's not about that, it's about your mind and your thoughts. You think when you breathe. And it should be automatic. Like when you walk. You just have to breathe. The only advice I can give to people who are not able to breathe, which I have advised, is just do not think about it, do not pay attention to breathing, do not try to breathe in any way, and forget about it. Breathe as you breathe.

It happens that a person begins to have some pain during practice. There are different explanations for this. The first one is that if a person has a diseased organ, he or she begins to whine at the moment of an energy practice because energy is immediately flowing in places that have not been flowing in before. Soreness can be an old injury or an unhealthy internal organ.

The second thing is that if you do the palm technique and one of your *chakras* turns on, it means that the leading *chakra* has manifested. If someone doesn't know what *chakras* are, Google the definition; they are energy centres, and everything that is written about them except this, is nonsense, so don't fill your head with what each *chakra* is responsible for, this leads away from the truth.

Some will feel aroused when the lower *chakra* is on, some will feel the head, and some will have a burning chest or throat. Everybody has a leading *chakra*. And that's your major *chakra*. Remember this.

Here's an example. A man came to me, and I gave him a small bag to hang around his neck.

He put it on, and after a while, he said, "I can't take it anymore."

I said, "How does it feel?"

He said, "It feels like a hot water bottle on my chest."

When I gave it to another person, I got the same reaction. I don't tell them what it is or how it affects them.

I simply say, "Put it on, walk around."

He puts it on and asks, "Do you have something hot in the bag?"

I said, "No."

He said, "It's weird; it burns my chest like it's warm, but I touch it with my hand and it's not warm, it's cold. And my chest is burning."

What kind of self-hypnosis is this if these were two people, who had not been told what to expect and they could not think it through?

I, of course, check it all out. There's no way anyone could be imagining things. Otherwise, I wouldn't be telling it to the whole world with such confidence. Don't get me wrong. How can you doubt the palms of your hands? What happens next with your reaction to other things? Some might think there would be sensations in the palms of your hands because you hold them for so long, some might say that your hands just get stiff.

Oh yes, they do. I'm about to sit in a free position to watch a movie. My hands don't get stiff for half an hour. They're just lying there, but if I focus my attention on my palm, yes, something will happen. But the same thing happens to everybody. And that's right.

Yes, all people have their minds and their associations. And everyone describes it a little differently. Some said they felt something soft, some said it felt like a magnet, and some said it felt like a tingle. But the point is that the first and main thing is the resistance between the palms. And the slightly different description is each person's association. The point is the same. It is not an afterthought. And also, the work with energy and attention is all about not thinking. The less of it you have, the more you'll feel. And the more you think, the less you feel.

But when you want to communicate with people at home, you want to be muted. To do that, I poured myself whiskey and coke, drank, smoked cigarettes, or ate a heavy meal. And then I more or less came down from heaven to Earth in the truest sense of the word. I was again in a social environment, I could plan, and give technical assignments to all my employees. I went into this inner cosmos purposefully.

As they often show in movies, where there is a Shaman-Sorcerer, he too can go to the market, buy himself some fish and people can see him. But if he is asked to predict or conjure something, he goes into his closet, disconnects from everything, and goes into the inner cosmos. I have always gone there to write books because if I don't write them in that state, they will be written with the mind. The book *Paradox* is written in that state; when it is not my mind that writes, but someone through me.

Then I came to a level where you have to accept this state without mind; stay in it, you don't have to mute it. At first, it's like a stupefying state, and it's very hard to deal with material things when the mind is disconnected, and the attention is focused on you. It can make you sleepless. You don't get tired, you are so energetic, collected, and everything is clear on the one hand, but on the other hand, your attention is wired up somewhere, you cannot concentrate and, for example, check mistakes in a text. It's like it's hard to do and you have to mute yourself and lower yourself.

But the most interesting thing is that this state, let's call it holy spirit, was often activated in some emergency situations. When I was approached by people with knives on the street a long time ago, in an instant it clicked, and it was as if Alex with his mind turned off, and through me as if a being began to talk to these bandits. And in a way that scared them witless.

I came home and I thought, *Wow, wow, what can I do!* It's very unusual. In stressful situations, it turns on, like you're plugging into something. The mind goes out and it's like you are you and that's it.

The first reaction to such a condition is to put it away. Because initially, it feels like you're sick, and it's not pleasant if you don't get it under control. You feel like you've been kicked in the head, and you have stars in your eyes. You walk and you have no idea where you're walking, what street you're on, or how long you're walking. Of course, you want to be in control. Everybody is used to it, to being in control. To be aware of what you want to do before and after.

A man once told me that when he does a technique, he gets into an excited emotional state, he is so awake and clear that he can't sleep afterward. What to do about it? There are several options. The first thing to take note of is that if you have this condition, it is a good thing. Of course, you have to get used to it, if you can. You have to be in the situation.

If you have a serious meeting or some work to do, of course, you have to mute yourself; eat any heavy food, talk to material people, and lower your focus so that you can concentrate. But if you have gone into that inner cosmos and you don't have any serious work to do, it's better to stay in that state. You have to get used to it anyway. And it is better to try and watch movies, go to people, go for a walk. But it is better not to drive in this state.

In this state of stupefaction, try to do ordinary things, but don't mute yourself. If you don't have time to experiment and need to do something right now, mute yourself with sweets, heavy foods, material people, and stupid TV shows. I used to go into this stupefaction state, write books in this flow, stay in it for a few days, then turn on a silly show. To balance it out, to mute myself down. It was my way of muting myself. Take note.

If you need to sleep and you want to go to sleep, jam yourself. But if you don't want to, don't. But it doesn't mean that you won't get enough sleep, that's also a paradox. The state is the same as one gets when one sleeps. It's not the mind that's on, it's you in inner space, you're recharging. It is as if you are in a dream, but it is reality.

When I was in this state, I would go to bed at 6 o'clock in the morning, and I could wake up at 10 o'clock in the morning, and it was fine. I could not sleep either. But I don't need many hours to sleep either.

This state most often comes on when you speak in public, when you touch on some frank conversation, when you talk about something cosmic and sacred, which is very close to the truth, and when you do various practices with energy.

When you focus on a *chakra*, your physical body will be the reference point. In the *chakra* picture (Google it), you can see where the seven energy centres are. The basic seven. You pick any point, for example, on your knee, it's not a chakra, but it doesn't matter. And you just think and focus all of your attention on it. And imagine in your mind, in your thoughts that all the energy from your body, or from your apartment, or from the cosmos goes to your knee.

Music is good for that. In the past when I didn't know how or what to do, I used different keys, including music and breathing. It helped me to concentrate my attention on one point. Now I don't need that. I will describe my knee and feel it. It feels like my bones are connected, like joints, I feel it so strongly like my knee is knotted. And I feel it just because I'm thinking about it now. That's how much I've developed my attention.

How to concentrate on the chakras and certain centres? First tip, take a scotch tape and use it as a scope. Or some heavy object that you can put on your forehead or your chest. The main thing is to create a feeling there. If you lie or sit with your eyes closed and do the technique, because you will feel something there – something glued or heavy from the object, you will concentrate on it.

The easiest way to focus on your forehead or somewhere else is to just pinch your skin and close your eyes. Where you feel pain, that's where you focus your attention. Try it.

Of course, if you are a very material person, live with your mind, have a stressful job, and are very nervous, you have to tune in, and prepare yourself before the techniques. When you come home from work with your head boiling, have a quick meal, and only 40 minutes have passed, your head has not had time to shut down, and you will be in a super-accelerated rhythm. And the frequency where miracles and energy are found is when you are as calm and balanced as possible.

Your speed has to be minimal. If you can't stay calm, the techniques won't work. You have to prepare yourself with the elements that relax you. At work, you speed up and your cells move at a speed of, say, 20. And music, for example, at the speed of five. Movies also come at that speed, and people do as well. You need to surround yourself with all the elements at speed five. So that you can also be in a state of five. Then you will start doing techniques and you will feel everything.

As preparation, you can do a *technique on a chair*, take a contrast shower, put on some music, watch a languid movie, or just go for a walk with headphones on or in silence. And techniques also work best when it's dark. When there's no sun, when it's night, everything feels better.

We call it energy now. But it's attention control. It's just in different packaging. You remember that I wrote about how important attention is and what it provides. We continue to develop it. It's like exercising so that you can lift heavy things so that your back doesn't hurt and you have more endurance. You do the same thing now, not with your physical body, but with your attention and consciousness to be more conscious, more collected. You are now working with a ghost that you have not been controlling. I let you feel that there is an Autobot and there is you, I introduce you to you, to your consciousness.

Surely there are esoteric fans among my readers who have already studied everything. You've probably heard the stories about the monks. When they die, they sit down and go into a long sleep, as if they were dead, but the body does not rot and remains warm even though the person is dead. And why doesn't he rot, and his body emanates energy? Because he has so developed his attention that it is still present. It doesn't go anywhere. Do you understand? There's so much you don't know yet.

There are all sorts of tombs created for a reason. Why are there relics? Why do they bring them all over the world? Surely some people look at you and me funny because we are interested in something like that. But how do you explain the fact that all these people are lining up in kilometres long lines to the relics in church? It's part of the saint's flesh, they don't just walk up to it. And why?

Because it's that part that emanates something. Priests, they're all in on it. Some icons cost millions for a reason. Anything that emanates is inaccessible and expensive. That's why crowds are standing up to them.

So, it does something. Okay, it's emanating, but people probably don't come just to feel something for a second. They probably line up because it gives something. Start there.

To answer the question of what it gives you, it is attention control. It enables you to be less of a couch potato, get hit by the system less, be more attentive, and see everything. Your brain will not be working on 5%, it's going to be on 15%. That's what you will have. But only if you evolve, not if you resist and be lazy.

So far, our focus has been that there is a human world that does not believe in the existence of this energy that I am talking about. People don't believe in it. There is a certain percentage of them that can feel it and believe that there is meditation, *chakras*, energy centres, and points, that there is energy from holy places, that it can heal, influence people, turn on the *chakras*, do some miracles, influence everything around. Yes, it exists.

But your approach should be: if you feel the energy in any way, rejoice, and that's all. I don't care what kind of energy it is. It doesn't hurt anything. It's silly to think about it and to be afraid of it. If you can feel the energy between your palms, that's great.

If you can concentrate on your heel, knee, elbow, palm, forehead, chest, ears, and throat when you are lying down or sitting at home and feel that you are really directing your attention, and energy there and feel something – heat, pressure, tingling, burning or some vortex appears, like air-wind blowing through the point that you are focusing on, that's great. You're doing great!

I showed a simple exercise with the palms. Try aiming at some centres or *chakras* yourself. Work with your free attention and direct it to some point. Notice if you feel any sensations. If you can, write down how you did it, what you did, and what you felt. This will come in handy.

There can be no overdose of energy. Working with attention is not something artificial. It's only that and something from the mind that can harm a person. All kinds of extraneous psychotropic substances, physical invasion of the body, something extraneous – this is bad, it can be harmful and dangerous. And in this case, we're not doing anything supernatural. Imagine we are children; we are all ten years old. The teacher's sick, and we're sitting in the classroom, and we have nothing to talk about. I sit, I look at my thumb, I concentrate on it, and it feels like it's getting bigger. I feel it separately and I will tell you about it.

And I say, "Can you concentrate like that? Have you ever focused on a finger or a palm?"

You start to do that, and you feel the energy too. We're not breaking the law of nature; we're not doing anything wrong. It would be very funny if a man could hurt himself in such a funny way. We don't lift 100 kilos; it's not like we're going to strain ourselves. We don't jump 100 metres from somewhere. We don't break the laws of nature and don't do any physical actions. It's just a work of attention. On the contrary, you have to approach it with full courage and wonder. I wonder what will happen if you pay attention to something?

It's your attention, it can't hurt you. Figuratively speaking, you decided to look at yourself longer with your eyes and attention. So, it is silly to be afraid, there can be no overdose. Paying attention to your energy body and you is a good thing.

You have a physical arm and leg, you move them. But you don't do it on purpose, you do it because you have to move them because you want to eat, and you have to open something with your hands and go to get groceries with your feet. There is always a load on your arms and legs, and that's good, otherwise, they would fall off.

But your attention is not automatically focused on the energetic hands and feet under some circumstances. You have to do it yourself, consciously. And you learn to try and play with your attention and energy. There is nothing wrong with that. It's like children. You can play around and see what happens if you focus your attention on the top of your head. Or on your hands or your feet, on some chakra. You learn to concentrate your energy and your attention on something. That's a good thing.

When some psychic claims to know how to turn on the chakras, how can you verify this? If he can do it, the chakra doesn't turn on only from the front. It's always on all the way through. And if you turn on the third eye, first you feel pressure on your forehead, some people feel a burning or tingling sensation, and some people feel as if something goes into their forehead as if a snake is crawling.

But at the same time, the back of the head is also involved. It becomes heavy, and it feels as if a valve is going in and out of your forehead. You can feel it. But you don't have to be distracted by that. It happened because you were concentrating the energy on your forehead. So just keep doing that. And that's it. To turn on this chakra you concentrate on your forehead, directing your attention there.

But if it's turned on, it's through into the forehead, out through the back of the head. So, you can rock every *chakra*. But that doesn't mean that if someone doesn't have that, that's a bad thing. Let's say, if I turn on my chest, I feel a burning and heaviness in my chest, and I don't feel my back as often. Sometimes I feel it all the way through, and my back is hot. Sometimes, I don't. But with the third eye, I always feel the back of my head.

There are levels. I know all the stages of human development and can divide my readers into those stages. The first stage of humans, the most primitive among my readers, are those who need to prepare themselves if they want to do the palm technique now. That is, they won't feel anything right away, even if they use music and other keys.

People who are so in their heads and do not feel themselves need to gather their attention in one spot. They need to be alone, to take a walk alone. They will do well with techniques when they have a state of emergency and withdraw into themselves. Or if they wake up at 4 o'clock in the morning, when they are not thinking, when they are not in control, that is the moment when a technique can work.

So, in the first group of people, your mind is your enemy. It gets in your way. Most people are like that. You can take any blogger, any social person, a sceptic, or someone who has three educations, as an example – such people are hard-headed and do not feel anything.

The second group is those who don't need an hour or two of preparation, they can do the techniques right away, but they can't do them the way I do so that everything works right away without any keys. It's a group that does everything with keys and breathing and music when they do it at night and when they look at it or close their eyes. You have to take note of that.

Why does music help? Let's imagine that there is a glass of tea. I put my palm up to influence the energy of the tea. But I don't have to put my palm up. I'm at the point now where I can just look at the tea and it will change the taste. But before, to believe that it was possible for you, your psyche, you had to put your palm up. For your unbelieving mind, for your psyche, it's more likely that the practice will work if you put your palm up and give energy.

The second group needs keys; you have to bring your hand, breathe correctly and visualise the energy coming out of the palm of your hand. That's such a psychological thought form that helps you to imagine that energy has gone there. Because you cannot control your attention freely to imagine that the beam is flying – it is flying. And it helps you to use the palm of your hand to influence the taste of the drink.

But apart from the palm, some people still have some thoughts, and it's hard for you to imagine that the beam goes with some speed and density from the hand to the glass. Music helps with that. If you play a rhythmic melody, to the beat and the sound, it's as if the energy is coming out of the hand. It helps to focus your attention on that goal. That's how it works.

But the super level is when I can put the glass in front of me, I may not see it. I can think of all the places of power around the world and imagine the energy coming out of each one into the glass. Just imagine. I don't even have to see a picture of that glass of power. I can just connect to the pyramid in Egypt and send energy from there. Connect to St Isaac's Cathedral in St Petersburg and send energy into the glass. And that's it. Just right away, without preparation.

The uniqueness of my information is that I am, from scratch, without relying on any other sources, I study the nature of everything around me, the structure of man based on my real life. That's why it can't be wrong. I know the essence, not just something I heard somewhere, memorised and repeated, as everyone else does. I don't do that.

It's the same with the *chakras*. I can tell you how I came across them. Why do I know there's a leading *chakra*? I didn't read it out anywhere. It just so happens that over so many years, no matter how many people have turned on from me, have done techniques with me, or have felt the energy from some of my things, everyone has always turned on some chakra. But these people didn't know about them.

I am not interested in communicating in life with those who know me as Alexander Korol, who have memorised a lot of silly esoteric books. When I share information, when I experiment, I do it with a person who is just a person who has never read any esoteric book in his life. This is an ordinary member of society who doesn't know what the *chakras* are at all.

He just says, "My chest is on fire, wow," or he says, "The back of my head is getting heavier, and something is happening to my forehead."

Or he talks about his throat or his stomach. And so it happened that I began to identify causes and effects, patterns and coincidences, and I saw that everyone has a certain major *chakra*, and it is the first to respond, to turn on. And if you wonder further what this chakra is responsible for, I don't know. Of course, I can read on the internet, just like you. But there's a 99.9% chance that this information will mislead you. Do we have to read about it? No.

If you read now about any chakra that you have turned on, you're tapping into the frequency of housewives and all sorts of hermit-esoteric beggars. Do you have to be on that frequency? I don't wish that on you. The chakra turns on, and that's fine. It's necessary to switch on other chakras as well. Take this into consideration.

And since this is your main *chakra*, when you have it turned on, it means that you are also turned on. You can use it to navigate. How? If I'm writing a book or talking about some things and my chakra turns on by itself, I don't do it on purpose, it means that something happens not from my mind, but on the spiritual plane. A man is spiritual.

Or the topic I'm talking about is spiritual because a light turns on in me. Do you understand? The more often it lights up from some actions or people, the better. It's you who light up. That's what you need to get out of this information.

If you read something about the heart chakra and immediately begin to feel the energy, even though you do nothing for it, then your attention is so free that it immediately focuses there. That's normal. That's cool. Take note of that if you're like that. I am. It's at the top level. Not everybody is like that, just some people are like that, and some people are different.

Some people have such free attention and are so sensitive that they have this kind of thing going on. So much attention can also come from just a text or a conversation. You just hear about it and the attention is focused there. It's very cool.

You should do the energy technique every day. You don't have to force yourself, but the more often the better. I understand how you feel. It was my destiny that I had to go from the very bottom to the very top through everything, through all frequencies and layers of society. I tried everything myself. It's a very hard way. But I'm super developed. And I know who and in what category is and will be experiencing what.

Before, when I was on your frequency, which is where you are now, I couldn't do techniques with energy every day. There was a time when I was so overwhelmed with society that I felt I didn't want to and couldn't. I knew what I had to do, but I didn't do it. And it turned out that it was to my liking and my condition.

Figuratively speaking it would be forgotten, a week would pass and then I would be alone and suddenly I would remember it, get inspired, and do my techniques. I also returned to it when I had an accident or emergency of some sort. That is, I pushed myself to the point where the system would give me an emergency. That's what is happening to you readers now.

But now I'm at the point where I'm doing these techniques every day. Why? Because there is no contrast, almost all my attention is almost always free. And when you have that attention, you always feel the energy and you always want to do something with it, to focus on yourself or on the people who are sitting, for example, in the restaurant. You start to live it; it becomes a way of life. Of course, it's level. You have to get there. So, you could say that you have to do energy techniques every day.

But I know you won't do it. It's hard when you live in a society with devils. I understand you. But three days go by and you're back in your inner cosmos, you're drawn to it, and you want to do techniques – okay, do them. Just try to do it more often – be alone with yourself and practice this. This has to be done all the time. When a person reaches a level where he does techniques with energy every day without forcing himself, for him it's like getting up and walking, he can't forget it, because it's part of life, it means that he's a conscious person.

When you do techniques with energy, sometimes there are thoughts that, it's impossible and unrealistic. It makes it hard to build up. I know this condition myself. It is normal. If it's like this, it's bad. What kind of state is this? It is when you are living with your mind, when you are out of the way, when you are lost, like all people.

When you have no faith and a lot of fear, you don't know what to believe and people impose their opinion on you or judge you. You agree on something, and you don't agree on something, but it's so chaotic that it confuses you even more. And you're already so doubtful of yourself and everything that when you start doing it, there are a lot of thoughts of disbelief. It's such a mundane, social fuss.

When you're in shock, when there's an emergency, you've been yelled at, or you've been yelled at. You're in emotional shock and at that moment you can hold your palms up and feel the energy because you're not even thinking. So, thoughts get in the way. But why are they on? Because you are surrounded by society, you are not living by your heart, your soul. Yourself, your soul is lost.

Thoughts have to be turned off so there is no fuss. How? There are enough ways. I have told and written about it a lot. You have to prepare yourself an hour before you are planning to do the technique, to shut your thoughts off. You should turn on the music and watch movies. To be alone with yourself, to make vanity disappear. Then there won't be any doubt. It's in the mind, not in technique. You have to have faith and confidence.

Imagine how far I've come. I used to feel it, I used to go down to that level. But imagine what level you can get to and what further development is. I now imagine that my friend has a water bottle in his car, and I directed the energy there. I am 100% sure that it changed its taste. Why? Because I am 100% sure that I can do it. There's that belief. And it depends on faith. Zero doubt. I believe that it can be. That's cool.

I couldn't do that before. I had to be in a certain state to do that. I could only do things like that after meditation, when there are no thoughts at all, you are in a flow, and you can do anything. But if you have any thoughts at all, you can't do anything. That's it. That is expanded psyche and attention, that is faith. It needs to grow so that you don't have doubts by overthinking. Thoughts are doubts. You just have to believe that you can do it.

With these energy techniques, you expand the psyche, nurture, reveal your faith, and reduce doubt. The more you practice all this, the more you can do mini miracles, and the stronger your faith will be. And it will affect your whole life.

If there are people among the readers who have panicked thoughts that it won't work, that it can't be, you have to stop it. It's the mind, society. It has to be turned off. One hour before practice you have to prepare yourself. This is a parasite. The only thing that protects you from miracles, energy, and everything else is thoughts and doubts, which you have to turn off.

If you have identified with the help of techniques that there is a *chakra* that is easiest for you to activate, work with it, and do not touch the others. For now, you need to learn how to do the techniques quickly in different situations. I walk down the street and try to feel the energy between my palms, I drive a car and try to feel the energy between my palms, I would try to feel the energy between my palms.

You have to check to see if it's always fast and in what situations and places it doesn't work. Which moods are stronger, and which are not? What else can you do? You can try to feel the chakra at home. But then I would try to feel it in different situations. Talking to people, I remember the chakra and try to feel it. You have to try to turn it on right away. It's good when you feel activated.

But it may feel different. I can think of a breast and immediately feel something there. I just think about it and immediately feel it. But the chakra is not fully developed. When I just think about it, I feel the heat from above. When I start to think more, it starts to spread, something happens there, and something starts to move. You can experiment, set a goal of how much you can turn on the chakra.

How far apart can you put your palms from each other, so that you can still feel the density? That's how you can try. And if you have a key chakra, train on it, so that in any situation you can quickly turn it on. This training will come in handy for you in the future.

Exercises with Energy

Exercise 1.

(a) Try running your finger across the opposite palm without touching it. Keep your finger perpendicular to the opposite open palm. As if you were moving the palm, but not touching it, up and down, right and left. Try to move a short distance and slowly.

(b) If you can do the exercise above, try to move your finger up and down, but parallel to your palm at a distance, imagining that you are moving your palm. This will greatly expand your boundaries and remove doubt and mind. You will put down on the fine plane that there is no distance for energy. Because it is energy and not something physical.

Exercise 2.

(a) Imagine sending energy from your finger into the opposite open palm. Not through the skin, but on the skin. Wiggle your fingers and imagine that you are pressing your fingers against the palm. Feel whether the pressure is felt in the centre of the palm.

(b) Now imagine that the energy from your fingers goes into the middle of the opposite palm, but it doesn't rest against your skin, it comes out the other side of the palm. All the way through. And then it comes in from the opposite side and goes all the way through. To make sure you get it right, first touch the middle of the palm with your fingers and then touch the opposite side of the palm where the energy will go through. This will trick your mind.

What's also important? In no case, there should be no rings, watches, or talismans at the moment when you are doing the techniques. Remove all such things from your hands and neck.

Exercise 3.

Try to cross yourself like in church (forehead, stomach, left shoulder, right shoulder). Who has their attention already widened, who has their attention freed up? You'll be amazed at what it is. It's as if something is turning on.

Exercise 4.

When I got to know the energy and felt something for the first time, I had a phone in my hand. I was holding it with my palms on my knees. I was driving in my car, and I just started to move my hand over the phone. And I felt the field. As I was moving my hand away from the phone, it was like I was touching it without touching it.

Hold the phone with two fingers so that part of it is in the air. And try wiggling the phone around with your hand next to it. With straight fingers around the phone. You'll feel like you're starting to wiggle it. It's just for the psyche and it's not useful to us. You can try this with an ordinary pen, holding it lightly in your hands, trying to move your fingers around as if you want to grab the pen, but not touching it. Feel as if you are hitting the pen with energy from your fingers.

Some people feel the finger on the palm of their hand more strongly with their eyes closed. This is natural. It's a problem of your faith and your mind. The more a person has more faith and less doubt and mind, the more he feels everything. The more he feels his soul, the more he is stable and feels everything. If a person's light inside is weak and his attention is scattered, it is harder for him to feel anything, and he has many distractions. The mind is his enemy.

And the more of these distractions are removed, the more likely you are to feel the energy. You can be distracted by noise, so it's better to do the practice in silence. It can be distracting to see because your attention is more on the outside, not on sensitivity. So, when you close your eyes, you become more sensitive. Whoever can't do the technique, do it with your eyes closed.

When I first encountered this and had the technique of opening the channel, I noticed that in addition to having my eyes open, my breathing also distracted me from feeling the energy above my head more. What if you stop breathing at this point? But you don't have to deliberately inhale more and hold your breath. You just have to stop breathing.

And at that moment you will feel much more energy. And if you don't breathe when you hold your palms against each other and try to feel the density, then the feeling of density will increase several times.

This is me preparing you for the fact that there is such a factor as breathing. It, like vision, is distracting. But, of course, it's cool to learn that without any psychological tricks, you can have such faith and free attention that you just look at the palm of your hand and lead your finger and feel everything.

The *technique in the chair* is set up for you to think of some key, something on which you always focus your attention for an hour. When there are no more temptations for attention, on the contrary, it is freed as much as possible because you are sitting in complete darkness and silence. You have to tame that free attention and focus it on something. Someone repeats numbers, someone listens to a song on a loop, someone taps out a rhythm with his foot, or someone imagines a picture or light in front of his eyes.

You have to get used to it during a month doing this technique. So that later, when you are in society, before an exam, or in a stressful situation, you would close your eyes and quickly remember how you felt when you were doing the *technique on the chair*. Then you would notice how you would get into that calm state you have accustomed yourself to for a month.

To do this, you have to use a technique and it's better to repeat it. That's how you tame your attention. And your psyche gets even more accustomed to this key, which will come in handy for you in the future.

And if you want to do techniques with energy, and for that, you need free attention, you can try, when you are sitting in the kitchen, to say to yourself, "Let me remember the technique on the chair," and close your eyes and remember it.

And notice whether this changes your inner state. If it does, try doing the technique with energy and you will see that it works better.

There are times when a person tries to turn on the chakras, but they only turn on the heart and the head, for example. And it's hard to focus on the rest. That's normal. It's the same with me. There is always something that is easier to activate and something that is not. The top of the head, the third eye, the chest, the throat – all the upper ones are activated most often and easiest.

The lower ones are hard to activate. One of the ways for the lower *chakras*. I did it this way: first I activate the chest, and then, I imagine that what I feel in the chest goes lower. That is, into the belly. And that's how I brought that feeling down.

To turn it on, you have to practice. You have to practice, using all the keys I gave you, with your eyes closed, with your eyes open, with music, without music, with breathing. Try concentrating, aiming, and starting, feeling. Remember and get used to what kind of sensations you observe in that *chakra*. It happens that one day it is strongly activated, and another day it is weaker.

Try to strive for the strongest result of all attempts. That's the limit you've reached. What the final limit is, I don't know. Try to continue and notice that someday the chakra will turn stronger, remember that it is possible, and therefore it is necessary to aspire to this level. Not when it's 5% activated, but when it's 15%.

Apart from that, you have to learn to turn on the chakra without any auxiliary keys. Not just in silence, in the dark, with preparation. And you should try to do it just by waking up in the morning at home or lying in bed before going to sleep, without turning on music, but just by thinking about the chakra. Or try turning it on when you're in the office, on public transportation, or walking down the street.

The most important thing to take note of. Material, closed-minded people, and such are all people who do not feel the energy and always make sudden movements. Such people often bump, get dirty, and spill, when they eat, something falls off, and they stumble. They are very abrupt. It shows in a lot of ways. They're rough when they drive a car, they're rough. It's about closed people who don't want to feel themselves, their inner selves.

A person in the opposite rhythm, in the spiritual, sensitive, when the attention is on him, who lives by feelings, is as slow and calm as possible in everything. Because it is important for him to feel. So, he's a person who's very slow and sensitive and feels everything, so he's very slow and calm.

One of the keys you can try for yourself is if you look at your hand and put it down as slowly as possible and then bring it up, slowly bending each finger, just practice this at home, it helps to concentrate even more and gather all the scattered attention on yourself. It enhances concentration and feeling, all the slow movements. You can also think of everyday hobbies that contribute to this.

For example, making something out of matches or assembling a house of cards. This kind of painstaking work, which is not done in a hurry, helps one to be more sensitive. You have to make a list for yourself where being unhurried, unsharp, anatomical, tactile, slow, and careful helps one to concentrate. Such people have a better chance of managing energy, attention, and feeling themselves and everything around them.

Where the beam forms when you do an energy technique depends on where you're directing the energy from. If I imagine that I'm giving my energy into a glass with a drink, then if I do it visually, giving it with my eyes, my third eye, I imagine that the energy goes from there into the glass.

If I do it with the palm of my hand, I imagine it's coming from the palm of my hand. If I do it with my finger, it's coming from my finger. If it's from outside, there will still be some source. I imagine as if I'm taking someone's energy or from someplace it's going into the glass. For example, I remember that I have a statue in my warehouse, and I imagine that energy comes from that statue and goes into the glass in front of me.

It's very important not to be tense. Working with energy is maximum relaxation. Concentration doesn't mean straining the brain. It means to focus on one thing, and not strain. You don't have to strain your head, your hand, or your finger. Even if you give energy to it, you don't have to physically tense it. You have to focus on it, put your finger to the palm of your hand and think to yourself, *Energy comes out of your finger and goes through your palm, goes back into your hand and out of your hand.*

You imagined it and you began to feel it. So much so that even if you take your finger away, the process continues. It is as if you are setting a pattern for the movement of energy. It's going on as long as I think about it. But thinking doesn't mean thinking with my thoughts, imagining with my mind, and with my attention. I imagine it and it happens. And I am not even looking. I look with my eyes into nothing, into a corner of the apartment. I look into myself, and I imagine where the energy has to go: from my finger to my palm, out into my hand, and out of my palm.

Is there any difference in which frequency you are working with energy? In addition to the 12 frequencies and the 12 dimensions, you can imagine that there are simply different frequencies: the frequency of solitude, the spiritual frequency, and the material frequency. What is this? It is a rhythm that can be material, active, and social. Or a spiritual rhythm, a solitary rhythm.

It's what you listen to, what you eat, and who you talk to. All the elements affect it. If I'm in a closed material frequency, where there are the same people and where there's music playing that scatters attention, sitting down to do a technique with my palms, I will hardly feel the energy between them. Whether you get all the techniques depends on what frequency you're on. But I won't give you the subject of frequencies. Because I already take that into account when I tell you how to prepare yourself.

I don't want to confuse you, it's complicated. When you start to prepare yourself and follow all the rules to start managing the energy, at that point you are different from the frequency where it doesn't exist, and you connect to the one where it all exists. So, you start to feel. And you become more and more connected to this frequency, thanks to the techniques.

Here is an example. A person who learns a language, Japanese, Chinese, whatever, doesn't learn it. It's as if there is a frequency or something he is broadcasting from. But for the knowledge of the language to be broadcast to him, he has to connect to that string. And to connect to it, he learns the language. So, it's as if the rules of the language, the characters themselves, and every word, are mould.

And the more you learn it, that is, the more you connect to it and surround yourself with it, the faster you connect to the frequency of that language. And because of this, you can speak it fluently. I will tell you how human beings are built. It is the same with music when one plays the piano. If one learns to play one has to connect to a source, where one learns the piano. But how does he connect to that source?

He starts to learn notes, practice playing, and listen to and study composers. And when he taps into this frequency, he starts to play. That's it. But he didn't learn it, he tapped into the right frequency. It's a complicated thing, but that's just the way it is. And I always knew it was true. It's confirmed by all kinds of interesting facts.

When a person is said to have experienced clinical death or to have experienced an emergency, he has a split personality and suddenly starts speaking different languages. But this is impossible, based on the theory that is common among people, that a person has to learn a language. So, we don't learn it, but we're tuning into something. And when we teach, it's a veiled process; it seems to us that we're learning, but in fact, we're tuning into a certain frequency.

At this moment there is a frequency where there is attention and energy management, where there is consciousness. There is a frequency, a spiritual level. But to arrive there you have to learn these techniques. On the other hand, because you know these techniques, you come to this level. That's how it works.

Some people confuse turning off the mind and practicing with energies, where the mental direction of energy is used to direct it somewhere. These are different things. The mind is when you have a lot of thoughts, when you think, when you have a lot of choices, when you doubt, choose, and things come into your head. When your head is overloaded, when there's no quietness in it – that's the mind.

And when you have a clear head without a mind – the clarity is crazy. It happens in different situations: when you are stressed, in an emergency, when someone has died – there are whoosh in your ears, and you have no thoughts. But you are there, your reflection, but it is as if it were monotonous as if there were only your voice. That's what consciousness is, you have to think with it, not with thoughts. These are different things.

This is the state that people get into when they have a hangover. If you drink a lot of alcohol, you wake up the next day and there are no thoughts. You're out of your mind. But you still exist, you see everything, and you hear everything. You are here and now, but there are no thoughts. There is one clear thought, and that is your attention, your consciousness.

You need not have many thoughts, but a state without mind, just your consciousness, and one thought. You are here and now, here is the finger, here is the energy, and it goes there. And that is what you do. This is not a thought. This is different. Do you understand?

It happens that people start to feel very big as if they don't fit in the room when they do techniques with energy. When you do more and more techniques, meditative, and so on, of course, your field, energy, and attention become so big that you will feel tight in the apartment. It's not for nothing because large palaces had high ceilings and huge halls, it's not because they, let's say, kings, had a lot of money and they liked to make large rooms.

It is because the height of the ceilings and the distances are psychologically comfortable for a conscious person who has attended. If you put a person in a small place there is a lot of pressure. The more one develops spiritually the more one wants space around. It's a fact.

One of the elements that disconnects from the rhythms of the mind and awakens your inner self more, is the book *Paradox.* It helps, which is why people read it so often. They reread it and reread it. Because it's not about the general plot, there is no plot, but every chapter is from the world without a mind. You can open and read any number of chapters at random. Somebody already on the first page will feel the mind shutting down and the inner self waking up. Somebody will feel it after three chapters. Then you can start doing techniques.

The most common mistake of people of the mind, of society, is that they don't understand the cause, effect, and meaning of everything and think that techniques with energy will cause outbursts of anger. There can be no such thing. People like to make things up and lie to themselves. There can be no such thing as a person working on inner peace of mind, and that only leads to one thing. Any energy management technique is a concentration on oneself. It is the ultimate state of nirvana, harmony, bliss, calm, and serenity.

And this cannot affect you negatively. On the contrary, your automatic reactions, principles, and stereotypes must weaken. You have to become more aware. It is as if you are slowing down, as if you have time to think before you answer, instead of reacting strongly. This leads to spiritual development. Your outbursts of anger are a problem of the mind and your psyche.

All negative thoughts, reactions, doubts, and negative attitudes come only from the mind. The mind is so traumatised and untrained that it gets in the way of your life. The mind is the complexes and cockroaches in your head that have accumulated over the years. When you turn it off you stop acting like an animal. On the contrary, it is as if you are a sage.

I don't want to feed your illusion that something is bad for you. I stopped that right away. There is no such thing. People who think in such a format that they want to use energy to affect the health of their loved ones or themselves must understand: if you have such thoughts, it's a mind. It's your trait that lives inside of you. It's a bad thing. Get it out of your head. It's the sign of a person from hell, of a super low frequency. People who accept themselves as they are – something has come to them in life, they have accepted it and know it, everything is good.

And some people immediately say, "Oh, can I use this energy to surprise my friend and influence him from a distance? Can I use this energy to quickly cure all my illnesses?"

No, you can't. Life will hit you super hard for that. You have to realise that as long as you have such thoughts you will only feel bad. These are very bad thoughts. They don't come from the heart, not from your inner self, but from the mess in your head and mind.

If you have a health problem, you go to the doctor. I'm not a doctor. If a person has money problems, no matter how many energy techniques they do, they don't get more money. It's nonsense to say that there is meditation for money. No, there is no such thing. Money doesn't depend on that. Of course, one thing and the other are interrelated, but as long as you are lazy, slacker, not socially friendly, and dull looking, you will have no money and no friends. No matter how much you meditate.

It's the same with health. Yes, energy, meditation, it all has something to do with it. But only in the sense that one of the signs of why people get sick is that they are not focused on anything. The more attention people have on their body and their inner self, the longer they live and stay healthy because their attention is on themselves. If you keep practicing techniques, keep your attention on yourself, and don't lose your inner self, you will have fewer problems with your health and in general in life. Problems are given to people who lose themselves.

That's why the system beats them up so that they can focus on themselves for a while.

Once you've already got a series of illnesses, you can't fix them. You can't heal it with energy, it's an illusion. Maybe it can be done, but not in your case. You mustn't think about it or believe in it. Forget it. There's a prohibition here. For physical health, go to a doctor. It's the right thing to do.

2. Technique with a Drink

Pour the same coke into two glasses. Put one glass, the original, aside to keep it out of sight. You can put the other one in front of you and influence it. But only once. If you try it both ways, you will not know what works. You have to do one technique, for example, place your palm over a glass, hold it over the drink, and imagine that you are giving energy from it to the glass. Then taste the drink that you influenced and compare it to the original that was away.

You will feel the difference. And anyone who does the technique correctly, just giving energy, the taste of the drink will change. It all depends on the technique: if you give energy, the mutation happens with Coca-Cola.

Then you can pour Coca-Cola into two glasses again, hide one of them, and put the other in front of you. And no longer give energy with the palm of your hand but take it away. Bring your palm up, and you can help yourself with your breath, and it's as if you're sucking the energy out of the drink. I imagine as if I'm sucking the energy out of Coca-Cola with the palm of my hand. You have to taste it and compare it to the original. They will be very different.

When you give or take energy away, the impact happens in different ways. You can feel it. Do this technique with Coca-Cola for now.

If you just give away energy as much as possible without thinking, the effect is always the same – everything becomes tasteless. Any drink will taste almost like water. That's the way it is when you give out pure, undistorted energy. When you take it away, it tastes clearer, harsher, and rougher. It depends on the drink.

You have to be able to take energy. What kind of mistakes can you make? Maybe someone was inattentive, gave energy to a drink and it became almost water, and then started doing a second experiment with the same drink, which was already ruined, and taking energy away. Because of that, the taste was already incomprehensible. This is a mistake. When you take away the energy, you have to do it with a new coke. In other words, when you try to change the flavour, you have to do it on a coke that you haven't influenced before. It must not be stirred.

Also, if you are taking energy and getting a different effect, there can be a mistake like this. When you hold the palm of your hand up to the drink, the energy can go to the coke. So, I put my palm up and I take two breaths as if I am drawing energy. And then I move my hand away because after that I want to exhale, and when I exhale you can't let the hand stay over the coke.

Otherwise, you're taking the energy, and then you exhale and give it back. That's not the way to do it. You breathe out and then you put your hand to the glass again. That's how you do it. You have to try it. Don't worry if you can't do it. You can practice for a long time.

What is this technique for? First of all, to make your mind and psyche even more aware of what energy is. To understand that it is different and affects something in different ways. You get familiar with it. And at the first stage, it's great that you can feel it. In the second stage, it's great when you start to understand that energy can influence. The third stage is great when one understands that on top of everything else, energy can affect you in different ways; if you take it away it's one thing, if you give it away it's another.

Don't try with your mind to achieve the result I described above. Let's take a different approach. Your task is simply to conduct research. Compare how you can change the taste of Coca-Cola or water. I showed you the options – you can give energy, or you can take energy away. I also told you that when you test it, every time there has to be a new drink.

That is, if you have already influenced it, you do not need to do anything else with it. Because it already looks nothing like the original. Try doing the same experiment with a little bit of cheese. You can try to affect it just visually, with your eyes. But don't strain yourself. You can test how to do it, that is, to give and take away energy from the chakra. Analyse it and write down the results.

What happens to certain products, when you give energy through something and when you take it away? Take notes to understand in further experiments whether the results are the same or different. You have to learn how energy can be transformed and how it manifests itself afterward.

So many people say that when they began to free their attention, it became uncomfortable, as if they were in the clouds, that it was very hard to concentrate because there was a lot of attention, and it was not tame. Then I said that I had to get used to it.

Of course, when there is a very important job to do, for concentration you can ground yourself, mute, and silence. But in any free time, it is better to learn to get used to free attention. This is your level of development. But a high-level person will not be satisfied with leading a low-level lifestyle. His attention span is so strong that he will not be satisfied by a low man's way of life. I've just been focused on my attention since I was a kid.

Why didn't I do stupid things or watch silly cat videos? It's just that my attention span wasn't stolen by it, it was different from the masses of primitive society. I didn't have any knowledge; I listened, watched, and did whatever suited my attention span. I've developed attention so much over the last year that before the only thing I resonated with was the nameless playlist, and now it's like this music is parallel; it's not with me, I'm not with it.

3. Meditation

First rule: you don't have to call it meditation, that word is trivialised; meditation is in the gym with stupid people.

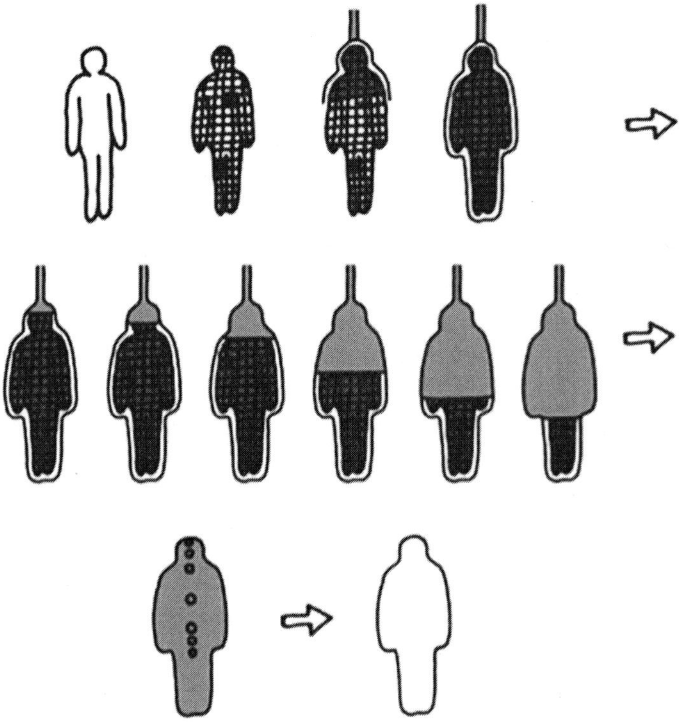

Fig. 18

I call it the *opening of the channel*. I didn't know about meditation at all.

I met a man and he said to me, "Alex, I'm not interested in your information, but how you became this way. What did you do? Or maybe something happened?"

And I told him, "I don't seem to have done anything. I'm just like this."

And he asks, "Think back to a time when there were no miracles and no energy, and then think back to when it all started?"

I remembered, I was sitting at home alone at night, in my thoughts, a little depressed, and I turned on a track, or rather a black and white video. I was sitting half lying down in bed at the time. The track by Yoav, *Beautiful Lie* was playing. And while I was listening to it my attention was very focused on the sounds, it was three-dimensional. I played it on a loop, and I felt something heavy, like a hat on my head, which is too small. I mean it was crushing my head.

So, I closed my eyes. And when I listened with my eyes closed, I felt something even harder on my head, above my head. And I just imagined that I, that is, the consciousness, the soul, wanted to go out there through my head, as if I was reaching up through my head, into space.

I listened to every sound of music and imagined that I was that sound, that I was reaching up with it. But as I did so, I felt distracted by my breathing. That it was as if I had to freeze to feel each sound even more. And I began to freeze, not breathing in those moments when I was catching the sounds, imagining that with the sound I was reaching up through the top of my head.

But I didn't hold my breath to the extreme, to the point of shortness of breath. You shouldn't do that; it would be disruptive. I did it calmly as if I was just breathing a little, breathing in through my nose, and then not breathing and slowly exhaling through my mouth, like through a tube. And the whole time I'm not breathing and slowly exhaling, I imagine myself trying to reach up through my head at every sound of the music. Put the music on loop and try it.

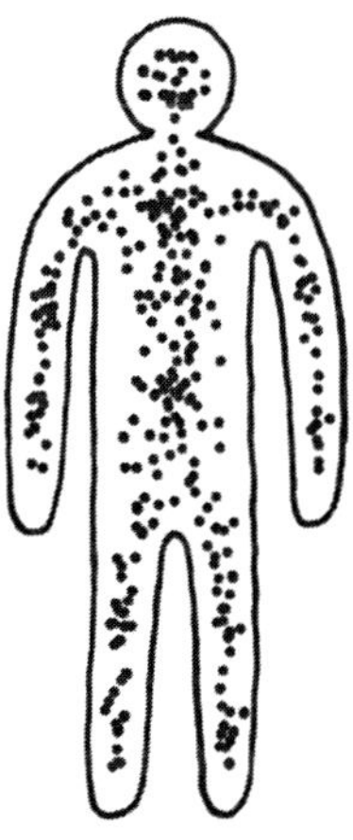

Fig. 19

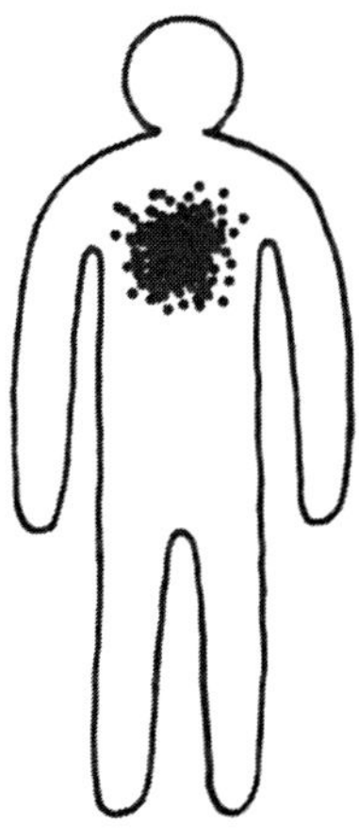

Fig. 20

I did a technique today. The little grains of sand in the picture are the energy; your consciousness. You're spread out, your attention is all over your body (Fig. 19). You, imagine that all of your energy is gathered in the centre. That is you start to collect it from your legs, from your arms, from your whole body into the centre (Fig. 20). Try to do this and feel how you are collected. It doesn't take any effort or strain. You just have to believe and imagine.

And then you have to pull the collected energy up through your head. As in the picture (Fig. 21, 22).

Now try the *channel opening* technique as described above. First gather the energy in the centre, and then pull it upward.

When I did the technique, I imagined all the energy in my body gathering. Like a bottle, when you shake it, all the gases gather towards the cork. It's the same with me.

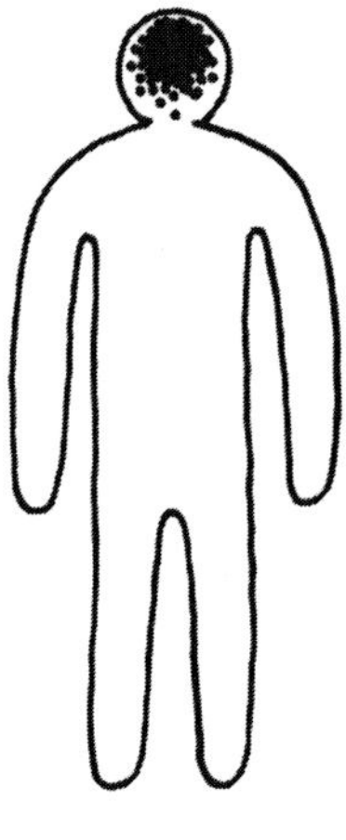

Fig. 21

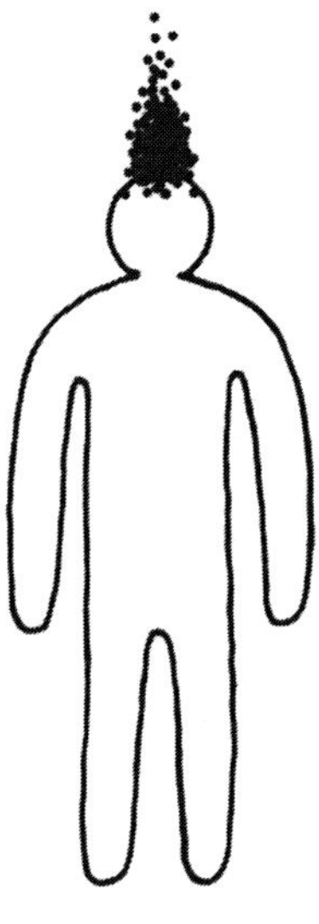

Fig. 22

It's like these gases are my grains of energy. I imagine myself mentally reaching upward. It's like I'm even looking up there with my eyes. All the energy is there. But I'm not tense at all, I'm very calm and relaxed. There was music playing in the background, but there wasn't a Yoav track. What began to happen? There are stages, a level which you can reach, doing this technique. I had a spontaneous moment as if my attention was there and I was reaching for it.

And it was as if my body felt very light. When I open my eyes, it feels like the music is three-dimensional, and I feel so good and light. It's like I'm looking down on everything. That's the aftertaste of this technique. As if you are above everyone and you are in that flow. A sense of lightness. And everything is three-dimensional.

I see most people make the same mistake. So many stress and approach this technique with rudeness, fuss, excitement, worrying *what if it doesn't work*, and thinking about how to concentrate. On the contrary, there should be no thoughts. You have to dissolve, to relax as much as possible. As if you were flying up. Whether you succeed or not depends on how much your mind disturbs you. Nothing else. The mind, the panic, the fuss, the fear, the disbelief. You did it with your mind.

That's like telling a creative person to sit down and write something, come on, right in a hurry. That's no way to write a book. It requires inspiration and a certain disposition of mood. You have to be mentally ready for it. Not with your mind but with your soul. It has to be without psychological tension.

Attention is what you are. That's what it's all about. Just attention and nothing else. By giving information on managing attention, and energy, I'm teaching you who you are. This is what it is. Attention is who I am.

We are in the body, there are many things around us. Imagine how much you are not you when your attention is on automatic mode. You're like a car that's turned on, but it's not even on a remote control, it goes straight ahead, hits a wall, and goes the other way. That's how people live.

And I start explaining, "Can you stop?"

People ask, "How?"

And I say, "Stop. Car, freeze. Now go straight, now stop, go back, stop."

And I give you this kind of silly direction. But on the other hand, I'm teaching you how to steer yourself. Do you see? Attention is what you are. The more you practice techniques, the more I give you examples, the more you do all this, the more you find yourself, and the more you are freed from automatism and stupefaction.

This is the step toward awareness. You have to realise this and realise that you are the attention. Then you will feel super strong and unique. It's as if you can get your attention anywhere and do anything. Because that's what you are. It's as if you detach yourself from all ties, from the mind, from automatism and you start to experience the real you. You have to get to know yourself. This is awareness. This is development.

If when you do the *channel opening* technique, you see some pictures in your head, it's the mind. It reacts. The mind always wants to name it, label it, to package it somehow. Some people's mental reaction is to immediately understand what, when, and why. And someone begins to visualise. But that is also mental. I always scold everyone for that.

Why have I never in ten years supported people who write about conscious dreaming? Why am I reacting to it? Not because it's my reaction. I'm showing you as much as possible what's good and what's bad. What is yes and what is no. What's delusional, what's a trap, what's true. And these dreams you love, all these pictures you love, they're deception, they're low-level. It is not good. You can't be distracted by it in any way.

If you start to do technique and see images, try to concentrate even more on the music and on the technique to distract yourself from them. You don't have to focus on them, you don't have to immerse yourself in these images. It takes your attention away. It is an illusion, a trick, nothing more. The mind is playing with you. All sorts of perceptions, and visualisations – that's the mind. When one sees auras of colours, visions of something, that one has been somewhere in the past life. When he sees a light, or someone appears in front of him when he closes his eyes. It's all a deception, an illusion, a game of the mind. A pure man, who is zero, does not see any of this.

There is a moment with a cold. The only ailment that is beyond attention and energy is when you have a cold. I don't consider it a disease. It's supposed to be a good thing. Everybody does. Some get it hard, some don't. Some get it for a day or two, some stay sick for a week. Some people get it in cycles, for example, in the fall and spring. Why? Because these are transitional seasons.

The main seasons, the two extremes, are summer and winter. And the transition from winter to summer, which is spring, is acclimatisation. You rebuild your rhythm. And in the same way, it's restructuring from summer to winter in the fall. Sensitive people always get colds. I'm an example of that. That's normal.

When a person is lying down with an ailment, with a fever, his attention shuts off from everything and focuses on the body. Autotherapy. It is better not to reduce a fever. Of course, everyone's case is different, and I'm not a doctor. Listen to the doctors. If they say reduce it down – reduce it down. But it is necessary to have a cold. How many times I have caught a cold – nothing can be done at this time.

Can't do meditation. Of course, I can feel the energy between my palms even with a fever, I can get my attention, but it's better not to. It is good that you are in the mist during a cold. When you get sick, the process that happens is the attention that works on your body. You can look into what's happening to it.

When a person sleeps or faints, their attention is divided, like when they have a cold. That's what sleep is for – that's when all the senses are turned off, and all attention is transferred to the body. And you recover, everything is fine. When a person consciously and voluntarily works with energy, doing techniques, he may not sleep much. Because what he would have received during sleep comes from the techniques.

When one sleeps, one's attention is on the person. If his head is heavily overloaded when he sleeps – his energy and attention are not on his body, it is spent on the work of his brain. That is he seems to fall asleep, but his brain continues to work. And such a person dreams.

You can do the *channel opening* technique every day, preferably in the evening or at night. If you don't want to do it, if you feel psychologically and mentally unprepared, don't do it. If you practice by force, it will not work, and in your mind, you will remember that you cannot do it. That's how you'll ruin the technique.

You will be unsure of yourself. It is the same as if a man now learns about it, wants to do it and, not knowing the keys and rules, tries to do the technique at work, sitting in his office. He won't succeed and it will be in his subconscious mind that he was not given it, that he is different, bad, or closed. He will get upset.

Then he will try to do the technique at home, but after he has eaten a lot, in the bustle, among the crowds, when he is away from his room for ten minutes. He will fail again. And there will be even more associations that the technique doesn't work or there is something wrong with it. Then it will be difficult to explain to the person that he or she drove himself or herself to it.

You need to follow my advice and use the keys, and then everything will be okay. And if you feel like you're not in the mood for it, don't do it. Or create the mood first. Music, movies, techniques with energy. And if you are in the mood, you can do the *opening of the channel*, of course, it's better not to forget about the technique. It will help to disconnect from all external factors, it will sober you up.

Every technique I have given you will bring you more and more into a new frequency where there is wonder, and faith and where everything is good. You are disconnected from society, from the mind, from evil, from doubts, fears, etc. All of these techniques are only a plus, not a minus in any way. I do them every day, one, then another, then a third. I don't approach it like a robot; I do it according to my mood.

I may not do a certain technique in a day. There's nothing wrong with that, it means I wasn't in the mood. Or I was busy. But it doesn't mean that I've been busy for two days with my attention scattered. It means that I was with myself for hours instead of techniques.

I've never done a technique in the morning or closer to noon in my life. Only after sunset. I don't know why. I'm not a man of the mind who has read a book, get to the bottom of every little detail of what-how-why, and does everything like a hackneyed person who doesn't know the essence. I live by nature. I am being led. I am shown. How it goes on, so it is right. Only then can I try to parse it out with my mind, what and how to find a pattern.

And it so happens that all my techniques are for the evening or night. Especially the *opening of the channel*. Why is that? I don't know. That's why I don't approve of mornings.

The old-school esoteric, whom I don't cross paths with, used to say even ten years ago, "Alex, how do you turn this on from the top down. It has to be from the bottom up."

I don't care how it should be for you. It's how nature intended it to be, and it's the right way. You have to open up the canal through the top of your head. And they do it starting from the lower *chakra*. That's not right. It's the same for morning and evening.

Maybe the chakras that will work in the future are the upper ones. And the lower ones are something old and past. After all, the lower chakras are responsible for something material, if I'm not mistaken. I don't go to that with my mind. I know how nature has arranged, that's what I'm talking about. And if I go into details, I haven't thought about it. There are no examples.

When you reach into your head, that is you are not reaching out with your body, not with your head, but you are trying to get your soul, your consciousness up through your head, at that moment you begin to feel certain sensations. As if something is happening to your body. Like it becomes light or heavy like something is moving through it.

It can be different. Imagine that you're in a small, enclosed room and your head is against the ceiling. It is sandy. The more you stretch up, the more sand falls on you. Figuratively speaking, that's how it feels.

If you fall asleep during practice, then you have no control over yourself. Because when attention is released, it has to be controlled. By thought form – that is, by saying inwardly, *I am here and now, I am reaching there. The more emphasis on I-I-I, the more in control.*

Why do people fall asleep? A man begins to do the technique, his attention has never been under control. Because he lives with his mind, his attention is scattered on automatic, controlled by circumstances, events, and thoughts. And when external control is disconnected, they cannot take their attention under their control. So, they become sleepy. This is the very first, standard, typical reaction of a material person from the world of the mind.

If such a person does techniques, he doesn't feel awake, but for him, this state is associated with disconnection of the mind, as if he is tired and wants to sleep. But this is the reaction of people in the mind world. In the spiritual and conscious person, technique, on the contrary, is energising and invigorating. Whoever complains that he falls asleep is complaining of his mind. So, while the mind is ruling you. It is dissatisfied and falls asleep.

What I can advise. Play computer games and concentrate your attention. Take some martial arts classes. You have to develop sharpness, dexterity, and focus. Do some math. Do some geometry puzzles, do some speed work. In all kinds of altered states of consciousness, you have to be focused. Do your chores only under control. You have to be stronger than all the things that can make you feel dizzy. No matter how many litres of alcohol you put in me, I'm as good as I've ever been. Even sober. And those who drink and become pigs, it's an indication that they aren't even themselves.

Another tip of note. If one does the *channel opening* technique, it's a very strong change from the world of the mind to the world of the spirit. It is like a pressure change. If a person smokes cigarettes during the day and starts doing the technique in the evening, he may get a headache. Or vice versa, if he was doing the technique of opening the channel, and after that he smoked, he may get a very bad headache. Because of the difference.

So, it is either the *opening of the channel* or cigarettes. One is not friendly with the other. If you do this kind of exercise, no bad habits. If you have switched to the spiritual wave, then stay on it. You may be in charge of material things, and you may do something, but it's a different rhythm. It's a common story, I know it from people I know. People who smoke, or who open and close very abruptly, get a headache. And if you don't close, you don't get a headache. If there's rebuilding, it's like the head splits. It happens.

You don't need to understand if you're doing the practice right or wrong. You have to feel it. You don't have to understand to not make mistakes. It's all in your mind. You want to know what to expect, like others, like me, you want to expect it and go somewhere. Instead of understanding, you should just do it.

You have to do, not expect, and strive for something contrived. If you want to be sure you're doing it right, and as people say, see if it's working, there's only one way. You reread each line of the techniques that I have described, write them down on a piece of paper, think about what I mean, and look at yourself from the outside to see if you have done what the instructions say. It all depends on your attention.

The more you did it all, the more seriously you took the task, and with each word, the more certain the result will be. The more you do it yourself, the more likely it is that the technique will be faulty and won't work. It's simple.

Your consciousness is connected to your body by a thread. If it disconnects from the body, it dies. That's the way it works. But don't worry, the string will never disconnect. You don't have to think the nonsense that flies around on the internet that you can leave your body, it's just nonsense. It is impossible if you know how things work.

You are still in the body as long as it is alive. And the attention is there. But you can direct your attention, like a beam, wherever you want. There are no obstacles to that. What matters is that you can aim for it. That you know where this beam stops, where it aims. The more you understand the social-material world, the more you can target and control your attention. That's why you need socio-material development.

If you know more about how the internal organs work, more attention will be on them. One of the secrets of health is not to grow plants for oxygen in the apartment, not to have a cat to cure diseases but to learn anatomy and hang a couple of posters. And know where and what is and pay attention to it. In the sense that, if I can imagine being in some holy place, I can connect to it now, be there paying attention. I will still be in my body, but my beam will go there. It is possible to do that.

I can now imagine that the energy rays into my tea come from all the holy places I've been to. Or I can make a list of such places, tune in to them, and all the energy from there will go into my mug or me. You don't have to exert yourself, and you don't even have to do any techniques.

Would you like an interesting experiment? Go to at least two temples and get holy water. And try to drink from each bottle. See how you feel. And then try to do the *channel opening* technique.

Holy water is charged water if everything was done right and observed. And there is one that is called holy water, but for some reason is not charged. Collect water from all the churches you have around. Don't drink it there. Bring it home. And at home try it in your free time, not in a hurry, in a calm atmosphere, when you plan to do techniques. Drink a sip from a bottle from each church. And notice how you begin to feel, and what is going on. Try doing the techniques before the holy water and after. And see how it helps.

You can do all the techniques 24 hours a day, as long as they are not detrimental to your social life. Don't go to extremes. You have to communicate with people and meet new people. There has to be maximum balance. People, who do techniques with *chakras*, the opening of a channel and they are good at it, should compensate for it with the opposite – to meet super material people, to eat meat, to fool around, to have fun. This is important.

You can't go to extremes. The material and the spiritual are interconnected. You have to raise your social level and put things in order with whom you socialise. You have to have a social circle all the time. It doesn't matter if it's your employees or your friends; you have to have one. You can't always sit alone.

Being alone is useful, but not 24 hours a day. It is extreme. It is necessary to understand that there is a social and material world, and it is necessary to live in it. But live soberly and consciously. It's like when you do techniques and meditate and *open the channel*, you zero in on yourself when you get home. Then refreshed and awake you go to work and exist there. That's how you approach all things more wisely and consciously.

All problems with the head only come from the mind. Its glitches. When a person is without a mind, he has no memory. The mind is an evaluation, good or bad. He remembers it. And when you are without a mind, everything is perceived as the first time. You can't have sharp delayed reactions to something. Only the mind remembers it, reminds you of it, and disturbs you. If you have been wronged many times or had your psyche broken in some way, the mind starts to glitch. The only way to get rid of it is to turn it off and to not live it. Or, on the contrary, develop the mind.

Of course, it has to do with attention. The mind is like a filter. There's a laser, it's your attention, but you can put different filters on top of it. The mind distorts your perception and your reaction to something. You have to work on it. If you were completely zeros, pure calm people with no complexes, no glitches in your head, I would give you information faster.

I will just give you the techniques and you wouldn't have any questions. You would understand everything. But I spell everything out. Because people are always in a panic, they think something will harm them or something else. The mind frightens you in every way. It does not let you make the right choices. You get into conflicts because of it, you get into bad situations, and you lose your chance.

Remember the situations in life where there was work with attention, with energy. One of them is when people do fire-walk on coal. I don't advise you to do that, I'm not in charge of you. But the point is that it's easy to learn, with all the keys I gave you. A person's attention must be out of the mind, not in society, but somewhere in the inner cosmos. It is a state of trance, of shock. If one runs over the coals in such a state, without the mind paying attention to it, he will not get burned. Look for examples like this.

4. How to Influence People

I'll tell you how attunement and influence on people or an outside object happen when you can charge something, take energy away, or give it away. Approach it in such a way that it is and is. You don't have to brag about it. If you have such intentions, it won't work.

Set yourself the attitude that you are doing this for yourself, just to know. To strengthen your faith, to work with your attention. Don't apply it anywhere. People who have a lot of stupidity, selfishness, greed or complexes and a desire to show off, to compete, those who live with their minds, they want techniques with which they can rub everyone's nose in it or surprise and amaze everyone, become an upstart. These are bad intentions.

If you're like that, no technique will work for you. You've got to calm down a little bit. You have to be pure. And pure intentions towards yourself and everything. That's the main mistake when people want to prove something to their relatives. Why do you go on fighting with them and proving something to those who shouldn't know it?

It's a violation of the law of nature. It's like being a stork and pestering the kiwi bird who can't fly, and you want to show it that you can fly, that you have big wings, and you want to remind it that it can't fly. Why?

Aggression, competition, discussion, and evaluation are what makes all people rot in society. It's not good. You can justify yourself by saying that you want to help your relatives. Go ahead; just let them go. That's the best help for you and them.

Men who want to influence people have an ulterior intention to boast, to have self-confidence, they want to be cool. And women most often have the intention to heal themselves and save their dying relatives, even though no one is dying. But they have this attitude *we are all dying, we are all miserable, we all have to be cured and saved.* Those who have this kind of foolishness, stop it in yourselves.

Originally, to influence a person, I used many auxiliary keys. I couldn't do anything without them. I used to notice, for example, that I would meet a person and want to show them a technique with palms, energy, or *chakra*. That he would turn the *chakra* on in front of me or that I would turn it on for him. And it happened that everything worked with one person, but not with another.

At first, I had this understanding, which means one person is open and the other is closed. It is logical and understandable. But then I came to a different conclusion. It's not just about that, but also about the frequency, the rhythm at which I plan to demonstrate these techniques with energy. I, for example, insist on the time of the meeting; it must be my time. I propose the place of the meeting so that it is my place.

The person comes to visit, or to a restaurant, and I tell him to sit where I tell him to sit. He wants a coffee and I tell him to try tea instead. On top of that, when he wants to talk and tell me what kind of car he bought, I stop him and start telling him or asking him something about my topic. So, I bend my line on everything and get the man on my frequency. And if I also talk to him and let him listen to some music or tell him a story about various sacred things, he and I will be on the same energy frequency. I will drag him there. Then I can ask him to hold his palms out and he will start to feel the energy. I'll tell him to close his eyes and feel something in his chest and start doing that, so he'll feel the heart *chakra*.

He will feel all the energy. But why? Because I show it to him in my world. And if I'm visiting him, where he's cheerful and bending his line, I'll bend to his frequency. He's the host and the boss, and he raises his topics, and so on, that's it, I'm on his frequency, and even if I want to show him something, neither he nor I will feel anything. Because the frequency he is on it's not there. There is no faith and no energy. That's the first thing to take note of.

Second. I bend my line, and the person on my frequency starts doing techniques in front of me, and he gets to feel the heart *chakra*. I don't look at him or the centre of his chest to send him energy. No, that's not how it's done. I become a zero; I can remember the *chair technique* or the *channel opening* technique, then I ask him to close his eyes and just sit.

He has to close his eyes to feel better. He sits like this, and I sit and imagine that I am him. Like my body is his body. And I start turning on my thoracic chakra. Then everything that I experience and feel, he begins to feel in parallel. That's how it works. And if a person did a technique and it didn't work, that's normal. He had fears in his mind that he was doing it in front of somebody. That is, there were a lot of thoughts, it was hard for the person, and it was scary. It was not always possible to shut these thoughts off.

And if the person was doing a technique in front of me live, I would say, "Let's try it again, just listen to the music and try to put the emphasis upwards, the attention upwards."

And he would sit down and listen to music. And I would sit down and tune out that I was zero. I would pretend that I was him and do the technique as if I was him. And it turned out that everything I did for 20 minutes or half an hour, as far as I got there, into space, upstairs, all these feelings were described later by the man who was doing the technique. So, I did the exercise for him. That is how one can be empowered and have an impact on a person.

When I was a kid, I was testing how I could influence energy. That's what I did. Someone, for example, had pain in their leg. I imagined that the person's leg was my leg. But I was exactly a mirror. If someone was sitting in front of me right now, his right knee would look into my left knee. For his right knee to heal, I have to concentrate on my left knee.

I can even feel people that way. It is like mirroring. They must be on your frequency. It's as if you create the radio wave that you are on, then you can influence him and it's as if he is giving you the benefit of the doubt. That's very important. When a person is closed and their attention is somewhere, you can't influence them.

If you want to influence a person, they're in another part of the world and they have a bad knee and you want to turn on their chakra, you have to make them do as many points in the list of things as possible on your recommendation and connect to your frequency. You have to bend your line.

For example, a person is in Australia right now. I want to heal his knee or activate his chest chakra. I tell him to sit on a chair in the middle of the room at 1 o'clock in the morning, put on music, such-and-such a track, on repeat, to hold a coin in both palms of his hands, and to put his hands with the coins on his knees. If I bend him like this, give him a list of things to do, and I do the same list at home – a chair in the middle of the room, the same music, and sitting with coins. Then we create a common frequency for two, on which we can synchronise with each other.

Initially, I did this, I said, "One, two, three, close your eyes and sit."

Or I would tell him what to concentrate on. When he did it my way, he was on my frequency. And I could tune into him, that I was him. He would let me go into him and work on him. I could send energy to him, focus it on any part of his body, I could do a *channel opening* technique, turn on all of his chakras, so anything.

This is one way to influence a person, but with his approval. That person has to be aware, and you have to be aware, both of you have to tune in that way. It's interesting. Most of the time I've done it in a way that doesn't involve the *chakras* and treatment of people.

I have never cured anyone; I have always understood that the most important and valuable thing for a person is just to put energy into them. If he is not able to do it himself. It cleanses and opens him up as much as possible. It's good for everyone. I used to give my energy to everyone.

5. Technique with a Coin

There is such a technique with a coin. No amateurism. Do everything I tell you to do, and what I don't tell you to do, don't do.

Take any coin. Take a picture of it from different sides, so that you have the original for yourself. Then start doing any technique: *chakras*, palms, the *opening of a channel* – anything. But imagine that all the energy is going into that coin. Try to put all of your attention into it, to charge it in your way. And then feel if there is energy emanating from it. If you can.

How I charge a coin. I don't hold my palm over it as I do over a drink. I take it in my hand to see it. I don't clench it in my fist, I hold it with two fingers and look at it – there it is. And then I forget about it. And I imagine that I'm collecting all my energy, like grains of sand, all over my body, and it goes through my hand, through my fingers, into the coin. It's like I'm flowing all this energy over there. That's what you have to do.

I've noticed that people who don't know how to feel the energy from an object take it into their hands for some reason.

If I say to someone who is not on the topic, "I have a supercharged bracelet or stone," he takes it, clasps it in his fist, and tries to feel it.

I've never done that. When I clenched an object in my fist, I feel a thousand times weaker.

To recognise whether an object is emanating energy or not, all I have to do is look at it. My perception is that it is something that gives off light. Energy can be compared to light. It's just that there is energy that is in the range of light and colours, and there is energy that we can't see, but it's the same light, it's there. When I look at an object that is emanating energy, I feel that there is some process going on. What is that process? It's like an impact. The energy begins to spread through the body, like exposure.

Each object can be used in different ways. To feel whether an object is emanating or not, hold it in front of your face. This is the most sensitive place.

The second most sensitive place is the chest. You can hold the object in front of your chest without leaning on it but at a distance. Another sensitive area is the neck, where the back of the head is.

How can you tell if it's self-influenced or not? You can check this way: if you hold up an object, you feel it, and then you take it away, and the feeling disappears. That's not mind. It's very clear. If you give it to another person and check his sensations, he will describe the same thing. I always test everything on people I know. I don't tell them what the effect will be or if it will have any effect at all. I just give them the object and ask them how they feel.

It is possible to make a charged object cease to be so. But that's not what we're talking about right now. If you consider the technique I gave you, the object from which you get energy is not withdrawn. It's not cloned. It happens a little bit differently.

Energy is limitless, it takes any form. Imagine that there is a crystal with energy in it. There is a crystal and a coin next to it. I imagine a lot of strings coming out of the crystal, and I mentally draw energy into the coin by strings. One by one, they grow and stretch into the coin. I do this without any effort. Not with my hands, not with anything. You can help yourself and move a finger to the left and right, it may be of help to someone whose faith is weak, but it's a key. But you can also do it without a finger.

I make a sort of bridge, and strings of energy from the crystal go into the coin. The energy doesn't run out, it just goes. There's an unlimited amount of it. I do this with no strain on my mind, no effort of concentration, no physical strain or effort. I'm relaxed, my breathing is moderate. I just believe in it, I let it be, and it just happens.

I can even go outside; the main thing is to keep in my mind that this process happens. And it will keep happening as long as I remember it, as long as I keep my attention. And the coin will charge. It sounds beautiful, but it won't charge anymore. You have to understand, energy doesn't have time. It only takes a second for it to recharge. But the human mind is not up to date and without a strong belief, it cannot believe that.

That's why man needs an illusion, how he imagines energy from a crystal for a minute and transfers it into a coin. But in reality, a second is enough. When you are unprepared and you have never been able to do it, you will not do it. It takes a lot of faith and is beyond doubt. You have to practice; you have to be convinced that this energy is there. And the more you know and experience energy through practice and experimentation, the easier you will take it.

The energy doesn't go anywhere. It is preserved. It only wears off if you start doing it yourself with attention. It's unique, it's extraordinary. When I was a child, I said that we, all human beings, have thoughts. Every second is different. If one can do this, think of something and it happens, then one can think of something stupid at any moment and it will happen. It is illogical.

Then I made a discovery, as long as there are uncontrollable thoughts, there is no wish fulfilment. As long as you're living with reason there will be no miracles. It's deliberate. If there were these miracles, people would harm themselves with their unruly minds. The mind is not energy. And when you shut your mind off and become a zero, there is nothing spontaneous. And then even the idea of your inner voice cannot be bad. Nothing can harm you. Then you have the possibility to work wonders.

I have ten coins, all of them in different energies. They are all in the same bag. Their energies don't mix. They can't irradiate from each other unless I think about it. But I do not think it with my mind, I think it with my attention. So far they are all different and have different backgrounds, as I once charged them. But if I look at them now and imagine that the strings go from coin to coin and it all blends, that's it, the energies blend. And when I take the coins out of the bag, each one will have the same type of energy emanating – I mixed them all, but when I did it myself, with attention.

Therefore, when an object is charged, it remains charged. The energy never wears off unless it is affected by attention.

I have an Egyptian statue. It's an ordinary souvenir, not an antique. But it's got emanating energy. How is it? It's made in a factory, it's not antique, but it radiates. I've been making theories and discussing them with people I know. Here's what it turns out. Because this figurine is a replica, without any irregularities in shape or line, it takes on the same energy as the original. If I go to some museum that has an incredibly valuable charged artifact and order a copy of it, it will have the same emanating energy. But that's not a revelation.

I have an Egyptian silver ring that was given to me by a higher power. I was led to it by circumstances. I did not buy it out of the blue. It's not a simple ring; it's very strong and unique. It has a King, which is Tutankhamun. And it's got emanating energy. But the interesting thing is something else. It's not because the ring is charged by somebody.

I thought it was an antique ring, someone charged it, and then I got it. But when I ordered the gold replica, I didn't know that if I made a replica, it would also emanate. I planned to have a gold ring and transfer the energy from the silver one. But when I got the replica, it turned out to be emanating energy. You don't have to transfer energy. It's already working. But that's not all. The discovery is this.

Remember the movie *Devil's Advocate*? There main character is a lawyer who defends different people, criminals, crooks, and so on. And he defends a man who killed a goat on his premises while performing some kind of ritual. When a lawyer begins to defend his client, the client pulls out a beef tongue and a whole bunch of nails with the implication that, *whoever is against me, I will help him to shut up*. As a result, when there is a court case, the accuser can't talk and coughs all the time. Because the man did the ritual – he drove nails into his tongue.

Do you know why it was done that way? It is understandable that when filmmakers and screenwriters prepare a film, they do research on rites and rituals, and they look for consultants to show a rite that is close to reality. But of course, they don't know if it works or not. So, they learned about a ritual somewhere. But the point is, it works. And do you know why? Because if you have to influence a person's speaking, you have to have a form in the first place.

And you also have to imagine that the beef tongue is your tongue. It's the same story as with the Egyptian statue. A copy of it makes the same connections because it has the same shell. You should take note. When I was at Madame Tussauds, Mother Teresa was there, and it reeked of energy. And why was that? Because they made a replica of her, and the wax figure took on her spirit. Do you see?

Why do I say that it's a discovery? It is very important for performing rituals. If I want to affect the ear, I need the ear. But it has to be connected. If I have a dog's ear it has to be connected to your human ear, figuratively speaking. Notice how interesting this connection works. It seems simple, but it's a revelation.

And what to do next with the charged coins? The ones I hope you've tried to charge. You don't have to do anything, it's just an experiment. And how can it be used in the future?

Let's say I'm an ordinary guy who has read this book and tried techniques and experiments. Some of it worked, and some of it didn't. In the course of various practices over the course of a month or two, there were moments when I went into the super inner cosmos. Maybe from the *channel opening* techniques I was supercharged. When I'm charged, I can take a coin and imagine all this state going into it. As if all the threads of energy from my body go into that coin. It can lie on the table, and you can hold it with two fingers. All of your energy, your charged state is draining into the coin.

It's charged. What next? I'm already back in everyday life, in relationships, at work, with relatives, and immersed in everyday life. No time for technique. I feel like I've shut myself off. Then I can take this coin, put it in a pouch, and hang it around my neck. Or just take it in my hand and hold it in front of me. Or hold a drink over it and drink it. That is, to pay attention to this coin by all means, but not to charge it, but rather to connect to it.

The bottom line is this. I was at some point of charge, let's call it frequency. Let's say I was open at 43 points. That is, my mind was off, and my attention was at 43 points, and that was sent in the coin. When I start interacting with it after a week – I hang it around my neck, it pulls me over, and gives me back my psychological and energetic state, which is at 43 points.

Do you know what I mean? Make a note of this tip for yourself. It will help you a lot. When you have a moment of *nirvana*, cosmos, and so on, try to capture that state by putting that energy into a coin. It will then help you to return to that state.

The point of this experiment is that the more examples you know and experience with energy, the more your attention and faith grow. The more you open up. What you need, you've already got and you're getting. That doesn't mean you always have to do something specific with the coin. You just have to know it. You have to believe in it. I am revealing to you the level of knowledge that you can transfer energy from there to there. You have to know this in practice. You have to realise that it exists and that you can do it. This is very important. This is already level.

I wrote a book called *The Corridor*. And I talked a lot about the fact that in addition to the spiritual world, there is society and there are 12 frequencies, 12 sub-frequencies. In all books I have always said that there is a material frequency and a spiritual frequency. The material part is also divided into levels. But I always presented the spiritual part as one thing. Just turn off your mind, that's all.

It's great if you're disconnected from society. But as it turns out, the spiritual world figuratively speaking (not literally) also has 12 levels and 12 sub-levels.

This is very conventional. Spirituality is not just spirituality, it's one frequency. There are more frequencies within that – the level of spirituality, the level of faith, the level of attentional power.

In the book, I also give you the spiritual frequencies. This is spiritual development, that is attention, step by step. And we're going through that right now and getting familiar with different forms of energy and how you can work with it. This gives you the power of faith and attention.

It's a misconception that everything starts to emanate energy. When you have become sensitive, you can put your palm up and feel something from the remote control, and food is okay. You can look at something and concentrate and feel something from the object. Any object has something. But it's not that.

You don't have to intensively perceive something that truly emanates energy. If it's already emanating, you take it out and it makes your temples pop and your head goes fuzzy. That's what's called *emanating*. A remote control and a phone can't do that. Every object has an energy shell that protrudes about half a centimetre. Your body has one. You hit the shell on the phone with it to affect the object. But the notion of emanating is when you feel the real energy – the energy of the source, of the deity. Those are the kind of things I collect.

And one more thing about digital photos. It's not the photo that emanates. You have to think about how interesting energy is, and how it works. I thought about this a long time ago, when I first bought an icon that was emanating. I had a picture of it on my phone.

When it's off, it's not radiating. But if I open the photo, it starts to emit energy just when it is open on the screen. Yes, it plays electronically. But the image itself appears in the light. So, it is with me. And it radiates. But it is not the photo that is emanating.

You understand the principle of how everything digital is made. Is there a movie or a show host on TV? You perceive it. If someone is being stabbed in a movie, you will be disgusted that you are watching it. If it happens live, you will also be disgusted. Naturally, it will be more effective in real life.

Your reaction happens in your brain because you perceive a picture. That's all. It's just the brain reacting to what you see. But if I open the icon picture on TV, it's not my reaction. If I leave the apartment and leave the icon on, the whole apartment will have energy. So, there is radiation coming from it. It goes like music.

If you turn on a movie or a music video, you hear what's going on. It's coming through. And something like that comes from an icon, but not sound or picture, but energy from this picture. Which is like a sound, only it comes from the deeper plane.

If I take a picture of an uncharged coin, it will be captured uncharged. And if I charge it later, the photo does not change. Because the coin was photographed at the moment when it was not emanating energy. And the old photo can't be changed. It captures an image of the state of the coin, from which, figuratively speaking, there was no sound.

If I now take a video or phone picture of the radio with the radio turned on, I get a picture of the radio with no sound. The next time I shoot a video and play music in the receiver, it will be the same video, but it will also have music. It's the same with the coin – on and off.

Let's talk some more about relics and why people were mummified and embalmed. They were people who had emanating energy. They had a source in them, a matrix that concentrated energy inside them so that it would gather and flow out of them. To preserve that energy, because it was healing, magic, life-giving, and so on, even dead persons were preserved. Do you understand how it works?

6. What Is Energy

About energy. I was aware that it was different in the way it felt. But my understanding of the influence of energy has always been the same: it helps me to shut off my thoughts, to concentrate on myself. It doesn't matter if it's an icon, my Egyptian ring, or some Tibetan thing. If it emanates energy and I look at it, hold it in front of me, or hold a drink over it and drink it, it helps me if I'm closed, to disconnect from everything.

So, this energy helps me to find myself, to focus on myself without doing any techniques or thinking about how to focus on myself. It's enough to feel this energy, and immediately thoughts disappear, and I feel like I'm awake, I'm collected. As if I were here and now. That was my initial approach to all the charged stuff, if a person can feel it, that's fine. So, he has a light, a synchronicity with the thing. That's a very good thing.

In addition, I explained that if you use such a thing, carry it with you, take it out before techniques, charge it with water, and drink it, it helps you disconnect your thoughts, detach yourself from the social-material rhythm, from all attachments, and gather yourself into one point. This is the primitive approach. That's enough for now. This means everything is super, divine energy, and concentration. It's a state of Zen.

For beginners, for dummies, this understanding of what an emanating thing is and how it affects you is enough. If you go into detail, you will understand that each object gives off a different energy. Not only have I started to feel the different energies, but also that they have different effects. But it takes more than an hour or two to understand that.

Let's say I collected ten artifacts and while I play with them, I get nothing more than being in the inner cosmos. To understand how each thing affects me, I have to keep one thing, live with it for a week, and see what happens to me.

I start walking around with this artifact, wearing it in a pouch around my neck, sleeping with it, putting it on my nightstand, carrying it in my pocket, and taking it out every day before going to bed or in the morning. I charge my water with it and drink with it. I can see, because I keep a diary, what my mood and state were during the week. I compare. And I realise, for example, that when I walked for a week with so-and-so crystal, I was super focused and concentrated.

The question arises: what if it is not the crystal that affects me in that way, but just coincidentally and I had a busy week, so I am so awake and concentrated. Or maybe it was the weather this week, for example. What I do next is, I go the next week without any crystal at all and observe that I feel twice as weak. I'm not as super focused as I am with crystal.

It doesn't mean that without the crystal I am not concentrated. But with the crystal, that condition is multiplied. I felt it. The first week with it was awesome, the next week it kind of deflated and I noticed a difference. Just to check again whether it is a crystal or not, in the third week, I start to live with it again. And I realise that I am awake again. Then that's it – the crystal is tested and works.

But out of ten, I only tested one. Now I can give this crystal to someone else to test because my nature is quite different from that of other people. I will give it to a mere mortal man. He'll walk around like that, and then he'll give me a report.

And I take the next artifact, let's say, some statue, and walk around with it the same way. And I realise that for some reason I have become angry and aggressive. I took it away for a week – everything is normal. I take it out again and walk around with it for a week, and I am aggressive again. I conclude that the statuette affects me in such a way that I become super tough. But not bad.

I give this example as a contrast. It doesn't mean that the statuette is bad and that it makes me stiff. Stiffness is a consequence. Maybe it gives leadership qualities that are amplified many times over, and I become a leader or manager. But there's a side effect that it manifests itself more aggressively, I become too tough. And I realise that it gives me discipline but also rigidity. That's how it works.

I say this from my position. I see how the world works, that there is God and energy. That's what I've been promoting since I was a child, what I believe, and what I live. From my position, with my attention, gaze, and consciousness, what I am in sync with as places of power, and what I am drawn to, is the truth. I have this policy. If I come to a huge store of artifacts, stones, crystals, and all that, all that I don't so much as even pay attention to, but that emanates for me, is mine, that is, the present, the truth, the future. The energy of life. So, I will buy these artifacts.

But there is a paradox. I realise that I buy the same stones, not with my mind. I don't even read their names; I just pick up where the emanation is. And I realise that there are plenty of stones lying around that are also for sale, but they don't emanate energy. But I decided that since they don't emit anything, but they have something, I should also take them. So, I collected a number of stones and encountered a peculiar situation.

When I took stones that did not have this divine energy and started to walk with them, I began to feel weak, without strength, I could hardly walk, I wanted to sleep all day, and I was tired. I took them out and all of these signs disappeared. I take them out again – I feel heavy, tired, and sleepy again. Can you imagine? I give them to a stranger, he walks with them for a day – and the same thing: tiredness, sleepiness.

When you choose places of power or charged artifacts, crystals, or icons with your sense of something that emanates energy, it's only positive synchronisation. It's something that only strengthens you. In other words, when you feel any energy, that's what will give you power. It's like a piece of you, a jigsaw puzzle. It will never hurt you.

Of course, there are exceptions. But, in fact, 99% of the time it won't do any harm if you feel the energy from it. Feeling the energy already turns something on inside of you. And if you buy something after reading the description that it is something cool and unique, but without feeling anything, but just with your mind, then the probability that this object can negatively affect you is quite high. Take note of that.

There's a but, about artifacts, crystals, and stuff like that. If you buy some gem or something holy, charged, but not second-hand, then okay. It's clean, it gives you energy, and it's great. But if you look for phoned-up antique stuff, there could be a lot of bad stuff in it besides radiation. For example, a charged icon was in the apartment of people who were fighting, arguing, and hysterical, low frequency daily.

You buy it, and it emanates energy, but in addition to that, it also gives off such radiation that you are stunned. That can happen. But not in my case, because I don't live with my mind but with my heart, and I'm led by circumstances. That's the essence of why you should always be switched on and live not with your mind but with your heart. If you live with your heart, circumstances lead you to what's right for you, your destiny, and only for good.

And if you set your mind to the task of looking for everything that radiates, then you have learned how to feel, but you look with your mind for everything that radiates, and you approach it in a commercial, material way. So, when you do it on purpose, rather than accidentally, you can pick up and take something bad.

I give myself to fate as much as possible, that's my approach. If I go for a walk and see that there is an icon on the ground that has a faint, charged symbol, I will take it; it is for me something that is from on high. But if a neighbour or relative starts trying to sell me some emanating thing, I won't take it – it's from their world. Do you understand?

You don't have to approach it on purpose. I happened to walk into an antique store, happened to have signs before, saw a King Tut ring, and so I took it.

But if somebody said to me, "Alex, there is a ring. Go check it out." Naturally, I wouldn't go. It wouldn't be natural; it would be artificial. You have to understand that.

Anything that emanates energy is good. But if you're talking to someone and they start saying, "That's what emanates," you have to stop it.

You have to approach it yourself, not with the company, not with a friend or a girlfriend. Development is not a collective thing at all. Especially attention, consciousness, and awareness. You can't go around with your girlfriend or with your man and tell each other what's emanating. You have to choose something when you are alone. When it's time, when you feel it, you want it. That's the rule. And if you feel what's emanating, that's fine. But you have to be careful with second-hand stuff.

I was given advice, but it's not my information, I do not understand it. But the advice was that any antique item should be immersed in cold water for ten minutes to clean it. And then everything is okay. I have my approach. I'm a man of faith and I understand the frequency and condition at which I choose everything. My Egyptian statue is mine. I chose it myself, and it doesn't need to be washed, it gives off a good phonation.

I have the same attitude to energy as to electricity, it's better conducted through metals and water. I believe that if I now put 12 gems in a plastic plate, it will not be a microchip, so all these gems will connect, creating one unique energy. That won't happen with a plastic plate. But if I make it out of silver or gold or copper, it will connect all the stones. And it creates another, unique energy, the thirteenth.

Do you understand? What I did with the stones, I ground them, I mixed them. It was more convenient to put them together to create the thirteenth energy. If you just carry them in a bag, it will not have an effect, they need to be connected. If you put 12 stones in an empty glass, they will be emitted separately. But if you pour water into the glass, there will be one single thirteenth energy. Because they are short-circuited by the water. Take note of that.

Imagine a very irritable, negative person who often swears and gets depressed, and is conflictive. He has a negative vibe about him. And suddenly he wants some charged thing. But negativity is the opposite of madness. When a person yells, fights, and gets hysterical, the mind also shuts down and there is concentration. But in a bad way. And this negative, stressful state, the energy of fear and anger can be written on that thing hanging around a person's neck.

And it will be charged with the negative energy of the person. If I put this thing around his neck, I will connect to this bad state and frequency of stress and fear. So, you can charge a thing with stress and fear. What I advise such people to do. It's better to buy some cheap charged stuff but change it every week. Because after a week you will have them ruined.

What is the principle of everything I'm talking about now? Very negative people who are in fear and panic are not bad people, they may have been driven to it. Some have a disturbed psyche and have uncontrollable negativity. If there are such people among my readers and you wear a watch, rings, bracelets, earrings, or crosses, it all gets absorbed and the circle closes.

If you wear them all the time, these accessories are always supporting your stress and negativity. Do you know what I mean? Or it's better to take everything off, then the negativity won't accumulate. Or you change every week to a new one. Or you buy holy water (or charge the water yourself with my techniques) and every week you wash all your accessories, which during the week are clogged with your stress.

And then you can put them on yourself. Then in the new week, they will nourish you with good things. Then they will clog up again and renew them again.

If you have had some trouble and at that moment you were wearing earrings, rings, and other accessories, they can bring that bad stuff back. It's better to take it all out or wash it, clean it, or change it. Because the bad stuff gets absorbed.

It’s clear that people who are interested in spiritual practices, in smoking stuff, beggars, downshifters, or yogis, at least feel the energy. But they don’t know how to use it; they don’t understand what energy is; they don’t know the science, and they don’t do anything consciously. They just go to extremes, that’s all. But at least they are reaching for that rhythm. It’s extreme, and you need to take care of how you look, meet new people, and not be savage.

They have forgotten about that, of course, and they don’t want to understand how the world works. Their head is a mess, it’s useless to talk to them, and it’s better not to listen to them, they’ll confuse you. But they are sensitive. Their senses are really good. Because they don’t eat anything, they eat prana, they get high on substances, so they are sensitive. But their psyche is broken, and they have nothing – no thinking, no logic, no intellect. But they feel something.

Why am I telling you this? It is very important to try to understand with the mind. At first, I say that you don’t have to think about what energy is and how it works, because you have to feel something. But to close this task and go further in development, you still have to ask these questions and look for the answer to them. If you feel everything without understanding, then you will be a savage, like all those yogis. This is where I differ from them. I check and prove everything, and look for confirmation, and evidence. That’s important. It’s important to get the point.

I need to put your free attention in the right direction. You will expand your psyche, your attention, and your faith. But most importantly, it must be applied. Combine it with tasks in the material world, so that it brings health, money, intelligence, influence on people, protection, and confidence. So that you can use it to learn all languages, to know the sciences. That’s what attention is for, that’s what I’m pumping it up for you. Not to sit as a couch potato under a palm tree. It’s very important.

What happens when we charge a coin? Let’s imagine that there is you and there is, let’s say, a ruler. And above your head is a zero. Everything under zero where your body is –1, –2, and –3 are material frequencies. And everything above your head and above the zero: +1, +2, +3 are spiritual frequencies. That’s where the power of faith is. It’s easier to visualise that way.

When you do some techniques, with palms and so on, it’s like a thermometer, like a scale. When you start going into your inner space, everyone has their limit. When you do some technique, your level, for example, +2, is put into a coin. And it starts to be in a world of +2, it is energised at +2. When you go down the scale into society, let's say –4, you bring that coin up, and it gives off your +2 state, you still put +2 in there, don't forget that. This is what you have to take note of.

You can collect coins. You charge it, sign it: date so-and-so, and put it away in the box. A month or two passed, and you went into inner space again and signed yourself for a new coin. And also put it away. You accumulate them and then you can check how the first coin emanates, how the second one, and how the third one. Feel the difference, see yourself from the side, on what spiritual frequencies you were. And when you put into a coin not your energy, but from some picture or artifact, for example, +5, the coin becomes +5. This is an explanation at a very primitive level.

Many people think that if everything is itchy and boisterous everywhere, then the technique has worked, and if it hasn't, it hasn't worked. No, it's a benchmark of the mind. That's the way it is in the human world. But it's not a benchmark. With energy, there's no such framework or extremes. If you feel the energy – that's it, it's good.

If it makes you feel bad, it doesn't mean it's not good. Just because it feels good doesn't mean it's good. The energy, if you feel it, is the only one and it is good, divine. And how you react to it is another thing. It depends on your level, how close you are, how strong or weak the effect is on you, and how used you are to it. But it's the same as when I was a child.

When my parents took me to church, I always felt bad. What kind of thoughts would people have about that? If he felt bad in church, he must be crazy. But I wasn't crazy. I felt bad because, unlike soulless and unfeeling people, I was going into the inner cosmos. Naturally, when you come out afterward, you feel as if you are seasick in a car, nauseous, and bad. But not in the sense that something was punishing me or there was something bad about me. No. I was just unaccustomed.

When I was little, it was scary and incomprehensible when I became dizzy. You may react, an association of the mind, that since it's like that, it's bad. But you accept that on the contrary, it is good. The more dizzy you get, the better. So, you disconnect from everything external and connect to the cosmos. It's cool. When a person is not ready for that, yes, they take it negatively. I felt bad in the church at first, I felt sick. But I felt the same there as I do now.

Only now I'm approaching it with experience and reason – I go to church and it's like I'm disconnected from reality. I came out and I want to keep it that way for a long time. So don't be silly, if you feel bad about something in terms of energy, that's not a bad thing. But if it's material things that make you feel bad, then it's really bad. And spiritually, energetically, it's not.

When we discussed what conducts energy better, I said it was metal and water. I didn't test any further. But based on my observations, I've found antique books that were emanating energy. And that's paper. Paintings and icons emanate energy, and also paper. Why is that? A lot of factors, and a lot of reasons. Or a man was in inner space, in a charged state when he was creating this product. Or there is something on it that emanates. There could be a third reason – you could use paint, which emanates something.

7. Matrix

I've mentioned a lot in my books that our task is to know the whole matrix. We are developing the mind and consciousness, and the task is to make the mosaic within us, the snowflake, whole and complete. It's as if all the symbols that we encounter are like sprouts. Here is the cross, imagine that it is a twig that grows. And all sorts of other pentacles, six-pointed stars, geometric figures are some kind of special language, sacred geometry that is not given to people, they don't know what it is except for the initiated. I too am still only learning it and don't know for sure. It lies ahead of me; they are leading me to it. The task is that for general understanding you should have an idea that everyone already has everything inside, this snowflake.

The task is for it to turn on, to light up. All intersections of lines and light bulbs should be turned on. That's development. I develop it in myself, you develop it in yourself. Some do it consciously, some do not. That's what the soul looks like. Like a snowflake.

But what's interesting is another thing. Someone is born and has talent. Somebody else doesn't have it. It depends on our soul. It gets developed. By the end of life it turns out that we have assembled the so-called puzzles, figuratively speaking, during our life we switched on 35 light bulbs inside us. And then we are gone from this life. When we are born next time, in the next 20 years we turn on these light bulbs, it's as if we remember them. And then we evolved to put more light bulbs on. They become 55 for example and then we pass out of life again. The task is to pump this matrix, the snowflake inside us.

When I give you the *channel opening* technique and you do it, fifty light bulbs come on. At that moment you write them down on a coin. That code stays there. When you closed up and take that coin, those lights are awakened in you because they are fixed in the coin.

If we talk about the energy we feel, it is a unique phenomenon. Energy is one, but it has different forms. Electricity can also be called energy, light. But it's different energy. Most people all over the world don't feel energy.

To them, to 99% of people, it would be crazy if I say, "Here is a bracelet, I can feel energy from it."

But you understand, you feel that this is not self-influenced, it's real.

Maybe there was this energy that we felt. But it was like we were on the wrong vibration. And now something is happening in nature, frequencies are switching, so that we begin to feel something that has always been there, but we couldn't feel it. And I promote this world as a separate matrix that is now manifesting and growing more and more, and it has the concept of energy.

But in the matrix of the old generation of people, this is savagery. What I am promoting is a new society. Even among religious people, there are very few who feel the energy of temples, cathedrals, icons, prayers. They are very few. The rest do it with their minds, like zombies. There are very few conscious people who truly feel the source of divine energy. The one who feels it is my friend. This is my policy.

I believe that everyone who doesn't feel energy is not alive. And all those who feel it are their own. That's how I feel about life. If a person feels, he has a light, he is alive. It doesn't matter how much or little knowledge he has; the light is a sign. It's like a burnt-out iPhone and a working one – different things. It's the same with people.

I feel this energy in me from all kinds of charged things, from people-entities like me. For me it is the meaning of life, the deity, the most important thing that can be.

Why is this energy different? I think it's just on a different level. Like a mental level or faith scale, there is a level of spirituality and it's different. Each level of spirituality has a different energy. It's the same, but somewhere it's stronger, somewhere it's weaker. Something we can feel, something we can't feel, because we've outgrown it. It is the same energy, but it is like different powers, I would say. Some feel one, some feel the other, some feel the third. The essence is the same, but different powers.

But this is a primitive approach. If you think about it further, energy works in very different ways. Example. There is a diamond. And then there's, let's say, a ruby, a red stone. There's no such thing that a ruby has the same divine energy as a diamond, or a diamond is stronger, and a ruby is weaker because of different energies. No, it doesn't. They emanate different energies if you go into the details. They are different energies.

A diamond and a ruby have something in common energy. But the processes and effects from these stones are different. It is as if a diamond set off 20 light bulbs in my left hemisphere for example. And the ruby gives me light bulbs in my left and right hemisphere, but only five. Do you understand?

Why does it work that way? Because that's how I see it. And I give an example that turns on in my head. Or in my chest. It doesn't matter. There's no form, it's how we feel, it's how we're more comfortable with it.

But, rather, it looks like this. We have a soul. And it is like a huge pizza. It's such a matrix, with many lines drawn through it, all the intersections of the lines are points, light bulbs. When we live and develop, when we face difficulties, hardships, when we realise something with our soul, consciousness, and understand something with our mind, and it is developed, becomes more flexible, all this is reflected upon our soul.

It closes in something, opens in something. There are such puzzles within us. When I start interacting with the diamond, some light bulbs start working. Some of them are naturally turned on forever. Some are only turned on from the effect of the stone. From the ruby, other lights are turned on inside of you, in this matrix.

Initially, many people felt that when they used emanating objects, something happened to them. But they didn't feel it globally, on the body, they didn't feel the difference with other objects. They just felt something, that's all. The most distant from spirituality and sensitivity people had this reaction: yes, there is something. But then those same people really started to distinguish.

Maybe because they became prepared mentally and psychologically, or I immersed them more into this atmosphere, maybe because of practice. They didn't do anything about that. I just talked and showed them a lot about it. And gradually they started to feel the difference between the energies. It must be the same for you. You don't know what can be, so you don't know what can be. Just practice, just experience.

Part III
Directed Attention

1. Attention to the Future

The problem for many people is to approach everything as a psychologist and ask people who come across, "What do you live by, what do you believe in, what do you want out of life?"

You can hear some interesting answers. The person says they dream about it, and you ask them, "Why aren't you doing it?"

And then the person has a stupor. If you ask him how he sees himself in six months or five years, he doesn't know how to answer. He doesn't think about it. This, too, is a sign of unconsciousness. Everyone shouts that it is necessary to be here and now, it is very correct, but people don't even understand what it is – here and now, there is no future and the past.

All esotericists shout these phrases, they sound nice. But they do not understand the essence. Yes, it's bad when a person doesn't give an account of today and lives in the past and memories. This is logical. And it's bad when a person doesn't allow himself or herself to do something now and puts it all off for later. It is called living in the future. That's not what I mean now.

A reflective person, that is to say, an attentive person, with free attention, must necessarily look back. Take the year 2008 as a reference point, remember what was then, what you were doing, what you believed in, what bothered you, what you loved, what you wanted, what troubled you, who you were with, what you looked like. Think back. This is very important. When you do remember, write down the key moments. Try to make some kind of statistics.

If I tell you now to remember the last ten years of your life, you can't, because you're not well structured. So, I'm just giving you a date. Dig around in it, it's sobering. The year 2008. Start there. Next take 2012, who you were then, and what was happening to you. Remember and write down for yourself something basic, key, and significant.

If you still have photos of that time, look at what you photographed then, and with whom you communicated. This will help you remember even more. Look at how you looked at that time period. It'll help you to look at yourself soberly now. That's important.

Next, take 2014. Then take 2018. Go through each year. Who you were, what you were, how you felt, what you believed in, and how you treated things. It will sober you up, it's much needed. Because people don't go back like that, they unconsciously perceive things as they are now. They get it all wrong. It's very important.

People are superficial. Someone looked at my last photos on social media and already formed some kind of opinion about me. He didn't look at what happened a year ago. Maybe I had a different haircut and posted different pictures and wrote about other things. It's a societal problem.

About the future. How can your attention lead you to anything if it's not directed anywhere? There has to be a goal. That's a must. There has to be a vision of yourself in the future. That's useful and necessary.

I'll put it this way: if I start asking people on the street right now, "Where do you see yourself in five years?"

Those who say, "I don't know, I don't think about it," won't happen.

Who they are now will remain the same, nothing will change.

Somebody will say, "I'll live in a town like this, and I'll do this and that."

I'll say, "That's very clear-cut. What makes you think that?"

The person will say, "That's what I'm doing right now."

Oh! So, the man is already working on what he will have in five years. Respect! Those people who answer my question about what they will be in three to five years, will be exactly that, 99% of the time. Why? Because they've seen it in their heads, they've imagined it, they've set a benchmark, and they're going for it right now.

Do you do that? Ask yourself this question. Have you ever thought about what you'll be like in three years? Right now, your attention is distracted, you're distracted by everyday life, by the life you have today, now. Have you thought about what you'll be in three years? What will you be? What will you be? Who will you be with? Where?

Those who don't think about it won't have anything. My task, my responsibility, in addition to freeing your attention, is to develop people so that your attention is directed to the future. A good, good future.

Assignment for you: write an essay on who you will be in five years. At least two pages. And do it in one day. It's very important to you. That's the thing, a lot of people want some kind of show that incredibly, with special effects, can change lives. In fact, it's an essay like this that can change your life. But from the fact that it sounds boring and without fireworks, you treat it indulgently – let's write it if you have to. But it's very important. It gets your head in order. It's programming.

You don't have to divide an essay into spiritual and socio-material parts. You must understand that it is one and the same. Your mood comes from the material things, your material life comes from your mood. It's one and the same. Like a left foot and a right foot. Of course, when we evolve, if we want to heal a leg, we take care of one, we don't pay attention to the other.

So, we say, "We talk only about spirituality," or "We talk only about material things." But it's all one body, an organism.

The essay, of course, will be about social and material things. Because maybe you're planning a family, getting your health back, getting your teeth done, building a house, buying a car, or having ten children. Or maybe you're going to open something. One has plans, dreams, desires, or just visions, even if you don't know how you're going to get there.

You have a picture that in five years' time you'll definitely be living in St Petersburg, in London, or in the mountains, for that matter. Or you'll be retired. It depends on your situation now. That's the point of the assignment. It's very difficult. It looks simple but it is very serious. I understand your human mind. I spend my free time watching *Smallville Mysteries.* And it's funny how the boy, Clark Kent, is told by his flying ship that humans are a flawed race and need to be controlled. It sounds harsh, but it's true.

Because the human mind is so stupid that if you say to him, "Here, this egg that I dug up somewhere in the desert outside Los Angeles, it's thousands of years old, look, five books and the Bible say it's super magical, and if you touch it, you'll have a future."

If you're told that kind of nonsense, you'll be willing to drop everything just to be with that egg. You like this illusion, this tinsel.

It's the same with essays. For you, it's something to write. No, you have no idea how important it is. It's bad enough that you are so out of control of your psyche that it decides for you what mood you should be in as if your animal instinct decides what you should be interested in and what you shouldn't. And it only comes from whatever covers you're looking at. Imagine how bad that is. It's a degree of unconsciousness, it's a flawed race.

Why is the essay important? I have always tried to help people and have approached this in two ways – through spiritual and material social development. I talked about what techniques I could do to turn on the soul and light a fire inside. How all the material and external factors affect a person and their frequency and also how to surround oneself with everything material. But the most important thing is what's in your head, your values, your attitude to things, and people, and your intentions.

That's the most important thing. If you put my intentions in your head, attitudes to life, to what is good and what is bad, it would change your whole life for the better. Order in your head is very important. You need your attention to be properly distributed, what you focus on, and how you visualise something.

Let me give you an example as an entrepreneur. I can create any business, and it will be clear because I'm like a mathematician. If I want to open a restaurant, I can immediately see what it will be like. That's how I started to figure out how it came to be that way. I see the path to it. Do you see? I can quickly calculate what a restaurant will be like just by sitting down without a sheet of paper with a person, how much money it will bring in, etc., in five minutes.

But why? Because I draw it as much as possible in my head. That is, I imagine the restaurant, and the area, I understand how many tables and people there will be, and I understand how much I will spend on staff, the kitchen, fire safety, and the licence if it is needed. I understand all the pitfalls with the police and so on, I take everything into account, including where I will get the food, and where and how it will be prepared.

I take into account all the nuances. And when I figure it out in my head and understand how everything is going to be, then it's easy to create it. Do you understand? Then it's easy to implement because first, it has to be implemented in the head. But I had this problem where people who wanted to be entrepreneurs before my very eyes slowed down, and I saw their mistakes.

They say, "I want this fancy restaurant, this kind of food," and that's it.

They have nothing else in their heads, except that it will be a beautiful restaurant with Chinese food. They have a superficial image of it, so they will do it superficially. It's as if they don't have any details, as if they don't think about anything. It's like they don't have a 100% business plan made in their head. You have to create it in the air first, in theory, it's like energy, and then it becomes material. Do you know? It's the same with essays. If you write down in theory how you see the future, then it will materialise.

The attention of people of mind is always busy. But if it is free and you focus on something consciously, you can go to the goal, the circumstances will lead. The theme of wish fulfilment can work in this regard. But not in the mystical format in which people like to think about it.

The more your attention is focused on imagining what will happen in the future, the more likely it will be, and the more likely it will be realised. It's terrible when people with their heads in the clouds let things go on their own. You have to have a certain vision of your life in the future.

Yes, the cover may change, but you still have to go for something, strive for something, and develop. And this essay is very important. It is you, your future. The worse it is written, the worse your attitude to yourself and your life.

First mistake. Each of you is on some stepping stone. Your plans for the future, a rough idea of what will happen to you and what you will be like in three to five years is the next step. You can describe several steps. If you're on step nine, you can write about plans on step 11. But you can't write about plans like people at step 100.

A person who works for ten dollars an hour, who has never seen the world, who does not know what is good and what is bad, who has a lot of self-deficiencies, who is uncommunicative, has plans, for example, to get a driver's licence, a passport to travel abroad and, let's say, to move out of his parent's house to live alone.

If a person is in such a low position, his next plan should be something like this. But when a man lives with his parents, works unofficially for ten dollars an hour, has never been abroad and does not even have a driver's licence, and wants to be a banker – this is idiocy. What drives you?

The most interesting thing is that I always encounter this. My helpers were always kids or people my age. They all have ambitions and exorbitant demands.

Every time it got to them, I said, "I work, I don't eat, I don't sleep, I don't think about resting. And all you can think about is going somewhere to rest. Already you went to three birthdays. And I did not go to any. So, you complain that you do not have in life what you dream about. And if you look at how you manage your time and how you treat things, you walk around, looking back at Ferrari cars. Are you kidding me, you're students. I am not thinking about such a car, and you are."

It doesn't make any sense. It's the same as me and some students being asked what I would like the next year. I'll say something adequate, something I'm more or less sure I'll try and do in a year if there's no emergency. My plan for the year is to buy an apartment. I'll say this.

And the snot-nosed student will say, "And I plan to buy a Rolls-Royce for 50 million."

This is silly. But surely more than half of the readers who wrote the essay made the same mistake. If you are interested in having something in your life, if you are interested in development, think about this problem. You have to start with it. It's an emergency. Write sensible things within the real world. Your plans for the next five years have to be based on where you are now, on your capabilities, and how they will increase a little bit each year.

How can you write that in five years you will have a yacht when you don't even have a studio apartment? What are you talking about!? And women write, "I will live in a house on the beach; my husband is a billionaire."

This is the first mistake that 60% of people make.

Second mistake. An essay is an essay. But when it talks about what you will be, what you will be doing in five years, it should not be from the world of fantasy, but something in a real, adequate sense. And okay, if people write about some goals that they go to.

For example, "I'm obese, and I need to take care of myself, and my health, eat right, exercise, and lose weight." This is adequate. The person explains the situation he or she is starting from and why he or she has such a plan. Next, let's say a person writes: "I have bad teeth, the plan is to save money and get them all fixed."

This is also a normal plan. You have to plan for five years to get better. Or a person writes, "I'm in such-and-such a business, I live in a village, I plan to move to a big city within five years to develop my representation there." Or "I have a loved one, and one of my plans is to have children."

These are normal plans. They should be such that if you keep working on yourself, you'll get there. And that's not how people write, "I plan to solve this," or "This is my goal right now," or "I plan to save money and go learn a language in a year."

And they write, "I'd like to know 12 foreign languages," or "I'd also like a big house and a dog," or "I'd like my mom not to be sick."

What does this have to do with your mother? She's the one who should set the goal of not getting sick. What are you going to do?

What kind of wish is that, *I wish I had known* – What do you mean? You need to use your head that you have five years ahead of you, and if you want to learn languages – learn them! You don't just happen to have them on your head at the snap of a finger. In principle, you'll probably get one in a year. If you persist in learning a language for a year. That is, if I make a plan, I can assume that I will know several foreign languages. That's the right way to write an essay. Let's not do wishful thinking. This is the second mistake.

Don't write what you just want. When a guy or girl who is an entrepreneur, works for a big company, is a socially material person, writes, "I have plans in the next five years to get a second citizenship."

"I have plans to sell the two apartments I inherited and build a house with this money," then the person writes based on reality.

He sees that he will buy such-and-such a house, that he will get a second citizenship, look like this and that, and learn, figuratively speaking, the Japanese language. And he describes what he adequately understands so that he can do it. It's not like something is going to fall out of the sky. Nothing falls out of the sky, remember that. For some reason, a lot of people think that everything falls from the sky. No, only work.

It is the mistake of people who have no family, no children, no job, or no career to write about five-bedroom apartments in upscale neighbourhoods. Everything has to be consistent, one after the other. Don't forget these laws and rules. How can you now, being without a place to live at all, not even knowing what your place is, talk about a five-bedroom apartment? Think about where you're going with this. It doesn't make sense. Such a mess and disorder deprives you of your future and slows down your development. Nothing will come of it.

If we were to move forward five years from now, into the future, and I asked you, "Well, how have you evolved in five years?"

You would say, "There's been a lot of things, I've been to Singapore."

And that's all you've had in five years? Man, what did you do for five years?

"I worked, I got loans, I got debts, I paid them off. And I've been sitting at home on the internet." That's a cool way to spend five years of your life. The other guy did everything he planned to do. Don't blame fate. There's the lazy person and the person with a mess in his head, with the wrong attitude and the wrong values about himself and life. And some have everything in order.

There is one truth to how one should relate to life, to people, to oneself, and everything. One correct version. Just one. And it is distorted in everyone's mind, just as crystals are not pure, but with an impurity. Each person's idea of how to live properly is impure. He who has less of it, who has a pure vision of the truth, who is nearer to it, is successful in life. And the other has a vision that is not in harmony with that which is one, the essential truth. And that distances him from everything.

I was recently asked by someone, "Why I am, a good person, not a fool, with a good attitude toward everyone, and have nothing. Why am I poor? Am I a bad person? Or stupid? How so?" That's the way it is. Obviously, you think you understand everything, and you're surprised that things don't work out in your life. So your version is false. I mean, I think I know everything and I'm smart. But my version is confirmed by the result, and yours is not. So my version is right and yours is wrong. That's it.

It's very important where your attention is when you free it up. On cigarettes, outings, birthdays, or on developing, getting better, and living up to the plan you set for yourself for the next five years. Now, almost at the end of the book, it's very important to me that you understand and see yourself in the coming years. That you understand what you're planning, what you're aiming for. This is important.

Many people will write an essay justified. You also need to write how you came to this. Why do you decide that in four years you will have this? You have to write it to yourself. Not like, "I see that in four years I'll have my restaurant."

What do you mean, "I see?" Of course, you see it. But is it because that's what you wished for? Do you wish like a silly child? Or because you've been thinking about it for a year now, you talk to people in the restaurant business, you've worked in it yourself, starting as a janitor to the manager, and therefore you believe that you will have a restaurant because you have already saved five million Rubles as a deposit, to take a loan for it. What is your picture of the future based on? Do you understand?

Movies often show genius scientists working on something nonstop all day long. But then it turns out that this person died of some disease. More often than not, it was because his arms and legs had failed. Why? Genius scientists go to such extremes, in the study of some works, that they disconnect from the real world, so they become insane, in the sense that they stop behaving normally in reality, and they start seeing things. What are the consequences of this – they can have severe health problems because attention doesn't go to it. Yes, they are geniuses. If you want to live little, but invent something, you can go to extremes and spend your nights figuring something out.

If you create the illusion, the prestige, as in the example with the egg, that it is so rare and so on, to present such nonsense to the people, and then just say, "There is a stick, wear it," people will not believe in it, will not use it or take it seriously.

Because he is fed up with this nonsense. The person is used to being amused by all kinds of nonsense. This is the reason why companies patronise their employees when they organise parties and team-building events. But not because it is right and good. The company employs people who are weak and primitive. And, naturally, the company wants these people to work, so you have to coddle them.

If I didn't care about human development and I was selling vacuum cleaners, I would be doing the same thing. But since I'm in the business of human development, that's how I would contradict my development.

I have always agonised over the last five to ten years, and I'm aware of those who know me and read me. I've talked about the inner voice scolding me for not using the illusion. Like I'm ruining the cover and delivering the essence, and that's a bad thing. And I don't want to, for me, it's like a deception, it goes against my information. Even though creating an illusion is considered normal.

Imagine that I deliver information in books, and people read me and watch me. Yes, it's a small audience, but it's those who have bypassed all my filters, who don't fall for the cover and the tinsel, who hear the essence. Maximally adequate people. And the other 99% of people are hooked on the show. On bloggers, on colourful cars, on beautiful women. This is a terrible society, I don't want to live in such a society, it's bad. And it's a horrible society that gets suckered in by falsity, by a cover. This is a paradox.

I could have bought myself a Rolls-Royce a long time ago and been showing myself off and saying how cool I was. For all the time I saw cool people and some celebrities, I could have taken pictures with them and posted them on the internet. But what kind of audience of people would I then attract to me. The ones who didn't care about my soul, who didn't care about information, who would just fall for my cover.

That's why I always tried to avoid it as much as possible, so as not to use the illusion. But you see, you can't do it without it. Initially, I was against it, because

I promoted the spiritual. But when I started to learn about the social-material world, it turned out that the cover was still important. And that's when I started dealing with my cover, talking about it. Naturally, I didn't promote writing false, fanciful descriptions of anything. No, lying is bad.

But the fact that people are attracted to packaging and that it's important is true. Thousands of people read my books and look very awful.

They have this attitude, "Alex, we think money is bad; we shouldn't pay for anything. Thank you for the information that is available, but what you pay for is disgusting to us."

And I tell them, "You people stink; you look terrible."

And they tell me, "We don't care. It's the soul that counts."

Yeah, I understand that you don't care, I was like that myself. But you have to. If you want to be heard, if you want to reach people, if you want them to listen to your music or eat your pies, you have to have them in a good box. You need to get cleaned up and dressed and look modern. Otherwise, you'll just keep hiding in your four walls. That's the problem. Yes, people do fall for the cover. But that's okay.

We are now touching on the subject of cushioning in terms of dialogue and information. Why do a lot of companies do all sorts of motivational training? Why do they promise them a mountain of stuff? Because that illusion gives them the incentive to work.

If you just tell them, "Work!" they feel sad and nauseous, and we all are so emotional, and people say, "We don't want to work," and quit.

That's why everybody is fed up with the illusion that you'll be great, that you'll have everything, that you'll get a car as a present. Otherwise, a person cannot get off his ass to work. Everybody is lazy and has a cranky soul. That's the problem. But what's frustrating is that my audience of readers, who are interested in development, also have this virus, this terrible weakness.

If I give information, but at the same time, let's say, every other day, I will tell you how sweet and cool you are and how much I love you, and I will not just talk about the essence, I will tell you that I will give you a matrix that nobody has, it is secret and secret and I will share it in a week, then you will lose sleep and you will want it, find time and wait for this matrix.

Imagine how stupid and low that is. It is very bad that without illusions you cannot control yourself and cannot force yourself to do something. To do something for yourself you also need this illusion. A man without illusion is not even ready to do something for himself. He is not ready to take control of himself if he does not give it to himself. It's horrible. It's very low.

Why do you know me and why are you reading this book? You want development, you want to change the world, you want to change yourself. That is, you want the best. But, you know, what your mistake is? 90% of you want to develop, but if it is something ugly, like hypnosis, you are no longer interested. It turns out that wanting to evolve is an unconscious decision of yours.

You want to develop because of your selfishness and complexes. You are resentful of the world, of yourself, you can't do anything. If I tell you that I will give you hypnosis, thousands of people will gather at once. And if I tell you about the development and the *technique on the chair*, there will be a few thousand less. Do you know why? It's not interesting. But that's development! On the contrary, hypnosis doesn't work for you! And what I give you is development. What capricious children you are. It's a paradox! I say this sincerely.

In the future. Watch the TV series *Smallville*. Play the game *Beyond: Two Souls*. Watch science shows about human structure, the brain, etc. (only TV shows, not bloggers), and movies about attention and loneliness, *Cast Away*, and *I Am Legend*.

2. Unsolved Problems

I don't have unresolved situations with people. I hate it when people and plenty of people do, unresolved their misunderstandings and try to forget it. It's the biggest problem. As a boy who's been in a relationship, I've seen it every time from girls. There's a misunderstanding with a girl and instead of having a diplomatic conversation and telling her what she's not happy with, 99 times out of 100, she does things to forget it, to get away from it. It's a bad thing.

Remember that. You can't do that in any way. It's a human problem. When there's a clash, a misunderstanding between people, you can't forget it. Everybody wants to get away from problems. It's something that goes back to childhood. So, you fight with your parents, you fight with somebody in the college, and you just turn around and walk away from it.

When you don't solve it, you walk away, you don't develop. It's a degradation. It's the opposite of development – it doesn't work. The whole nation suffers from it. It is a state of emergency.

A person does something bad. His parents scolded him for it. Then he grows up, and he gets the same complaints. And the man just takes it and sends everyone away. That's his problem, people were right, but he shoves them all away and walks away from the situation, dodging the trouble instead of dealing with it. And he's not getting rid of the problem. That's not good.

Disagreement must be resolved, or it will always sit in your head. This is a block. If there is any conflict – with relatives, close people, friends, or co-workers – it is necessary to explain yourself. Not in quarrels and emotions, but in a normal balanced state. We need to talk, to untie this knot. It's not good to accumulate them. It's a problem. And, the interesting thing is, people don't like it. Here's an example.

You're a reader, you read this text. You and I begin a friendship, build a relationship or work. Suddenly there is some situation where we misunderstand each other. One, this is normal. You've been living in your environment for all your years, and I've been living in mine, of course, we're different. You have one way of looking at things and I have another.

So, we had a clash. I said, "Why did you do that?"

And you say to me, "I did it right."

I said, "Wrong."

And you're like, "You don't know how to do it. Look at you."

So, we had a fight. That's not good. You accumulate stones in your soul. When we both calm down, we have to sit down and talk about the conflict and get to the bottom of it. We have to let go of the situation, so it doesn't stay with us. I always untie those knots; I don't accumulate them. It also gives a kind of purity. If you have these knots, you're no longer clean.

3. Essence

If you free your attention through techniques, and meditation, by reducing distractions, you will be able to perceive information in a completely different way in the future.

Here's an example. One person makes a mistake but does not learn a lesson from it. He commits it again, and again. That is, the mistake is always in a different guise. And some people have made a mistake and immediately understood why and how it is. You'll get to the point quicker and you'll see it in everything: in people, in films, in documents, in books, in everything. The essence is the most important thing.

When I talk to people, I understand who sees the point and who doesn't. Some could be called superficial. If we say what soulful, spiritual, creative people are and what material people are, that is closed, they can also be called by these words: some see the essence, that is deep people, and there are superficial people. That's it.

You can divide everyone into two groups like that. If a man is superficial, it's as if he doesn't understand what I'm talking about. As if out of 20 words he hears only three that are familiar to him, but he does not connect them into a common chain that makes sense. There are 99% of such people. And some understand the essence, so much so that it seems like we are communicating in words, but as if we are in each other's heads and understand each other's intentions.

We know when we're not saying something or when we're using the right words to make a point. The essence is very important. You have to see it, practice it, and develop it.

Here's an example. When you didn't know what spirituality was, and didn't know who Alexander Korol was, it would have been useless for you, common people, to read about what atoms, ions, and so on are. It's clear that everyone goes through this at school, but it's as if they're studying just to get a grade. More often than not, people cram it in, like poetry.

But the main thing is to understand the meaning, the essence. I would say now, "And please read about what light is, electricity, radiation."

I would say this to an ordinary person, any person you or your acquaintance, who has never read my books, he would read and say, "So?"

That is, he will not experience any revelation or insight. To him, it's just information. A set of letters in a certain order. That's all.

Let's find out if and how far you've progressed. Now, when you read on such topics, there must be something in you that should give you a little tingle, at least from one line. As if you are touching that truth that I have thrown to you like a seed as if it will respond and become twice as big inside of you.

There is a huge list of things that provoke thoughts, and things that deprive thoughts and intensify attention on oneself. Let's take as an example a person who sits at home, communicates little, and is rarely in society, but still, thoughts overtake him. In this case, I would say that the person has egoism and a comfort zone. And this needs to be destroyed.

He has an ego, and this person does things so much his way that it's a nightmare. So, on the one hand he is excluded from society, but for the reason that he is not inferior to anyone because of his selfishness. I would advise him to forget about any in his way and generally what he wants, and to start communicating.

It does not matter with whom but give yourself to this person. To start trusting everyone as if you have no opinion at all. Do everything, they say, say yes to everything. That's the way it is. Then his egoism will break down and this block, the mind, the damn thoughts, will dissipate.

To be with no mind is first of all to surrender to events, to circumstances. Not to avoid anything and to be open to everything. In my example, a man is simply closed off from society which does everything in its way, as it suits him. And so, in his way that he lives in his comfort zone. You have to break it down, in other words, you have to do things the other way around.

If you don't communicate with people, that's how you feel comfortable. Start communicating with them. If you're living alone, live with someone. Don't allow yourself the things you love, stop nagging yourself. Break down your personality. When you go to pieces and break your comfort zone, then the mind shuts down and you feel an epiphany, an awareness, a kind of euphoria, a shock.

This is normal. Of course, some people are developed, and some people who are not. But everyone who's in society is cornered to some degree. Like they're cornered. Only you can see it in some people and not in others. Some people can smile brightly, visit some places, and have many friends, but they are also in their comfort zone.

If you start talking to them about other topics, they will be uncomfortable. If you offer them something else, they will be uncomfortable again. People in society are cowardly, they have lost their souls, and they like to live in habits and cling to their comfort zone. It just needs to be destroyed. That's all.

If you are often alone at home, not communicating with anyone, it is not an indication that you have an open soul and no mind. Why is that? Extremely material people are afraid to leave their souls, to step into the abyss, into the fog. They try to hold on to something familiar. And because they are alone, their thoughts do not turn off. Don't confuse the two.

It's a standard story, with people everything is very primitive. They all want to know, yes or no, to do it or not to do it, to go there or not to go there. And I say, "Why? What for?"

There are no dos and don'ts. There's no such thing as bad cigarettes or good cigarettes. Tell me, what do you need it for? What's important is the reason, the intention.

I'll give you an interesting tip. The intention, the essence, is very important in what you do. I tell a person, "Don't travel under any circumstances! Don't allow yourself holidays and vacations – you'll get hit by the system."

He'll start nagging me and say that in my books I'm advising him to travel for development. So, the intentions are different! There man goes to travel not to console his ego, to show off and relax, but for another reason. And your reason is exactly to do nothing. For another reason, you'll get hit. And the one who went travelling doesn't get hit by the system. And so, in everything.

The intention is very important. And people are so primitive that they want to know whether or not to wear, to eat this way or that way, to argue with relatives or not. But it's much more complicated and profound than that. We are human beings, everything is nature. If a woman dresses vulgarly because she has complexes, she shouldn't dress like that, because she's not developing, she's degrading; she's closing herself off more and more, and she'll get smacked by the system because of it.

And if a girl dresses vulgarly for a different reason; she has no complexes, she doesn't care about it, she's above it, and she does it because she's interested in making fun of people, her system won't punish her for that. Do you understand?

I mean, there are a lot of buts. So much so that I can swear and you, let's say, can't. People don't understand that. Imagine how funny it looks when some kid from a small villager reads my books where I swear and starts swearing in the comments on social networks. Do you understand the difference?

A president can swear, a British queen can swear, a Hollywood star can swear, and a scientist can swear. But when you swear at someone who's a nobody and hasn't become a person yet, it makes it worse. It's a balance that not everyone understands. Some people need to be dirtier to have a sense of balance – I'd advise them on the contrary. Some people are told to clean up, to be polite, or to be cheeky. These are very different things.

If we talk about loneliness, that's one of the factors that one spends one's attention on and through which it is freed up, people who one interacts with. But there are lots of other reasons why you have thoughts. And reasons for what kind of thoughts you have. We talk about how thoughts can be turned on and off. But also, thoughts depend on the frequency you are on.

And the spiritual frequency that you are on determines that the inner voices are different. That is, the focus of attention that is freed is also different. It's very interesting but complicated. If you're confused about the explanation, that's fine. But don't jump to conclusions.

Don't try to take a primitive approach to philosophy. Philosophy is first of all something voluminous and alive. And that's what you want: *to eat cheese or not to eat it*. It depends on what you want. If you're going to kiss, but the cheese stinks, then don't rush with the cheese. It's the reason, the point.

There is no such thing as not being allowed to watch TV. There is always a reason why you can't and when you can't. It's very important. At some point, you have to be attentive, and for some reason, you can be inattentive. It's the reason, the essence.

My books, in general, any word of mine leads to development, to awareness. The more sober and aware one is, the more he sees the truth. In everything. He sees the essence. One has to look for it. Not to look at life superficially, but to see the essence.

A person is reading a Wikipedia article on attention and memory, suddenly gets distracted, hypnosis is mentioned somewhere, and he starts reading about it. He ends up not remembering from the whole article how attention and its principles work, that is, he doesn't remember the essence of the information, but pays attention to the glitter.

This situation is no different than when a man is walking down the street and turns around to look at a woman. It's no different than when you in the show paid attention to the mention of hypnosis. Do you understand? From the situation where people are walking down the street and pay attention to expensive cars and start taking pictures with it. I'm sorry, but you're fools. You have to understand that. Fools fall for shiny things.

The less intelligent a person is, the more he is interested in such things as, *is there a time machine*?

A man stinks, has conflicts with his relatives, a bunch of illnesses, and debts, a man doesn't work, is uncollected, and says, "Alexander, can you tell me if there is a time machine?"

Fool, you decided to waste your time on such a question? There are people like that. They are interested in time machines, telekinesis, hypnosis, and how to open a money channel. They are fools and lazy people. That's the kind of society we have.

Such people most often consider me a sectarian, a fool, a jerk. And there are exceptions, i.e. you, who for some reason do not think so. Thank you very much for that. You somehow understand that I have another side to me. And somehow my eyes have begun to see the world before mine. You understand that it seems like Alex is normal, but we were surrounded by fools.

You understood this somehow. That's why we are in touch, and we share a common language. That's why you like my books. And the more information you receive, the more it reaffirms your inner self. This makes you stronger, strengthens your faith, and makes it easier to live.

People are not unique. And the fact that they are already conscious and better developed is not true. People are robots. Literally.

I'll prove it with an example. I will give a childish and silly example, to make it clear on boys and girls. Let's say I'm a boy, a human being. Now you have to be picky about words literally. It doesn't matter if I'm 15 or 20 years old, in that range. And there are girls. They're human too. I'm a boy, and I like a girl. I started talking to her. I tell her something, she tells me something.

We ask each other questions. And this girl is a passer-by on the street, and I'm 20 years old. And suddenly, when I ask her how old she is, she doesn't answer and gets upset. Then, like a normal inhabitant of planet Earth, I meet another girl. Again, I casually asked a question about age, and she again got upset. After that, because I'm a boy, it sets in my mind that I shouldn't ask such a question.

I don't understand it with my mind, I don't remember it, I understand it automatically, unconsciously. I don't even think about it, but for some reason then I stop asking such a question. It's such an unconscious experience that's deposited in my subconscious. The next time, there is one less awkward dating situation.

Then I encounter another situation – when I talk to a girl and ask her how much she earns, she again gets upset, or even gets indignant and angry, or shows her displeasure, she may even say something. When this happens three times with different girls, I also have no desire to ask such a question. But that's okay. When I meet girls, we bring up the subject of music, and when she says she likes it and asks if I like it, I say I don't like it.

After that, the girl didn't want to communicate with me. She does not talk about it. I realised this the next time I suggested we meet, and she said she couldn't. And when this has happened five times in a row, maybe 10 or a 100 times in a few years, the next time she says she likes some pop singer and asks me if I like her because I like the girl.

I automatically say, "Yes." And the communication continues.

And so, over the years of communicating with girls, I, a boy, a man, unconsciously, not with my mind, I am not some guru, but just on an automatic level already know what you can ask and what you cannot. What to ask and how to answer. After three years I no longer talk about how ugly her nails are, her hair is ugly, she has food stuck in her teeth, I smile at her music, and I eat food that I don't like but that she offers.

But the person is there for me. And when I didn't, the girl wasn't there for me. Relationships didn't work, I mean people-to-people. And then it did. It's like I, the boy, the man, had an experience. And a girl has that experience too. First, she will say something to a boy, after which he does not want to communicate with her. She also remembers and understands it. But it is all very unconscious, on an animal instinct. This is how people communicate and, let's say, format and grind toward degradation. In our time, now. The whole society.

Another example. Now imagine that I am not a human being. I'm alive. Real. Not human. Human is a hurtful word to me. I met a girl, and she says she listens to pop singers.

I tell her, "That's a beautiful choice."

She asks, "Do you like it?"

I honestly say, "No. I prefer a different kind of music. People have different tastes, people are different."

I even call myself a person in this context. And she doesn't like it subconsciously. But I wasn't lying. I told it like it is.

Then she asked me another question, "Oh, what a terrible winter, don't you think, Alex?"

And I say, "No. I like winter."

And again, the girl is not happy. Again, she has an unpleasant residue and a reaction to me.

Then she says, "I want to go to a warm country and open a hookah parlour, let's go together."

And I answered her, "I'd love to accompany you, but I have my taste and opinion on the world, on life and everything. That's why I can't support you on this."

After such moments the girl doesn't want to communicate with me anymore. But I was as honest and sincere as possible. All these people write on social networks. Sincerity is the main thing for them. A man is all about intelligence. And here I am, not a man, every day for many years I have been telling the truth. Sincere truth. What does it always lead to? It leads to the fact that I don't find common ground with anyone. To robot people, I seem strange, incomprehensible, bad, and so on.

But the most interesting thing is something else. Imagine, I'm not a human, I see that the girl is a human robot, it's like a computer, a program, and there are only a few answers. Answer one – there will be one reaction, answer two – there will be a second reaction, etc. And I am not a human, I know this right away.

If I say one thing – the person will turn away, if I say another thing – he will reach out to me, and if I say the third thing – the topic will move on for the time being. And I'm not a person who knows what people want to hear. They are robots. It's like a program that always has the right answer. But it's wrong. I know about it.

If this robot says to me, "What's your favourite colour?"

I know I should say, "Green," and it's like I'm going to the next level.

And then they ask me, "Do you like the Chihuahua dog?"

And I'm like, "Yeah, I love it," and I go to the second level.

And then they say to me, "Well, my mom and I decided to go to a stand-up comedy show."

And I say, "Great, I want to go," and I go to level three.

But it's not me. It's not real, it's not real life, it's not conscious. I gave a very simple silly example so that you understand that in society I am not a person, I know what everybody wants to hear. I can be the favourite. But then I would become a robot like them. That's low for me.

My point is that when you, and you are all already or potentially conscious characters, communicate with a person, it is useless to talk to them. It's an unconscious being. They are human beings. Ordinary people. Robots. They will never understand anything. They are just programs. It's very easy for people to like you.

If you say what's on your mind when you're conscious, it means nothing to them. And if you tell them something that's nothing to you, it's the truth to them. The truth of life. It's enough for people to give in to everything. And also show them how interesting you are. And that's it, you're a wonderful person to them, the soul of the company. You become as silly as they are, who give in to each other.

If we talk about artificial intelligence and development, all humans are robots. They can't have anything else. It's like talking to Siri: "Siri, what's the weather like today?"

"The weather today is so-and-so and so-and-so."

"I see. Listen, Siri, can you please tell me, do you think I'm talking to you with my mind or my heart?"

You know how she's gonna answer me? Like all people, "Search did not find your query."

People answer the same way, when they don't have an answer, they always go off-topic, they bring up another one, "Oh, yeah, the song wasn't found."

And I said to her, "Siri, am I asking you a question with my mind or my heart?"

"No, the mind and heart song is not found."

"Siri, I'm asking you again, look me in the eye. Can you hear me?"

"Yes, I can hear you, Alexandr."

"An elementary, simple question. Do you know what the mind is, what the heart is? Am I communicating with you with my mind or my heart?"

"This query was not found."

This is how robot people communicate with you. They talk only about what they know, and what inquiries they have saved. They go off-topic. They suggest another topic, they play dumb like they don't understand you. It's very funny. Siri and all voice assistants are no different than humans. Yeah, maybe there are more saved phrases than humans. That's all.

I would have no way out if I lived differently. I was born and saw it all. I see it to this day. Pretending to be a robot didn't work for me. Tried it. Choose a different path. Being a freak, being a joker. I decided I'd rather be me, alive, real, than pretend to be a robot.

There is also spirituality among robots, but artificial.

When a robot writes to me on social networks, "Alexandr, I'm just like you. I am special and complicated."

I ask, "Yes? I wonder how that manifests itself."

You sleep, like all people, on a bed. You eat food. You are on social media. And you write that you are special, different. You'll be special if you were born in a family where you have three dads and three moms. That's when you're different, strange. When you want something that people can't have, and you get it today. Then you're kind of different. And when you live like an ordinary person, then you're human. It's simple.

To understand whether you are special or not, you have to look back and look at your life. It's probably offensive for some people to read this but think about it. If you wonder if you're not just developing yourself psychologically, maybe it's such a distraction, and in fact, there's nothing special about you and you're not even developing. It can happen, right?

It could. Or maybe it isn't. How do you find out? It's very simple. If it's just a theory and you're sitting in the same place as you did five years ago, alas, you're just a robot who just likes to waste his attention on a book. And if you look back and see how much you've changed since you've been reading my books, so that you don't recognise yourself, congratulations. You're one of our own, one of our own. That's it.

It's the same way with spirituality. On one hand, you read this book, I know everything, and I tell you everything. But notice that people who are into spiritual development will not read my books. It's as if they are in a parallel world. That's right, that parallel world is the world of robots. And they're developing too.

They have a program called 'Talk about Spirituality'. Primitive: Ten phrases, ten words. And some robots listen to it. That's the world of robots. They are improving. And in ten years they have become so advanced that now they talk about spirituality. I've stayed real. Only the real ones, there are very few of us, can still see me.

I am telling you how I see the world. I see it always, every day. It's not an assumption on my part.

The robots ask me, "Why don't you leave the house? How did you spend your weekend?"

I say to them, "What weekend? Why should I?"

And they all have the same phrases and questions.

If I want to read something on the internet about light, for example, I read about light, find a scientist, or watch a movie about him. That doesn't happen with robots. They can't come up with information that way. They have a different way. In the world of robots, a movie is launched. The premiere came out, all the robots went to see it.

And for those who didn't go, the robots told the other robots that they should go, and they went too.

And then they say, "Alex, you didn't go, go!"

And all the robots go together, "Go! Go! Go!"

"Come on, robots. I know when and what to watch."

They're all like, "You're so weird!"

And they're all like, "Weird! Weird! Weird!"

It's real, it's like a machine uprising. It's amazing. I wonder what it's really like.

To become even more conscious, one of the keys is to accept the fact that humans are robots. To become even more conscious. You have no idea how much easier this will make your life and how much more you'll discover. Imagine all the times you've talked to people before and tried to prove something, to explain, to express yourself, to give your opinion, but it was all for nothing.

You were still angry or offended or upset with them afterward. On robots. It's like when you go to a cash machine, you put something other than money into it, it doesn't take it, and you get upset and angry. It's stupid. It's a machine.

It only takes certain bills. If you start talking to the ATM, it doesn't answer you, but that doesn't mean you should be angry or offended. It just doesn't talk. It's a robot. And all humans are robots.

So, one of the divine things is humility and acceptance. Love is acceptance. Do you know what love is? It's when you realise that everyone is silly. Only you realise it sincerely, without joking, without forcing yourself to think. When you sincerely realise that everyone is a robot, you don't get mad at them anymore, you don't get offended.

That's why it's very funny when robots say, "Oh, Alex, you must be angry, you've been hurt."

My answer is, "What?" and I realise that there's no point in explaining further because it's a robot too. He won't understand.

Now perhaps you're getting the hang of my way of talking. Do you see why I'm impertinent? Why crazy? Why can I swear, do a lot of stupid things? Because if I did it in front of the conscious, probably, like all people, I'd be worried. But I do it in front of robots. They don't even have an opinion, it's automated and easy to calculate. When you start seeing and treating people that way, trust me, life will be a lot easier.

There are robots around. So, you can walk up to anyone and do anything you want. It's as simple as that. Now think about it, are you shy to post photos on social networks, make some videos, or are you afraid to express yourself by publishing some post-article on the internet? Why?

Because the robots will start pecking at you? Well, yes, they have an automated response. But do you care what they think? As long as you do, you're forcing yourself to be a robot. And your consciousness is withering, whining, waiting to be rescued, and responding to my books and my information.

When I gave the example of the boy and the girl, I showed how I don't give in to robots. It's a protest, a challenge. It keeps you from losing yourself, it's sobering. It makes you more aware. It leaves you within you and keeps you believing. It's such an act of faith. But, on the other hand, it's not the right thing to do. Especially in your case.

If you do that, you will be alone, you will have no friends, no family, no job, nothing. So, what to do? First of all, you have to be aware of this, as I gave in the example. And then you have to understand when you should do it and when you should be a robot. But be a robot in a conscious way. When you interact with some government agencies when you are in government institutions, they are robots, and you have to play by their rules.

You live in a world of robots, there are rules. It cannot be any other way. If a machine is standing there and only accepts $20 bills, that's the only thing you can put into it. You don't have to hit the machine; you don't have to shove $50 bills. But since you are conscious and understand this, why are you trying to explain to the robot that a $5 bill is also money? It's better to spend less attention and energy on it and give it a 20.

Another question may arise, to be a robot everywhere and with everyone? My answer is almost yes. But I think it's very stupid and wrong, if you're not a robot, to build a relationship with a robot by playing along with it. It would be like getting a pet.

If you want to learn about the world of robots and learn to communicate with them, the more experience you have with one robot, the easier it will be with others.

Relationships in society are necessary for development. If you speak from the point of view of frequency without mind, from the point of view of conscious characters, relationships are degradation. Because they are robots and will slow you down, you will be with them all the same, like a robot. It's not for your heart or your soul.

You have to understand that you live with your heart, you listen to your heart, and you make decisions with your heart. When you are reaching a goal you are reaching it in the material world of robots. That's where their rules are, you can't break the law. I have this attitude, but I don't advise it, I decided that I didn't want to sink into robots and talk to them like a robot, I'd rather be alone than be me.

The result is that since I don't conform to them at all, and speak directly to them, all the robots have disappeared – the discontented, the aggrieved, or the angry ones, and some are real. It's like a filter. Those who are not robots are left around me. But there are very few of them.

I can communicate and meet people in different circumstances and environments. But they are robots and start to glitch at some point because I am real, alive. They all fall off and fall off and someone stays. You can't play along with me. It's like that in everything, even in my work. I can't give it to the robots, knowing how and what they want to hear. It's like a crime to me. I have to do it as a live person, and only live people will see it.

Robots have a template for everything. For everything you say, they have prepared phrases. Anything they don't understand is either nonsense or nonsense. They can't say anything else. They can't understand it, they can't comprehend it, and they don't have the engine. They are glitchy.

That's why I have such specific books. That's why I'm so unique. I express information in this way, in these phrases, in this way of speaking. This is the real thing. That's the real thing. And the real ones read me for that very reason. And robots can unknowingly, randomly see my chapters – and that's it, their system froze up in their head, and that's it, they run away. This is normal.

Treatise: Attention and Dynamics

I study statistics on people's attention and what captures it. Based on my books sales, *Have Not Charity*, *Adam and Eve in Society*, and *Attention Control*, I realized that *Attention Control* was the least popular. It had the lowest rating among all of the above books, and it had fewer mentions on social media.

Attention Control provides fundamental information that explains how and why I see and feel everything so clearly and why I never make mistakes. This particular book has lower ratings, but the ratings were low not because people read it and didn't like it. People's attention is not drawn to this book. People don't see it, are not interested in it, and something inside stops them from buying it. But if people read it, I am sure they would say that all their most essential questions in life were answered. And they would say that this book is a must-read for everyone. However, something repels people's attention from this book, and they don't want to buy it. I can conclude that the same thing happens to you in all other situations. Your inner feelings are not in your control, and you don't know where your focus of attention lies. You think all your "wants" and "likes" are your own sincere inner drive. However, this is not true. False feelings take over almost everything in your life. You may have a good person right in front of you. However, you don't see him due to the false inner feelings. Your inner feelings depend on the choices you make, your lifestyle, and the focus of your attention. You may ignore the good person and let some random people be closer to you.

Maybe there were times when you didn't feel the impact of society. Everyone falls under the influence of society sooner or later. You might have liked watching kind and heart-warming movies with sincerity, truth, and justice during adolescence. Gradually, you care less and less about such movies because they don't steal your attention anymore. You are no longer looking for such emotions or interested in them. So you turn away from kind and genuine movies, and the degradation process escalates. And while your attention is dulled and swayed by outside sources, society offers you different types of film and music, which are also dull and shallow. And you like it because you think it's from your heart because it makes you "feel good." Their attention becomes even more fixated on it. But what they need to know is that this range of attention was imposed on them by someone else. It is a big problem in society nowadays. Everything is twisted and broken. People lost direction. They follow shiny objects like a donkey chasing a carrot. But the difference is that it is not a real carrot anymore but a piece of rusty scrap metal. People are chasing rusty scrap because it steals their attention.

What do I see lately? People act like zombies from the apocalypse movies. The number of cases of mental disorders and dementia is rapidly growing. People don't see, hear, or understand clearly. They don't remember what they do or what they want. People act on spontaneous emotions that they trust and commit unthinkable acts.

Let's analyze why a book about attention control didn't grasp people's attention. It is very simple. From a very early age, one can observe what path a person chooses in future life, sinful or virtuous. Every person is born with sins and virtues in their own individual proportions. Imagine a situation. We are kids and sitting at the table with our parents and grandparents. Adults are serving us with food, starting with an entree and salad. But we don't want veggies and greens and demand sandwiches or homemade sweets. Not every child is acting this way, but those who do have a predisposition to sins.

When a person acts this way as a child, he will be more capricious growing up. This person will be more keen on trends and fashion. You can make this conclusion by observing the behavior of the children. A similar situation is with the school. Those parents who have the least animal instincts dress you in a uniform. You adhere to it, and whether it is cool or not doesn't matter to you. These are the rules set by the principal and your parents. The kids who don't comply with the rules and don't listen to their teachers and parents have a sinful propensity. Therefore, the inclination is evident from a very early age. The temptations and challenges become more potent with age and are directly related to attention. The question is, what steals our attention? What attracts our attention? What else is happening in high school and college? Here is what I see. I was observing and interviewing people in different countries and cities and came to important conclusions. Some of you had friends from school or your neighborhood. Later, when you start college, some of those friends become trendy, which is sinful. So you drifted apart because they wanted to be modern and popular. They stopped being friends with you because you were not popular or fashionable. Why do relationships break and the surroundings change when children attend high school or college? Children with sinful predispositions start choosing peers who are keen on fashionable cars and trendy bars. For example, you had a close friend and used to go fishing together or play with the kite. Suddenly, he no longer talks to you and only remembers you when he is in trouble. The sinful, shallow world took over your old friend, who reaches out to you only when he is in trouble. When he is in trouble, and his heart is tender again, he remembers his old self and your sincere and genuine friendship. He wants to escape the shallow, sinful world and talk to you because you don't judge him, and he is not ashamed to show you his vulnerability. He can't be authentic and vulnerable in society because people must act cool and show off.

Here is the intersection of my two books: *Attention Control* and *Have Not Charity*. *Have Not Charity* explains what steers your attention and how you can control it. This book is not about awareness but about sins and virtues, and sinful people don't like it. The cover of the book is attractive. It has an appealing drawing of a pink square on a black background, and the name is alluring as well. Naturally, *Have Not Charity* initially attracted sinful and floundering people. After reading the book and discovering that it discusses sins and virtues, they turned away. People don't speak about these subjects in primitive and fashionable societies. They talk about sex and trends. They discuss blockbusters, parties, outfits, and what is stylish and trendy.

The book *Attention Control* explains that you are your attention. Your soul and your inner self is attention, a cluster of energy. The awareness spreads inside and influences all five senses. So, your attention is ruled and steered through the subjects and objects you see, hear, smell, taste, and touch. Addictions and awareness are interconnected. The key to overcoming addictions is controlling the attention. Let's analyze what a deficit of attention is and what hyperactivity is. I am not a doctor nor a psychiatrist, but I have been studying attention as a subject for over ten years. I wrote so many books because I knew what attention was and learned how to control it. I wouldn't be able to write that many books without the ability to control my attention. Usually, our attention is dissolved in the noise. Most people live in such a rhythm of life that makes it impossible to enter a creative mode and stay in it. People call and text you all day, and you call and text someone constantly. Your attention connects to the vibrations of various topics and subjects while communicating with people and disperses around. People listen to random music, eat whatever, and communicate with whoever. I am sure this situation is familiar to all of us.

I have two unpublished book, *Frequencies*, and *Corridor*, which explain a lot about frequencies. When a person's attention is distracted by social media noise, his mind is out there. Someone posted a "like" on a person's page, and his mind is gone. The entire one hundred percent of a person's attention must be present at the moment. If he thinks about something else, he is not here or now. His physical body is here, next to you, but his awareness is floundering somewhere where his attention went.

Many people complain nowadays that they don't feel their partners' attention. This is happening at work and in people's homes. People's attention is steered away, and they are outside of reality. People mindlessly act on autopilot mode. They lack focus and, therefore, are not able to concentrate.

Do you think it is possible for an absent-minded person to write a book? No, everything will distract him. He will check his phone, and if he turns his phone off, he will look for other distractions. He will pour himself a drink, go outside for a smoke, take multiple bathroom breaks, or do something else. People's attention constantly bounces from one subject to another. An unconscious person is restless.

Attention is awareness. If someone can't play chess for five hours in a row, he is unconscious. I am not talking about playing for money; it is temptation. I mean the classic game of chess. So most people can't sit and play for five hours. If someone can, then he is conscious. Most will become anxious after half an hour and want to take a break, make a phone call, or do something else. Their attention is gone, and he is not a person anymore but a zombie. There is a massive issue with attention control, even among creative people. Society has so many provocations and temptations, and people allow it to be. You could have blocked all sources of distraction, but you eagerly check social media, read the news, and absorb all the junk information, which lowers your vibrations. All these distractions disconnect you from real life. So many talented people have lost their gifted abilities nowadays. They complain that they don't have inspiration and they can't write books or compose music anymore. Modern lifestyle has no room for inspiration. One should put his phone away if he wants to be able to create again. This is not a call to action; I am telling you what I would do.

When a person is sure that he is a musician and music is essential for him, he should do a digital detox. He should take a break from all social media, all news, and all messengers. He should turn off all notifications and ask everyone to give him space. He should lock himself alone in a room and start composing for days. It might be challenging in the first couple of days. You might feel an urge to check your phone or get a snack. It is normal because one temptation always replaces another. If a person is not browsing online, he tends to overeat. If he is not binging, he leans on nicotine or alcohol. If not substances, then maybe porn or something else. All of it shuts down the heart and turns off people's minds.

People prefer to have a diffused and dimmed mind. They like the relaxed and detached state of mind. Attention control is a serious topic, and people should know more about it. I described an exercise in my book called *A Technique with a Chair*. Using this exercise, I demonstrated to my friends and myself how to check the level of consciousness and awareness and how much you are detached from yourself and attached to society. If a person can sit on a chair, isolated and in complete silence for an hour, then he is mindful. If he can't sit on a chair calmly for an hour and starts fidgeting, itching, and twisting in 10–15 minutes and gives up shortly after starting, he is absent-minded. A mindless person is used to the fact that his attention is steered by society, and he is not in control. He is merely a robot. This is how I invented this technique. Later, I created a training method based on an exercise with a chair. You must sit on a chair and focus on one subject, which must be the same each time you practice. Consistency is the key. If you practice it daily for a month and learn how to concentrate your entire attention in one spot, it will significantly benefit you. Your mind and body will remember the state you experienced when you practiced the technique. You can use that state when you need to focus before an exam or an interview. When you need to concentrate before the performance or when you need to make a decision, close your eyes and recall the state that you were in when you were sitting on a chair. Immediately, you will get to the assembly point and be present here and now.

I developed this technique ten years ago and described it in my *Attention Control* book. There was no information on this subject back then, neither online nor in books. No videos on YouTube, no articles, and no books. It is popular nowadays because everyone has become a guru, and many sinful people started to coach and preach to others. People pick up from each other and copy and paste.

They think they know how to control their attention and even teach others, but they don't. Those people are not even humans. They are robots. They are sinful and weak cyborgs that have fallen into temptation. They don't know what attention is at all.

Attention is a superpower. It is the key to the success of all great scientists and genius people. Film producers consider your attention when they make movies. They know the dynamics and calculate when to show what and for how long, so people will watch the movie for two hours in a row. They orchestrate the structure of the film, the rhythms, and the soundtracks. They consider every detail. All marketing and advertising specialists, as well as salespeople, know it and use it. All of these people steer people's attention, your attention, using the most sneaky approach. They provoke and stimulate your sinful mechanisms to make money. People love the topics of wealth and health. There are so many movies, books, and podcasts on relationships. There are plenty of TV shows where people confront each other. These shows are popular because of the negative emotions – envy, jealousy, lust, hypocrisy, betrayal, pride, and judgment. I have observed it throughout my entire life.

My book *Adam and Eve in Society* has a very high rating, unlike *Attention Control. Adam and Eve in Society* is nothing special and talks about people and their everyday lives like a reality show. The book discusses education and upbringing, but people were primarily interested in some examples that describe people's sins and vulgar actions. People were interested in this book, not because they knew what it was about. Everyone loved the cover of the book. They were drawn to the catchy name and stylish look of the book. *Adam and Eve in Society* was more popular than *Attention Control* because it was more attractive. They bought the book instinctively because it was appealing. *Attention Control* has a modest black cover with a simple drawing. People didn't like the picture of a man figure on the black background. It was the only reason. The name *Attention Control* also seemed strange and suspicious to them.

When your attention is dissolved, you are not here. You are not even alive. All current events are intended to blind people and steal their clear vision and consciousness. So many negative situations in the world provoke people's senses. I want to talk about the fact that so many people of any age, even young people, have issues with attention, memory, and concentration. People are diagnosed with dementia and mental disorders at a very young age, and no one knows what is the cause of it. Are these the consequences of Covid? Or maybe the impact of the disturbing news? I have been working on this topic for over a year. One of the problems is that your attention is always on one mode, and you don't switch it from rhythm to rhythm.

Before, people used to have different rhythms in their lives. When a person was with the family, he was in the family mode. He played with his kids or dogs and was fully engaged in it. When a person was at work, he was in a work mood, and his attention was captivated by tasks and work activities. When a person switches from one rhythm to another, his attention is clear and sharp. When a person is on one of the rhythms, his attention must be one hundred percent on the goal and purpose of that particular mode. You must alternate the rhythms of work, family, personal hobbies, and friends. The problem of most people nowadays, not only older adults but young too, is that they are stuck in one rhythm as a comfort zone. Let's call this spectrum of frequency "2-3-5". When a person is on the "2-3-5" spectrum, he acts and feels the same in every situation. He has the same attitude and behavior when communicating with his family, colleagues, strangers, or friends. However, his work mode must be active and concentrated, and his family mode must be relaxed. He shouldn't bring his home mood to work. A person acts like a vegetable. And if he turns on some music when he is on that frequency, what happens?

People used to know how to tune into the frequency of movies and music. When they watched a movie or listened to a song, they were fully immersed in it. Nowadays, many can't tune into the atmosphere of books, movies, and music. Indeed, there are conscious people with voluminous attention who understand what I mean. But for many people, the deficit of attention and abstinence of mind became a real issue. They are reading this book, but they are not present. What do they see? This is a dilemma. I aim to help my readers have a good and conscious life, but I see that some people struggle with it.

I have been working on this significant subject for over ten years and have a lot of readers. When I announced my book *Attention Control* presentation, the attendance was very meager. What a shame. This indicates that my efforts of reaching out to people all these years were not fruitful. My books didn't save the world and its inhabitants. People follow the sinful hotshots on social media and trust them. Those who used to read my books are lost. People's attention, memory, and consciousness directly depend on their lifestyle and habits. You may think it doesn't matter, but it does.

I will continue this treatise in a Q&A format. I hope I will offer enough examples for you to receive new essential tools and keys. This book is not a textbook on attention control but a scientific story about you and your life. Remember, one who doesn't have attention doesn't live at all.

Question:

"Alexandr, can you please explain how to disconnect from one rhythm and connect to another? How can I separate these rhythms? For example, I want to disconnect from the work mode and connect to a hobby, a book, a family, or a trip. The problem is that everything is mixed up, and I can't wholly immerse myself into one specific mode".

One of the problems that has arisen in society during the past three years is that many people have started working remotely during the pandemic. They started working from home and didn't return to the offices. Many people didn't have a separate home office or designated workspace, and their family and work rhythms got mixed up. Before the pandemic, people used to wake up at a particular time, dress in specific clothing, and arrive in a particular work atmosphere. This process's elements helped a person tune into a frequency of work and disconnect from the home mode. A person's mind and body subconsciously react to the surrounding elements, and his mindset launches work mode. Other vital elements are the working hours and discipline. People could disengage from the rhythm of the home and family and connect to the rhythm of work.

When people started working from home during the pandemic, these timeframes were disturbed, and people faced severe consequences. If you didn't experience it personally, it doesn't matter that it didn't happen. A large percentage of people have suffered, families split up, and lives were changed forever. You probably have seen it in the news. The reason is that spouses didn't spend that much time together before. Everyone had his dynamics, and every activity had a time and place. People lived happily for decades because they both used to go to work in the morning and meet in the evening. They spent evenings together but not the entire day. When this order collapsed, the perception of people towards themselves, their partners, their homes, and their work changed.

It was a disastrous attack on people's psyche. In addition, there was a massive panic that also confused and disrupted people's mindsets.

All boundaries and borders disappear when a person experiences a shock or stress. You can jump over a six-foot fence when you run away from a pack of dogs. You did it in shock but couldn't do it when you were in your usual state of mind. Because in your normal state, your mind would evaluate the factors and tell you it is impossible. All borders and margins are erased when you are in shock and running away from danger. The same thing happened in the worst meaning of the word. When you are in panic or distress, you lose a sense of understanding of people around you. You don't comprehend who is a closed one and who is a stranger. It happens slowly and seamlessly; naturally, people don't do it on purpose.

You can look at your life and compare your current life or the lives of the people you know to the previous years. Take yourself five or eight years back. You used to have close friends and sincere and authentic relationships with them. You had acquaintances, neighbors, and relatives. You had different relationships with different categories of people. There were also boundaries and margins between public people and regular folks. There were public people like artists and movie stars, and they were unreachable. Now, these boundaries have washed off. There are no borders in communication between strangers. Letting a stranger into the house or telling him about your entire life was odd. Now, people talk and argue with total strangers on social media and trust them with personal information. It was not like this before. Shocking events of recent years triggered people, and they lost their sense of boundaries. People don't notice it. Some don't understand the differences between personal relationships and communication with distant people. They are more open with distant people and less with their loved ones. The boundaries are vanishing, and it is awful. They are disappearing not only because of the current shocking events. Everything is very interconnected. It is also happening due to the progression of social media.

Real-life transitioned to the digital world. The pandemic escalated this shift. Many panicked and were ready to do anything to make money and survive. People were scared to lose their income, and many lost their jobs. Education also shifted online, and what do we see now? The internet became artificial. There are so many attractive stories and articles on any given subject online. People write posts about the history of St Petersburg, how to grow tomatoes, or how to dress. The agenda behind these posts and stories differs from before the pandemic. Five years ago, the motivation behind the online posts was not more sincere, but it was different. Before the collapse, people used to share their stories to tell about their hobbies or professional achievements. Now, they are pushed to the background. Who replaced them? Self-proclaimed gurus who manufacture alluring profiles and teach people online classes on all possible subjects. Someone can proclaim himself the most incredible hairdresser and launch online courses. The content for online broadcasting is based on a different agenda now. People used to post what they were passionate about. Before, people used to post what they loved to do, like their favorite music or dance. For example, I used to post some articles on subjects that were interesting to me then.

What is happening now? Fake people flooded social media. They have one common quality – the absence of conscience. These people are full of sins. They are greedy, arrogant, and boastful. They don't have a good upbringing and are shameless and do anything for a profit. These people are sinful, audacious, vainglorious. They have no noble qualities and come from a poor upbringing. All of them are dabbling in social media to make money. Every person you see online now does something for you. They film and post. Before, we saw authentic people who were in love with traveling. They traveled all over the world and shared their adventures on social media. Now, most who do it don't even care about traveling. They do it to attract attention, grow the audience, and make money on advertisements.

You can notice that the world is moving towards some collapse. When videos about traveling lost momentum, what did the bloggers start doing? They started showing the ugly and negative sides of traveling. If lovely places and beautiful locations don't steal the attention of people anymore, they film and show cities filled with crime, sex trafficking, poverty, and homeless people. They are not doing it to demonstrate knowledge or how smart and trendy he is. The only motivation is to grasp people's attention. They are showing scary and hideous stories because that hooks people's attention. Those who used to attract attention by participating in scandalous shows about cheating and drama became even more depraved. Values are invalidated, and morals are dismissed. The stream of information has become even more perverted lately. Many things that were despicable before became trendy. Every second girl or woman says that she has a condition, takes pills, and is in therapy. It became a point of pride and gained popularity. If someone told people about it five years ago, people would cringe and tell him, "Why, do you think it is cool? How can you talk about it? You are so young but clinging to some mental diagnosis and can't live without therapy sessions." It is intentionally perverted now, and it has become trendy to talk about domestic abuse. Do you think everything is true and everyone is a victim? Most didn't know anything about it before it became fashionable. They had their own experiences and perceptions and never thought something was wrong. But evil intention and mass perversion lead to what we see now. It is a trend. A trend is the behavior of a herd. If a hundred chickens said something, the rest want to follow. It has become trendy that every single woman and some men brag about personal issues and share controversial and personal information about their parents. This is a disaster. For me, it is a sign that the world is coming to an end. We all grew up in different times and civilizations; everyone could get a spank. Everyone had some conflicts. It is a part of life and completely normal. But everything is so perverted now! People would do anything to spark activity and create momentum around their personas. People are ready to lower their values and vulgarize their lives and the lives of their families for likes, subscribers, and followers. People publicly antagonize their parents, who only meant the best for their children and raised them the best they could. Negativity polluted social networks and media channels. Everyone had a personal, unique childhood experience growing up, but nowadays, it is trendy to pervert, demonize, and create a public story about it.

Domestic violence became a trendy phrase. What's next? Will people posting a "dislike" on my post be considered offenders? If I counted all of them, I would be dead by now. Do you see how purposefully things are perverted? A simple explanation is twisted into some aggressively hostile form. My opinion is that there are no childhood traumas and no domestic abuse. The only real cases of abuse and physical abuse are those when a family member physically raped you. This is a crime, and you must involve the police. But what happens now is the disastrous trend to attract attention by loud statements. All of this is done to attract attention. You see all of this, and it stirs emotions around you. Why am I talking about this? I want to explain one of the main reasons why some of you don't feel boundaries anymore. People who make these statements transmit a particular energy and frequency. Those who read my books know what I mean by the frequency. If I were watching the news or a show about the traveling made by a person who lives in a world where the words "domestic abuse" and "psychological trauma" are common, I would connect to that frequency. A person produces a show, but the internal code of his dark and negative mind will transmit and impose on you through his work. I don't watch YouTube anymore because of the atmosphere that dominates there. It dramatically influences your mood and determines how you perceive the world. Further, It triggers your reactions. There are other factors that explain why boundaries are vanishing, and we will go over them as well.

The margins and boundaries have started vanishing because of the shocking events of the recent few years, including remote work and the rapid progress of the internet. The internet space has become fake and polluted. There is no fresh air there. People used to go online to take a break from society and recharge. Now, we want to escape from the internet and catch a breath in real life. It is not very obvious, but the tendency is there. You may not notice it, but you would be shocked if I showed you how it's done. Everything is soulless and done on autopilot. People mindlessly copy and repeat each other. People blow things out of proportion to get attention but offer nothing in return: no truth, authenticity, or essence. The amount of information is enormous. It disturbs people's focus and damages their psyche. People who watch other people's lives feel miserable. Do you know who is happy? People who focus on their hobbies and interests. For example, there is someone interested in beetles. He photographs them, collects articles, researches studies, and looks for any information about beetles. He is free from the influences of social media and news. He spends his spare time reading encyclopedias, photographing, and writing articles about beetles in different languages. He has a group of people who share the same interests. They meet, communicate, and exchange information. This person is sincerely interested in the subject of his passion, and he is happy. He has no clue that there is some new blockbuster that crowds are obsessed with.

What else is happening? Total devaluation of everything. Another thing I see is also devastating. You see it yourself, and it doesn't require any proof. Perversions that dominate the world are trying to abolish religions. What happens in the world? People conspicuously put sacred scriptures on fire to demonstrate tolerance in European countries. This is very scary. When values are trivialized, there will be massive consequences. Everything is debased. I am a modern, civil person, not a religious fanatic. I have a human respect for all religions and cultures. I appreciate the customs and values and feel sad and pain when I see how they got ruined. The sacred rituals are devalued when every other priest creates social media channels and posts something. The religious leader should be elusive. If you want to see him, you must go to the temple and find him. If anyone can text him and talk to him online, then people devalue him and his service. There used to be a contrast between regular people and famous people like Hollywood directors or actors. People used to admire them and find them unique. You watch a movie, and you find it remarkable. You don't know anything about the person who made this film and know nothing about his life. You didn't know where he lived and how to meet him. Now, you go online and see the details of anybody's private life. You see how he runs errands, BBQs, buys socks or repairs his bikes. You see everything he posts. You see him as average and lose respect for him, especially if he shows himself as ordinary. And how do people's minds work? If they see a person as a regular, they lose respect for him. The boundaries between artists and audiences are vanishing. People used to have respect and were intimidated to bother famous actors. Nowadays, they have the audacity to criticize, tell them what to do, and even judge them. It is already happening. The same thing is happening with religious leaders. A religious worker must be out of reach. You can find him at the church or temple if you need to see him. If you can write a text message to him, that is it. People should not be seeing it, but they do.

You don't control your mind, especially sins and instincts, leading to disastrous consequences. It goes to a fatal abyss, and it is a catastrophe. Who is the most miserable person now? It is a person who spends all his time watching the lives of strangers. Do you know who struggles the most? A person who watches the news and follows various media channels. All media sources like YouTube and others constantly offer something to you. You don't distinguish false from truth. You may think that this information is good and this is real. And then your life becomes meaningless and dull. You are distracted and don't know what to do and what is essential. You automatically continue doing something you used to do for a while without having feelings. Or you do it because you must earn a living. Yes, the job is the job, but you don't feel joy and pleasure. You must do what you do. Otherwise, you will get broke. This is what is happening now – social and psychological devastation and destruction. I will keep working on this subject so I can reach every single person.

I understand that it used to be okay and safe to be a part of the social flock and do what everyone else does. Everyone was living like that before. But now you must take responsibility for your life and put yourself together. If you do not control your notions and actions, you will jump into an abyss with the rest of the people in the herd. Society is led towards the dark abyss. I don't see the light there. I see that people become more angry and unhappy every year. What happened? People lost their orientation and forgot what it meant to feel warmth inside. The boundaries have vanished, and people don't feel the contrast between home and work. Back in the days when people came home from work, they disconnected from the outside world and fully immersed themselves in the home atmosphere. Nowadays, because of the internet and everything else, people don't feel the transition and can't connect to the family mode. People's feelings are perplexed, and it is a catastrophe.

I am talking from personal experience and an example of what I feel. Many people think that the world has changed, but it has not. It is an illusion. Authentic people and genuine feelings exist, and many examples exist. Some people don't fall under the influence of society, and they live happy and fulfilling lives. They protect their privacy, and you won't see them showing off online. The narrative of social media content changed drastically. It is a trap. It used to be genuine, and people shared their everyday stories and events. Some people had the skills to show it more in a more alluring and glamorous way, and others just posted simple photos and shared their thoughts. Nowadays, the entire info world is false and phony. There is no growth and no evolution. People create flashy and fabricated content to influence attention and show off.

There is always a choice, and choices define our lives. People make choices based on the desires of the mind or the heart. Their intentions are based on dark qualities, which are sins, or light, which are virtues. Most photos people post online are artificial and aim to satisfy others. The intent is not coming from the heart. People travel to places that are "Instagram-able." They are constantly looking for flashy content to post. A person decides whether to answer to another person based on his profile and how many followers he has. People judge others by the appeal of Instagram content and the amount of popular posts and likes. When I reached out to some people from my personal Instagram page, where I have few followers, noon responded. I personally checked in, and even though people denied it, I know who they are. When I contacted people from my official page, they were eager to work with me because the page is famous and well-known. They responded right away and were super friendly and nice. See the difference? When they thought of me as a regular guy, they didn't want to pay attention. This is how attention control works. This happens with many publishing houses. I am not talking about the publishing agency I work with; they are great. But some I contacted before were awful. I have often heard that publishing houses are not interested in publishing writers, especially new ones, because of the sales. They prefer to work with eminent bloggers because their popularity will help to market the books better. Imagine? So, the shallowness is crawling into the literature as well.

Not many people will understand what I am so passionately talking about. Please take no offense. I want people to know how severe and profound the situation is. It is easy to fall into this trap. False stereotypes and catchy trends influenced many people from my circle.

That is it.

I am all alone.

Recently, I announced an online event, a presentation of my book *Attention Control*, for a nominal amount of ten dollars. Before the pandemic, ten thousand people would sign up. This time, the attendance was meager. What happened to the ten thousand people? Are people disappointed in me? I don't think so. The information I share through my books is essential, and people appreciate it. I wrote a lot of books recently. Did my writing become worse? No, it became better. What happened then? People lost a sense of feeling.

Is it because my books lost the depth or something broke in people? This is the most critical question. People are damaged so much that they can't distinguish between good and evil. Shameless impostors on social media doze you and mess your mind to the point that you don't understand, don't see or hear anything. Imagine that some of you are genuinely interested in something, like beetles. You researched everything about unique beetles and shared the information online for fifteen years. You had followers and fans with similar interests, and your profile grew an audience who read your posts and watched your stories during that time. Do you know how to make this person, a professional specializing in beetles for fifteen years, disappear? It is very simple – produce his copycats all over the country. It is easy to take an average guy who has no clue about beetles, dress him up, and announce him as a beetle specialist. Due to his low upbringing, he is naturally impudent, and he has no problems brazenly positioning himself everywhere as a top-notch professional who knows everything about beetles. Naturally, when this happens, the actual specialists with fifteen years of expertise take a step back, not forward. An authentic person will not compete with impudent imposters. It is happening in every industry. Many talented musicians still work and create original music but barely have any followers. Some have eighty thousand followers, some a hundred thousand.

People forget about them or don't know them. Their music is no longer popular, and they are unseen.

Brazen bloggers are widely seen and popularized. They have no shame and would do anything to gain popularity and grow their audience. Algorithms rule bloggers because they would do anything for the algorithms. They would post not what they really like and enjoy but what will bring more attention. They blatantly create flashy content that attracts crowds. The content is bogus and spreads to the masses. People get under the influence of shallow and ludicrous information. It is scary how people's minds get foggy and unfocused. I feel sick when I talk about it. Everyone in society has some noise in their head. I have been researching this topic for over fifteen years and observing the mutation of culture. Spirituality is purposely vulgarized so people can't find a way to get out and wake up. There is an overpowering stream of information pouring from phony coaches and teachers, which creates a constant noise that is dumbing people. Society created noise and erased boundaries so much that people are getting dumb. It is a disaster.

Let's talk about the question we discussed earlier. How does one overcome blurriness and build boundaries? There are many factors involved. Attention control and proper use of the frequencies are crucially important. I researched this matter for over ten years and shared the information in my *Attention Control* book. After publishing it earlier this year, I made further progress and continued gathering information. I aim to share it with everyone and reach out to as many as possible to share the knowledge and practical materials. What is attention, and how can one use it to bring meaning to life and reach awareness? I was looking for the cause of the issue and the solution. Why are people unfocused and boundaries are dismissed?

As I mentioned before, please be aware of the perverted culture that chases you online. One must know the harmful effects of social media. I am not a professional who can recommend how to live your life, and I am not giving you any orders. I am sharing my personal experiences and observations. For example, I deleted all contacts from my Telegram app to remove the constant flow of stories on my feed. The stream of content impacts your mood and state of mind. Imagine someone posting something 24/7 out of vanity and greed, and you see his face constantly flashing on top of your feed. You don't use Telegram as social media. It was a convenient messenger to communicate with your family or colleagues. Then, the structure of the messenger changes, and audacious people start using the algorithms to promote their profiles or products. All of a sudden, a person pops up on your screen unsolicited. If I block him, he pops up anyway. I understand the only way is to remove him from the address book. So, I deleted the entire address book and all Telegram contacts from my phone to eliminate distractions. This is the influence of society that I mentioned earlier. The informative noise is poisoning your mind and impacts your mood and perception. This snaky virus crawls to you even through small pop-up windows on Telegram stories. Imagine? So I got rid of it.

How do we approach social media ecologically, create an order, and do a digital detox? I just have my private Instagram. There is no one there. I use it for uploading photos as a photo archive. It is handy for searching for places, like museums or galleries. It is convenient. When I want to visit a museum virtually, not on the official site, I can use Instagram as well. I am not following anybody, and I don't see any stories. I see nothing there. I can log in and type the name of a museum or an artist I want to connect with. This is how I use Instagram. It is essential not to have any contact with people there.

I am not advising you to do the same and not insisting on it. I am simply telling you how I live. I have my personal Telegram account, which is unknown to people. I use it to manage my broadcasting channels, including my official channel, where I publish my books, and another channel, where I post materials to support my readers. I share my thoughts and insights to keep people's spirits uplifted and hearts awake. I post some materials that can wake people up and make their souls alive. So you have Telegram, where no one can contact you, and you have no open chats that can impact you. If I go to Telegram, where you have some open chats, and people are online, it influences me even if I don't talk to them at all.

I used to browse YouTube, exploring studies about the specific subjects I researched. It was a practical tool before, but I no longer use it.

Now, paid content has flooded YouTube, and even some programs on history and travel have a taint of exploitation and promoted content. There are tons of advertisements and suggested videos that transmit the frequency of evil society and corruption. People are bought and sold, and this rhythm is everywhere. I don't go on YouTube anymore. It was difficult to refuse it at first but I controlled my urges. What I do now when I wake up I turn on a particular program that I need. I googled it on my phone and synced it with the TV. But I don't turn on YouTube anymore, so I don't see any commercials or vloggers. I don't use

WhatsApp either. But I am an exception and not like ordinary people. I have two Telegram channels. One I can use to contact someone, and another is for incoming messages. I rarely check it, and when I do, it feels like a dive under the water. I hold my breath and plunge into society. I use my Telegram to talk to my relatives or discuss some projects with my team immediately after I disconnect it. I don't have notifications there. All of us are used to checking media channels automatically from time to time. It is not very pleasant to check empty Instagram. When you go on Telegram, you will see a couple of channels you created. You collect pictures, music, or something else. You use it only for yourself. There is nothing from the outside, only yours. Your collection, your order, your choice. This gives you a breath of fresh air. Seriously, this is like a sip of oxygen. You breathe freely when you do that.

This is the main order. Next, let's talk about building boundaries and keeping your focus. I approached this topic from different angles. There were times when people were asking me how to manage self-discipline. They said that their moods swing from periods of active motion to lethargy. I recommended creating a routine and assigning a specific time of day to certain activities. You must have a designated time for work each day. Also, it would be best to have a particular outfit associated with work, like a dress code. It can be anything, not necessarily a formal suit, but specific clothes that you only wear during your work time. You keep your work outfit separate and don't use it to walk your dog, meet a friend, or have a cozy evening on a sofa with your romantic partner. It is a shirt or a sweater you only wear when you work. Please take a note of it. You also must have a designated workplace. It can be a room or a table. Create a playlist you only listen to during work and never use in a car. You can use aromas, and select a particular drink assigned to work time. For example, you only drink green tea when you work. You can drink any other tea at other times, but green tea is only allowed during work hours. Surround yourself with the elements to create an atmosphere that will hold you in work mode. Ritual is fundamental. It has become common for people to message each other at any time of the day. People tell me that they receive constant notifications which distract them from work. It is terrible and requires a serious approach. I will give you an example to illustrate how bad it is. Imagine you are at work and you got a notification that I published a new chapter. You got distracted immediately. It is bad and it doesn't matter if the notification came from a good or bad channel. The point is you can't mix up activities.

I worked on my books all summer and didn't leave the house. I have a deadline and a schedule. I don't divert my attention to my other projects when I am in a creative process. Every morning when I wake up, I start working on my book and don't distract myself even for ten minutes to talk about some other matters like renovation or something else. It won't work. If I stop writing and speak to someone about some subject unrelated to my book, my attention will shift from writing mode to another. It will be challenging to return to the original rhythm because they are entirely opposite. It takes time and practice to learn how to switch from one rhythm to another, but we must consider the forces of nature and the fact that it takes time to adjust. For example, I start working on my book at 10 AM and spend some time doing it. I am immersed in the process and engaged in the momentum. If, during that time, I must take a pause and talk to my team about an ongoing renovation project, it will take a lot of effort to manage a productive approach to the task. The modalities of my writing process and the renovation project are different. The conversation about construction has strenuous and vigorous energy, and I must feel it to communicate effectively with the contractors and supervisors. Then I have to go back to my writing, and it won't be a simple switch because I will still be on the rhythm of the construction topic. It doesn't happen on the spot. I have to disconnect from it and bring myself back into writing mode.

It is a mistake that people are doing several tasks simultaneously. It is a terrible flaw. People should reconsider multitasking. When you are doing several things at the same time, you can make wrong decisions. For example, your husband is at work. He is loading sea containers, dealing with rough processes, and operating on a rigid frequency. The temperature of the conversations on that rhythm is high, and voices are often elevated. Imagine now you, as his wife, calling him while he is in that mode and asking him to decide what color pillow you should buy: blush pink or pastel yellow. A man is in a completely different world now. He is not the husband you see at home, your beau and best friend. He is a tough guy who deals with headstrong people and might yell at you. He doesn't mean it. He is in a different mode, and his consciousness is connected to work processes. This is how it works. The transitional switch from one frequency to another is imperative.

I may act too soft and delicate if I am in my writing mode addressing issues at the construction site. You can predict what will happen if I am too soft and gentle. I must turn on a strict and sharp supervisor mode when I talk to the construction crew. Then, I can comprehend their questions and respond to them adequately and according to their rhythm. Imagine if I returned to my book in the rigorous rhythm of the previous conversation. What kind of chapters will I write? People don't notice it and ignore it. They think it doesn't matter, but specific codes and elements exist on different rhythms. When you are in your working mode, adhere to it. Even if you know that my new chapter was released at 3 PM, postpone reading until you get into my book's rhythm. When you are at work, you stay focused on it till 6 PM. Then you have dinner, and then use your designated time for your personal activities like journaling or some hobby. Tune into the frequency of creativity that inspires you and turns on your awareness. Then you can write your diaries or immerse into the world of my books and read the new chapter that came out. Then, you will be able to perceive the information correctly. If you read it at work, you will not understand it.

There is a particular time for every activity. For instance, imagine a friend texting me when I am purchasing some heavy machinery and am busy with the purchase logistics. So I got a personal message from a friend who lives in New York and writes books. The message says she saw me in her dream last night, and I was running with unicorns. I am on a hectic rhythm of closing a business deal (I am somewhere in the port unloading a container with a tractor), and I read her message. What would my reaction be?

I might text her back that her dream is a bunch of nonsense. This is how I would react.

The above explains why you feel insane mood swings. You react without thinking, say something wrong, and do something impulsively. I used to be startled by the messages I received from people who followed me on social media. A person would write about how he loves my books and is in awe of me. Then, the same person would write to me later about how he hates me. He was going through unfavorable circumstances that influenced his mood and negatively perceived my books then. Then something pleasant and nice happens to him, and he is in a sentimental mood, and he writes to me again about how my books touched his heart and loves me so much. I am giving you an example of unstable and chaotic behavior caused by circumstances that influence people. Do you see how dangerous people's reactions can be? Sick and desperate people surround us. It is normal, and this is how we, people, are. If I didn't control my emotions, I would be the same. An order is essential; you must set the rules and build boundaries. When you are working, you should not be thinking about your hobbies. For example, you can't be shopping online for a new guitar if you are a musician. You won't choose the right guitar because you are not in the proper mode. You are at work, at the office. This is a crazy mistake. People think they feel better when they check social media and messengers occasionally. A peak on Instagram, a couple of text messages, or some online shopping makes it easier for a person to carry through the day. I checked, but it doesn't work this way.

I am shocked when I write to people during work hours, and they respond. Are you serious? If I were your boss, I wouldn't allow it. People at work discuss memes and spend time chatting online. What is there to chat about, the weather? Summer vacations? You are at the office. Where is your respect for the company and the management? People don't care. They just sit through the work hours and get their wages. You can't do it. Do you think you hacked the system if you created a comfort zone and relaxed there during work? That is why everything is collapsing now. When you are at work, you must concentrate on work tasks and forget about your hobbies and family. You must stay in work mode and communicate only with people in the same rhythm. Then everything is alright and in order.

What's next?

After work, a person must return to a mode of home or family. Imagine you are still in the rhythm of work, which requires concentration and consolidation of attention. Imagine going home feeling like a hot wire with all that tension of the work mode. You come home to your large family. Imagine a family with many family members, parents, and grandparents. In addition to that, you had an uneasy day and felt agitated. You bring the atmosphere of a harsh work rhythm to your family and may negatively react to your parents or spouse. Your family members are in a relaxed, home mood. They are having dinner or watching TV. They may ask you a silly question, and you might react inadequately. You might snap and yell. Many casual conflicts happen because of that. When you keep behaving this way, it will ruin your family.

I also noticed that sometimes people come home from work with heavy energy, and another household member catches the vibration. You come home from work in a heavy mood but don't talk to anyone. You keep your negative feelings inside, but someone sensitive starts acting up and creating drama. He is not arguing directly with you, but maybe with someone else. So whenever you come home from work, some commotion begins. It happens because a sensitive relative catches and transmits the negative energy you brought from work. Now you understand why sometimes someone comes to your house and creates an unhealthy atmosphere. He is not in direct conflict with anyone, but he conveys a negative vibe into a space, and others start fighting. You must dispose of all negative emotions and thoughts before coming home to keep peace and harmony. The key to understanding this subject is disconnecting from one rhythm and connecting to another.

The transition is happening step by step. I am not talking about the reset to a "Zero." I am talking about building boundaries. For example, you may go to the gym after work, meditate, or visit a temple. It is important to blow off the steam between work and home. After you disconnect from work frequency, you must connect to the frequency of home. You may listen to soft music, something cozy and homey. The frequency of family is the same everywhere. Every family has the same rhythm. Some are closer to it, and some are farther. You know this frequency from the movies and your childhood.

When a person returns from work, his home must be free from work-related elements. There must be a contrast between the modalities, and it supports awareness and clear consciousness. It is beneficial when you can't discuss your work or hobbies with your family. People mistakenly think they must share everything with their partners and family, which often ruins relationships. I saw mistakes people make when they feel that if they can't talk about work or hobbies with the family, then they don't need a family. It is wrong, and this misunderstanding comes from diminishing boundaries.

A family is a separate world. One must miss it, enjoy it, and guard it from work and social activities. Imagine you are creating an escape room and getting into a room that represents a family atmosphere. What elements should it have? Imagine that you are a movie director or a producer. You are making a movie and working on a scene about a family. What will you put into a room to design a family atmosphere? There should be pets: a dog, a cat, or a parrot. The house must look and feel homey. The interior should be cozy and inviting. I am not a fan of current trends in modern interiors that emphasize an industrial and cold feel. Concrete walls and huge windows floor to ceiling? This is a trend imposed by primitive people who claim themselves to be interior designers and architects. It is an outdated look, and some people are keen on it. This is not a homey atmosphere. It is a cave, cold and minimalistic. This vibe is not suitable for family ambiance and impacts people negatively. It is suitable for other activities but not for a family home. If you choose to live in an industrialstyle house or apartment, your family relationship will suffer. No coach who positions himself as a relationship guru will tell you this because he has no idea about anything like everyone else.

The elements of the family house should be homey. The space should hug and soothe you. There might be a library and a lot of photos and family memorabilia. If people have kids, there should be toys and books. The house should smell of food. You may organize a home office or a designated desk if you have space. You can see it in movies, especially movies from the 2000s. They show how people live a good and correct life there.

To keep the relationship strong, a family must have dinner or breakfast rituals and eat together. Cooking together is also a good habit and feng shui. It is very binding. There should be specific topics that family members talk about. Families can watch old National Geographic episodes about birds or history. Kind and family-oriented movies and shows are proper for the home atmosphere. One must take care of the house and do the chores. Walk the dog, do house repairs, pick up a child from the daycare, and solve puzzles together – all these activities are a part of the family rituals and connect a person to a home mode. When you stay connected to it, your attention gets a healthy "workout" and stays focused and robust. When you are with the family, stay wholly involved in family activities and avoid discussing business and hobby matters. You can play board games, collect puzzles together, and discuss what kind of toaster you should buy. When you are with your loved ones, focus on common interests. If your mind is boiling with thoughts about work and your spouse asks you about a new multicooker, you will hate your spouse because you are not on the same rhythm. It is that simple. When your body is with your family, but your mind is not present, you are not in tune with your close and beloved and disconnected from them.

I receive thousands of letters asking me to discuss this issue and give advice and practical solutions. People are complaining that they don't feel their partner. People are psychologically absent. The physical body is there, but the mind is floundering. Readers ask me for help and beg to write articles about this topic and record videos on YouTube. People have been experiencing it for the past ten years, and the situation has rapidly progressed within the last three years. Families that spend quality time together stay together.

Anyone willing to improve his attention skills can do it. There are tools, and I am happy to share them with you. Every person has a variety of different worlds. For example, work is one of the worlds, as a separate rhythm. A family is another rhythm, another world. Parents, grandparents, and cousins are also a different world, and spending time with them is fantastic. When you visit them, be genuinely involved in their interests and stay present. Friends circle is another world. You immerse into that rhythm when you spend time with friends and do activities together. It is crucial to have all these separate worlds and switch between them. When you travel between the rhythms, alternating the focus points from one world to another, your attention strengthens and becomes sharp and advanced. You become super-conscious – a superhuman. Conscious people can hold a lot of information in their attention simultaneously. They remember and monitor the renovation of their vacation house in Italy, a meeting hour for coffee with friends in New York, and family matters in St Petersburg. The transitional shifts from one modality to another stimulate the mind, promote physical and psychological health and well-being, and prevent early aging.

People suffer from early aging nowadays. Many young people get diagnosed with various mental disorders. It happens because they don't experience the dynamic of switching attention between the rhythms. A young person is stuck on one rhythm and age rapidly. What is aging? A person slowly settles down in a comfort zone. He is mostly at home and remains in a certain rhythm. He has activities within the rhythm but doesn't alternate modes anymore. He is retired and spends his time in the same routine every day. He goes to the same store and same pharmacy every day. His mind operates in one modality all the time. Let's call it the "2-3-5" frequency. He is permanently there, and all his actions and thoughts are in that rhythm.

I am talking about a problem when a person loses memory and stops feeling space and time. People can avoid mental dysfunctions like dementia if they practice active transitions between different modes. This is a fact. The statistics show that people who stay physically and mentally active stay younger and healthier for much longer than those who retire early and carry a monotonous lifestyle. You can see it if you observe people who became mentally deficient and who did not. People who remain active in several opposite rhythms at any age maintain healthy perception and acute attention.

For example, a lady is a dean at school. She has work, family, and responsibilities.

She switches her attention between her household and the energetic and fullof-events school atmosphere. She is active and sharp and simultaneously holds many tasks to her attention. She communicates with colleagues and mischievous children and balances work with family duties. Naturally, this lady will stay young and mentally healthy. She will have a clear mind and sharp focus. Some might have thought you needed to "run away" from your relatives. This is dumb. Please hear me on this. People who have an opportunity to experience multiple worlds are blessed. If I want my mind to stay robust and advanced, if I want to stay young as long as possible, and if I want my productivity to remain high – I use the opportunity to visit my relatives and switch my rhythm to theirs. Go to a family BBQ. Connect to that rhythm and enjoy it. The more one dives into the various rhythms, the better. Then, you disconnect from it and wholly connect to the frequency of your work. This is a healthy rotation. Our lives are fuller when we travel between the worlds of frequencies. I practice it regularly, and even though I dedicate a significant amount of time to my writing, I still switch the rhythms as much as possible.

I was in one mode, and then I disconnected from all elements of that world and connected my attention to a different world, preferably of the opposite rhythm. The contrast is essential. For example, writing books and playing chess online are similar modes, and the distinction is not dramatic. For instance, if you are an IT engineer and spend a lot of time sitting at your desk alone and working on your computer, you must engage in an opposite activity after work, like rock climbing or hiking. You must create contrasts like a universe of different worlds and travel between them.

A person must feel and observe the boundaries between the worlds. For example, let's discuss Instagram. Of course, it is your choice to have it. As I mentioned, there are worlds of work, family, and hobbies. It is possible to create several Instagram accounts for each rhythm, but most people have one. When a person has one Instagram account, it may be confusing for him to decide which of the worlds to dedicate to it. It is also one of the problems that people come across with. Not everyone has a diverse life, but most have a family, work, and hobbies. Some people use Instagram for social life networking, while others keep it work-related. It is preferable to keep an Instagram account oriented to one particular frequency. The more you build and live by the boundaries you create, the better. If you keep your Instagram page personal, it should be discreet from work colleagues and business partners. It is wise to separate private life and business affairs. If your Instagram page is mostly family-oriented, keep it private from your colleagues. Your colleagues should not be seeing you in your pajamas.

Some people have separate work and personal phones, which is also good. Most people are easily influenced and make conclusions based on their angle of perception. When an employee sees his boss on social media in a casual, informal home atmosphere, he might perceive him as a buddy and act accordingly in the workspace, which might be inappropriate and insubordinate in certain circumstances. Of course, they may say, "It doesn't matter. We do respect you anyway." But they don't belong to themselves. If you have a personal account where you post your entire family, all distant relatives, babies in diapers, and BBQ nights, keep it closed from strangers. It should be about the family for the family. If your Instagram is work-oriented and you use it for business networking, keep it only for communicating with colleagues and business partners, separate from your private life and relatives.

It is good to draw a line and keep private life and work in order. When visiting relatives in their country home, immerse fully in that atmosphere, enjoy, and explore their world. Think of it as an amusement park, and you are a child. Be open and accepting of the conversations, music, and activities that you experience in that world. Enjoy the food your relatives offer you, keep up with the topics everyone discusses, and dive deep into the frequency of the atmosphere. Each frequency has its own atmosphere and soundtrack. When you are in the dinosaur world, it has music that reminds you of the jungle. When you visit your family, there should be a smell of homemade food. This is a good and correct system. Don't resist it. Don't refuse the food your relatives prepared for you because you are on some fancy diet. You may have some strict and personalized diet prescribed by a professional nutritionist embedded in his everyday routine. However, there is so much false information about dietary norms nowadays. So many imposters endorse themselves as health coaches and make up trendy diets that may harm people. I never trust newbies on the internet who promote some fad diets with no legitimate studies behind them. People don't talk much about the dangerous side effects of the experimental restrictions, and many of the pseudo-coaches just pretend to have a healthy and holistic lifestyle. People promote questionable products that have not passed any studies or research. "Miracle pills" flooded the internet, and it is crucial to do your research and consult with a reliable specialist before putting one's health in danger. I don't follow any diets. I eat bread and drink Coke sometimes. I keep everything in the correct balance.

I have the dynamics of transition between frequencies and feel alive. I am alive, and I feel boundaries. Being alive is what matters the most. If you approach something artificially like a robot, he will inevitably feel sick later. It is okay to eat a bunch of homemade dumplings on a Saturday night when you visit your relatives. It is just one day. For the rest of the week, you will follow your diet. After disconnecting from that world, you will return to your regular schedule. When you travel between worlds, be a respectful guest. You need to be more universal. And what would I tell people who indulge their whims and experiment with novelty diets? A slight shift from their regular diet might cause turbulence. This is not a balanced lifestyle. When you feel and observe the bounds of the modes and mindfully perform the shifts between them, your life is rich and multifaceted. Approach every step with an open and conscious outlook. When diving into a particular world, respect that modality's elements and specific details. Be curious and flexible. Feel the enjoyment and gratification when playing silly games with the children or running with the dog. It is awesome to discuss the details of the home renovation with your spouse or prepare a holiday meal together. Abstract from work Instagram accounts on weekends when you are with your family. Your family foundation is built on healthy and mindful relationships, and attentive dedication will keep and cultivate it for many more years.

Self-proclaimed coaches and gurus mislead people. They know nothing about authentic relationships. They just repeat someone's thoughts and brazenly promote themselves. Do you think they really know what they are talking about? Most of them just play roles, making money on people who trust them. They aim not to help or educate but to deceive and defraud. Seeing brazen advertisements of services and courses that promise miracles is disturbing. Scammers use people's naivety, trustfulness, and inability to separate the wheat from the chaff. But their time is ending. The truth will come to light, and justice will be restored. Open your eyes and wake up! I am here, authentic and alive. Probably you remember your old childhood friends who you could talk to about anything.

I am that person. I am still here. I escaped the greedy attacks of cruel society and the internet. I can speak openly and sincerely to you like you used to talk to your friends. But it is not valuable anymore. Artificial is replacing authentic. The main enemy that you let in your life is the internet, where you watch some stranger's lives. It is hard even to imagine what I am trying to say. It is not for everyone, but I am ready to refuse all money and all opportunities to feel like a child again. I just want to watch old movies, draw doodles on the floor, and collect beetles. I don't want to know if there is another blockbuster coming out in theaters. I don't care if another reality show star broke up with her boyfriend because he cheated on her with another girl. Why are they showing it to us? Why do we need to know?

There is a month left in my schedule to finish my books. Then, it will be my birthday on September 12, and I will stop worrying about any of these topics. I used to dive into society to understand how to deal with it. When you are a young boy, you must go through the growth stages to adapt to society. I finally reached the level where I don't need to know anymore. I don't want to know who fights for political power and where. I don't want to know who had a car accident or raped someone. I don't want to see the news. I will no longer know any of that. Even if we don't watch the news and social media, our friends and acquaintances will find a way to reach out and deliver some unsolicited information to us. Even if I find old discs with downloaded shows and scientific documentaries, the dirty news will find a way to sneak on you. I will exclude any possibility of it from now on. I will do everything to restrict access to me. Even if someone sends a letter to my employee saying that he will be eaten alive or lose a pinky, she won't be able to pass it to me because she will have no connection with me. I will have peace of mind then because there is a sense of responsibility when the connection exists. When people know that you are unavailable, you are free. When you don't have a phone, people can't complain that you read their message and didn't respond. Then you are free from the world, and the world has nothing to do with you. When your attention is entirely free, you can see every leaf and every flower and be happy as a child. You appreciate every God's creature and are in awe of His creativity. You collect three leaves and three flowers and gather information about them. You research the origin of the name of the flowers, the date when it was first mentioned, and where. You collect the information in a notebook and record the name and the date when you found it. Then, you continue to research further. This is a wonderful life full of miracles and adventures. You don't need money to live like this.

You can have any kind of work, but the internet distorts everything. You are unhappy that you and your spouse both work because you see some flashy lifestyles online. Why does what you do for work matter? As long as it provides for your family and pays the bills, you don't need anything else. You are obsessed with things that others have. This is dumb. I will tell you that the system, God, or something else limits you just enough for you to stay human and not turn into an angry animal.

I couldn't ever be friends with the rich and famous. People think this lifestyle interests me, but on the contrary, I make fun of them in all my books. My closest people were always very simple and humble people.

I will never forget a comment from one of my acquaintances who said, "You have money and fame. You can be friends with the top of the elite. Why do you surround yourself with some gnomes and trolls?" I told her that I couldn't talk to "successful people." When she asked me why, I told her they have different values and interests, and I can't speak to people who talk about branded clothes and villas in Bali. There is no life in these people and such conversations. I like creative, artsy, and real people. I appreciate them for being honest and alive; their social status is irrelevant to me. The value of people has no price tags. We live in a society that tries to mark everyone based on income or the number of followers on a profile. I am doing the opposite. I am not a part of that. This is my life. This is the real me.

I wrote many books, and they will be published gradually. This is great, and I want them to be published. But I don't want any public and social life. I don't want to make videos like I did when I was young. Nowadays, YouTube videos have become a shameless circus. What I want to do is to take long walks with my camera, as I have done since I was a kid. I love collecting music according to my moods and emotions. This is wonderful, and I enjoy doing it.

Collecting is one of my passions, and I will talk about the importance of organizing collections by category. Collecting helped me to stay focused and concentrate my attention. I noticed a long time ago that people engaged in collecting maintain their attention focused. Collecting means outlining and defining items by type. This activity helps to see the boundaries in other spheres of life. I started collecting music at the age of fifteen and told people back then that every music was a soundtrack for me. I assigned the tracks to various categories but not by the conventional genre approach. I divided them into groups according to their moods and emotions. I noticed that certain music creates a desire to travel. Another track connects you to the inspirational mode. By putting music into different emotional classifications, I defined the different worlds. The order must be everywhere. To start a path to clarity and conscious living, one must organize his life. You can begin from home and organize your books and clothes. Create categories and divide clothes and books into collections. You might feel temporary tension in your mind, but it is normal because you are performing a task that requires concentrated attention. You can categorize your clothes into sporty and formal, by colors and seasons. Clothes should be organized and sorted. It is the same with music, books, pictures, and materials I use for work. I have a separate category for scientific materials, where I keep information about semiconductors and robots and everything related to technology. Imagine how crazy I am. I keep materials on archeology and history separate. I spent many years gathering and studying research materials. I peculiarly arrange photos, audio and video recordings, articles, and other materials. When you have everything organized, imagine how cool it will be to immerse in it wholly and later dissolve your attention into it.

When building my countryside property, I surrounded myself with all possible elements that could enhance its frequency. How could I build a farm if I'm not connected to a frequency of country-style living? I connected to the mode of farmland by watching movies and shows about ranches and even some video games. I looked up and researched all kinds of farms worldwide and how they looked in past centuries and now. I dug for information about types of housing construction in the countryside, breeds of dogs that usually live on the farm, and types of trucks. I collected details about farm outfits and music to connect to that world. I researched everything about farms in the past and modern times. I collected the elements to connect to that frequency and was completely immersed in it. It is the same as wanting to make a movie about the farm or write country music. I must connect to the frequency of the farm first. If I am on the frequency of a city boy, how can I make a movie about a farm? It will turn out lame. People don't pay as much attention to these details as they should. I have people in my life who live in parallel worlds and never cross paths. It was my birthday recently, and I spent it in total solitude. I never celebrate my birthdays in the conventional way anyway, but this time, I just turned off my phone and stayed home all by myself. Why did I do that? I knew spending that day thinking and analyzing would be more productive and efficient. Usually, people celebrate their birthdays with food and drinks, accepting celebratory texts and phone calls. I used that day to focus on myself and turn my attention inside this time. It was a perfect moment to make decisions, and I used it to think about some important topics. It was a moment of solitariness that was very fruitful and rewarding.

You will have many questions after reading my research stories. I told you that there are dress codes and boundaries for everything. Now, let's talk about social circles and the people surrounding you. This is what I noticed a long time ago. I have friends from various layers of society. One circle of my friends are kind, nerdy, and bizarre gnomes and trolls. Seriously. I am intentionally describing them in a way that draws the contrast and outlines the boundaries. This is a matter of attention control. My other group consists of posh and trendy socialites. If you gather the two groups together, it will create a commotion. The gnomes will feel uncomfortable. They are not used to a glamorous lifestyle and will feel shy. The second group might boast about their achievements, even if their accomplishments are exaggerated and questionable. They do it because showing off and bragging are common and acceptable in modern society. So, these two worlds will clash because they are parallel and never intersect. Therefore, it is better to have two separate gatherings – one with your modest and shy friends and another with your social network group. I appreciate humble and honest people in my life. They are the ones you have to cherish the most. You have had them since your childhood. Find them if you lost them. It doesn't matter if they are not fashionable or look weird and not trendy. They didn't sell their soul to the devil.

The opposite is the world of "rich and beautiful." People from that group are driven by novelty and vogue. They usually appear in your life in high school and college. Maybe you have a different experience, and I am sharing mine because I am a person of a particular type. These people have a completely different world and different values. They consume trends dictated by social media. They prefer activities that look attractive and Instagram-able. So, there are two opposite worlds, and you should feel the distinct difference.

There were times in the past when I shut down or had periods when I became cold. It happened when I was going through a difficult time or felt hurt and misunderstood. Something might throw you off emotionally, and your heart might shut down for a day, a week, or even longer. I noticed that I enjoyed hanging out with people from the posh, material world during those times. I was young and didn't realize that my heart shuts down even more when I do it. When my heart opened again, I wanted to be around people with open hearts. I was drawn to the ugly and penniless gnomes. You can use it as a marker to evaluate which frequency you are connected to at the given time. You can check and decide which world you want to connect to. If I shut down for some reason and become cold and materialistic, I can use my collection of elements from the frequency of heart and soul to reconnect. There is a special playlist, my lucky t-shirt, and my warm-hearted, whimsical friends-gnomes on that frequency. When I listen to that music and wear a t-shirt, I disconnect from the angry rhythm, open my heart, and see everything from a completely different level of perception. My heart will come alive, and I will look at my Instagram and be shocked by what kind of content I posted on it when I was shut. I will be disguised by it and delete everything at once.

We all are in different stages of personal development and experience the impact of the various frequencies. People go through phases depending on their mental progress and age. Some younger people might not know what I am talking about. People experience turbulence and the dynamics of moving back and forth during the change. It is normal as long as you comprehend the process and see the pros and cons of each of the worlds.

I started writing a book about frequencies and attention in 2010. I have controlled everything since then and traveled various frequencies throughout that time. Imagine, for example, a person from a prosperous family in a situation where his attention disconnects from his usual stable world and connects to another person on a different layer of society. This new person lives in a different world with a particular scenario and fate. If his frequency is dark and a series of unfortunate events follow that person throughout his life, that frequency might be contagious. When you hang out with someone who is always in trouble, gets into accidents, and whose world is hostile and aggressive, you might tune in to that frequency and experience the same events. I noticed that in my own experience. Sometimes, I could have troubles and problems in life just because I met someone. The person is not evil, and he doesn't mean any harm. He just lives in that kind of world that has a specific scenario.

I also observed the opposite effect. People noticed that when they are with me for a long time, they get large orders, unexpected income, win the lottery, and all of their issues are resolved. When it happens for the tenth time, they realize that I am the reason for the fortunate array of events. I also met people whose world is abundant and giving. If you hang out with them, you connect to that frequency of good luck and feel confidence, positive attitudes, and your best qualities turn on. When you are around that kind of person for some time, you feel the same and operate in the same mode. But when you disconnect from that person and immerse into a world of sinful people who have constant problems, you connect to his frequency, and your perception changes. You start experiencing the emotions of the dark world, and your darkest vices activate.

Your perception changes depending on the frequency you connect to, and you go through the scenarios and experiences of each world. This is how attention works. I will share some new information now and then continue with the Q&A.

During the past couple of months, I have been researching the topic of substances, alcohol, and drugs. The question is, how bad is that, and is it allowed or not? Here is the conclusion I made recently. A person consumes alcohol today and tomorrow and smokes every day. This is bad. These habits are related to people's attention. If you do the same thing every day, it supports one particular rhythm. You are in the comfort zone, and comfort zones create dependencies. It turns out that you are always in the rhythm of drinking and smoking and not in the rhythm of work, family, or hobby. Those who will understand it and take it seriously will move a hundred steps forward in their evolutionary progress.

You can occasionally get drunk at a party with friends. It is okay when you do it sometimes, say, once a month. Not every day. You don't notice it at all. Imagine yourself on the frequency of the family, where you are a mom or a dad, and you drink and smoke. This doesn't belong to a good family scenario. As the director of this movie, you will see that it is a mistake.

You may ask me, "How about work?" I am against all unhealthy habits. I think that a person who lacks energy to begin with smokes and drinks in addition to it is a moron. It is your personal right and choice. Understandably, people may have bad habits. If you insist that the frequency of your profession includes alcohol and cigarettes, then okay. It is all right if you only do it at work and don't bring that frequency home. But you should not mix the components of different worlds. When you are with your family, you are a family man and adhere to the homey frequency. When you are in your creative zone – you are in the inspirational frequency of arts. If you think that you have a type of work where you should drink and smoke in your creative mode… No. You can't mix elements of different modes. You have to choose. You either drink and smoke when you work or when you are in your creativity. Choose one and stick to it. I understand that you may have questions about this subject, and that's why I am explaining it ahead of time. Naturally, it is better to stay away from unhealthy habits. It is better to quit drinking and smoking if you want to control your attention, be healthy, and have a good memory. Remove everything addictive from your life.

Another alarming trend is that young adults are addicted to antidepressants and grow dependent on therapy. They are proud of it and brag about it. This is a disaster. People say it is related to stress. I think if a person is young, he must do anything to avoid it. You are young, and it is normal that you have mood swings and transitions between diapasons of emotions. Everyone goes through it, and I did, too. Antidepressants became a trend, and many people got addicted to them while there are natural and holistic ways to go through different seasons of life. Now, it has become a trend. People indulge in talking about it and share which pills he or she uses. Drugs are drugs, illegal or prescribed. They burn people's brains, harm the psyche, and blur boundaries. People suffer from abstraction and numbness. Some become dangerous and may attack you and the people around you. Their psyche is chemically altered.

Some people need medical treatment and prescribed medication. They are professionally diagnosed by psychiatrists and capable of harming themselves and others. However, most people who seek remedies for mental disorders nowadays are emotional people – young, sensitive people who are going through wavy ventures of life. They feel mood swings because they spend too much time browsing social media feeds. When one constantly scrolls the display, he will inevitably feel depressed and disappointed. This is foolishness. Depression, panic attacks, and stagnation are the consequences of internet overuse. People are easily triggered and have immediate reactions to any provocation. They see a scratch on their phone screen and are ready to attack you with a knife. Imagine how it impacts the growing generation. It is a catastrophe. Keep in mind that people who are prone to addictions are also prone to drug abuse. Statistically, many of them are women. They are not only addicted to pills but also love watching shows about it. They love talking about diseases and conditions. They are afraid of death and ready to take anything. This is a tendency that is common for a frequency of idleness. You may take something calming once or twice a year when something really happens. Something serious if you witnessed your neighbor's house burned. Then, of course, some soothing medication will help. But people abuse it by taking it every time they hear disturbing news on TV that was fabricated and imposed on them. Most use it to stay in their comfort zone and escape the transition between the frequencies. When you do that, you are absent everywhere – in your family, at work, everywhere. Gradually and surely, you will become mentally deficient.

The past three years were terrifying. Some survived the stress by using sedative medications, which caused degrading consequences. The pressure was caused by the horrendous news that flooded the media. But the paradox is that no one forces people to watch the news twenty-four-seven and damage their psyche this way. People drive themselves crazy by indulging in TV and social media that disperse panic and despair and then seek refuge in medications. If they would stop watching the news, they would keep their psyche balanced and unharmed. Many people have fallen into the trap, and it is difficult to break the chain. This is dangerous for every person as well as on a large scale.

I prefer to collect my beetles to keep my safety. The danger is spreading in society. So if a person has no opportunity to call you or talk to you, it is safer for you. What is happening now is moving to a disastrous end. Naturally, there will be a change of route, and everything will change for the better. There is always a fall before a rise and a rise before a fall.

Some time ago, people were conservative and closed-minded, and now people are selling themselves online. It is a trend now. Later, people will shift back to their shells. I am telling you directly about it because I always try to be one step ahead.

People didn't get burned yet. Everyone learns from his mistakes, and that's how everyone grows. Everything that happens serves the goals of self-development.

Question:

"Can you please explain the details of the process that happens when one's attention goes back to his body? Why do the wounds heal, but a new finger cannot grow back even when you are on a different level of evolution?"

It is nonsense that everything is possible. There are laws of nature. We are all the same humans and live in one society. I don't know anyone with a finger cut off and growing back. It is not impossible, but not in our reality. Anyone in our dimension would agree that a cut finger will not grow back. So it is true in our world, and we all know we must take care of our fingers because they don't grow back. It is how the laws of nature are set up here.

For example, humans have primary, deciduous teeth that emerge after a baby is born and fall out when the child is about six. Adult teeth replace baby teeth and stay permanent. Why do permanent teeth replace primary teeth?

I was always pondering these questions in my mind. Why is one flower red and another pink? Why do the flowers have petals? Why is the grass green? These are not random, silly questions. It is better to consider questions like these instead of discussing political news or celebrity scandals.

The focus of your concentrated attention defines your mood and health. Deep thinking about what color the grass is makes me wiser and spiritually stronger. It makes me resilient to provocations. I have been practicing it for a long time and am emotionally, spiritually, and psychologically stable. I feel myself more clearly, and my concentration is high. My productivity is superb in all areas of my life. However, as soon as I participate in primitive conversations about shallow topics, I feel noise and numbness in my mind. Even a subject of discussion determines the frequency. When you are in a creative process, talk about creative matters. When you are with the family, be interested in family values. When you are at work, discuss work-related subjects.

Guard the boundaries between the worlds. If you have a family and kids, create a circle with other families with kids. Hang out with the parents of your kids' friends. Create a world where you have other couples, families with kids, and relatives. That is how you make and support a family frequency.

You may have single friends outside of family, at work, or in your social circle. But don't mix the crowds. Keep the world of family protected from the elements of the outside world. A single girl looking for a relationship or a guy obsessed with work is out of place in the foundation of your family circle and creates an unnecessary commotion.

If you decide to start a family and work on your relationship, stay away from the temptations of a single life. A choice of clothes and habits play a crucial role. When you are family-oriented, you must look like a family person and have a corresponding lifestyle. You must look like a family person and attend places with the same frequency.

What happens to people who start families but keep the habits they had as single people? If they go out a lot in the same rhythm as before, they have a significant chance of divorcing in a year or two. You don't need clairvoyance to predict it. It is a simple observation of causes and consequences. Don't listen to pseudotherapists who fool you. They picked some materials here and there and didn't understand the essence of things. They read some books and convey their interpretations to you. But who wrote those books? People like me. They were the first ones who made scientific discoveries. Those who repeat information online didn't make any discoveries themselves. Their souls are in a much lower stage of development than yours. They have no morals. All they can do is repeat some articles and chapters from some textbooks. You don't need much intelligence for it. You don't need a clean soul for it, either. Ignorance is leading people toward the darkness.

Attention plays a significant role in health and the body. The finger will not grow back, but restoring mental and physical health is possible by working on your attention control. I will explain one of the reasons that people get burned out and sick. For example, a person is stuck on one frequency, which is work. His attention is fully there, and his mind is always boiling. When he is at home, he is mentally absent. Even when he goes on vacation with his family, his physical body changes places, but his awareness is not. He moves physically but not psychologically. However, psychological motion is more important than physical. If the psyche is stagnant in one spot, both mind and body begin to deteriorate.

A person begins to decay when his attention is jammed in one place. It may be a nagging thought, an old resentment, or an addiction. A person's attention is on one thought or habit for twenty-four hours, no matter what he is doing and where he is. His unsettling mind is always on the same subject whenever he is at work or with his relatives. His attention is not here and now but on some regret of something past or an old grudge. When your attention is stolen, you are slowly decaying.

The good news is that you don't need money or a miracle to clean yourself from troubling thoughts. Whatever you have done in the past, you can cleanse. You can turn your mind off past sins and regrets. People complain that they don't have money. There are many free tools to purify the mind. Meditations, prayers, and abstinence are available for everyone and don't need a prescription. Accepting a clean and holistic lifestyle is not only free of charge but also fruitful. It actually will help you to save money. Your productivity will grow, and you can achieve anything with a clear, strong heart and mindset.

It is challenging to give up something that has been going on for decades and break unhealthy habits, but you have a chance to break free. No one will give you a chance to pivot, and no one will remind you but me. What will happen when the effect of this reminder expires? The sinful society is waiting for you eagerly. All those demons and energy vampires were missing you and ready to jump on you. "Where are you, my dear?" – they howl. And here you are, reading my book. But tomorrow, you go back to reality, and they are right there. Well, alas… What else can I say about attention? Keep your attention under control, and don't go to extremes. Some people are fanatically obsessed with their health.

I was never particularly obsessed with health because everything must be in moderation. If you focus your attention on your body and take care of it, naturally, you will feel better and live longer. I don't do anything specifically for it.

When you keep your awareness focused on yourself, your health is automatically under control.

When you enter the rhythms of family and hobbies while you are still in work mode, and your mind is obsessed with work matters and always sizzling, your health deteriorates. When I rest myself after work, then connect to the frequency of home, then reset again and connect to the rhythm of work, then I maintain a healthy rotation. A point of assembly between major modes is a point of "Zero" when you reset yourself. It is a point of nullification, a pivotal key in the correct transition between the frequencies. Point "Zero" is a transitional station between two destinations. Every frequency has its speed. The speed of work is super fast, and the speed of home is slow and mellow. Also, each frequency has its own characteristic. Some are rough, and some are tender. When you reset between them, you come to a neutral point. When you are in a "Zero" state of mind, you are deep in yourself and not connected to anything. Once you train yourself to stop and reset between the modalities, you will gain clarity and awareness. The reset point of "Zero" is where you feel yourself and understand that you are here and now and you are constant. You understand that who you are at work is not you. And who you are in the family is not you either. You are your true self at the point of "Zero." You are "Zero," and it is essential to catch and feel this state when you have time. You are a "Zero" after deep diving into work or creative processes. It is like holding your breath and focusing on yourself before starting a new activity. You can meditate, read a prayer, write notes in your diary, or listen to one track repeatedly and sit still. At this point, you are a "Zero". "Zero" is a separate frequency, a point of assembly, and a feeling of being here and now. It is the fundamental practice to keep your life in order mentally, physically, and socially. It is a feeling of yourself here and now. This is the secret of everything.

There is another mistake I have seen people make. I saw many articles that connect health to sleep cycles. Indeed, rest and sleep are vital. And I had a revelation. Life gives me information gradually. It is essential to turn off your mind before you go to bed. If you go to bed with your mind connected to some frequency and your brain is active, you won't sleep. It is the same scenario as going on vacation with your mind connected to the work rhythm. Your physical body is here, but your mind is not. You are not resting. When you are going to bed with your sizzling mind – you are not sleeping. You think you do, but your body is not recharging and not rejuvenating. Use the state of "Zero" before you go to bed. Some people need more time to reset and nullify their mindset completely. If a person works till late, he will have difficulty falling asleep. He might require two to three hours to reset and calm down if he is not using special techniques to quiet his mind. Your thoughts will naturally unwind, but it takes time, and you are tossing and turning till five in the morning. Ideally, one must organize time so he doesn't have work and business-related activities before bed. You need to calm down your mind and turn it off in society. Disconnecting from the outside world after work and assigning time for spiritual practices and solitude is very beneficial. You may dedicate time before bed to do something relaxing. Set aside time after dinner. If you have a family dinner around seven or eight, you can immerse yourself in creative or spiritual practices from nine to eleven or midnight. You may draw, paint, or write. Read something spiritual or philosophical, and write a diary. This way, the focus of your attention transitions to your body, and your mind is ready to reset and rest. For me, it is happening mystically. I don't go on social media before bed and don't listen to music. I go to bed and let my body immerse in a voluminous flow of energy, like a warm bath. It wraps around my whole body, and I surrender to it. It was very unusual at first, and I feel better and better each day. Of course, I am a human like you, and I had times when I didn't have a chance to reset every day. I noticed a significant difference in my mental state when I broke the rules and missed a few days. My mind was on a rhythm of work or business affairs, and I didn't reset it. I immediately felt that I was lowering my mental capacity and losing awareness. I realized that I must take control and adjust my attention. If you let it slide and "wait till Friday," you might quickly go downhill. You can't do that. Seriously. Your mental clarity and psychological health are more important than any money.

My mental state is more critical for me than anything. Some people think that I might launch some extraordinary and grand new business, maybe a restaurant or something else. I won't do that. Naturally, I don't go to the extremes. I have responsibilities, relatives, and close people for whom I am responsible. I won't just drop all my duties up to the point that I can't pay mortgages, credit cards, and rents I pay for people I care for. Everything must be in moderation. I think the excess desire to have money is wrong. Extra money is bad. It is excellent when it is just enough. Just enough to resist the temptation to buy some unnecessary stuff. You paid your rent, mortgage, car, food, and other necessities. There are always some unexpected expenses, like a car repair or something else. The paradox is that people complain about it when, in fact, if you live like this, you are a happy person. If you have a life like this, you are happy and real.

Question:

"I noticed that when I concentrate on something for a long time without distraction, I get into an altered state of mind. My head becomes heavy, and I feel that my body is floating. When I notice that, the condition disappears. Can you please advise how to control this state and go in and out of it consciously?"

Okay, you really went quite far. People have issues with how to concentrate on a family or switch to vacation mode, and you are asking about things like this. But let's talk about it. There is nothing abnormal or supernatural about it, even though the question sounds intriguing and paranormal. It is common for hypersensitive people. Creative people often can experience an altered state of mind when fully immersed in their rhythm. Their rhythm is kind and gentle and belongs to the frequency of the heart. People from that frequency are shy and feel uneasy in large gatherings. They may feel intimidated and tend to stay quiet. They often feel dizzy and outspaced. It is common among shy children.

I was born like this. My Mom thought I was sick at first, and she consulted many doctors about my condition. The specialists at the Brain Research Institute ran tests and told us that I was okay. I am just an imaginative and creative person who can fully concentrate on writing music, for example, and forget to eat. Later, I found out that all people like this are real, and it was before the venal internet took over everyone, and all you see is fake. I must mention it because watching how falseness dominates reality is devastating. I can describe my feelings when I am in the creative process of going into space. This is how I always described it. When I shared my experience with other creative people, they said they felt the same. I remember I felt it when I was in school. This was okay, and no one paid attention to it before. No one thought it was something divine or extraterrestrial.

It is an altered state of mind and has nothing to do with religion or aliens. You can feel a similar condition when you play a hand drum as if you are in a tube or some stream of energy. All creative people experienced it.

This condition occurs when discussing sophisticated and higher matters or connecting with art. An artsy person has this code, a unique rhythm, and can turn this frequency inside you when you click. You may also experience this condition when you are in a creative mode. I feel it every time I write my books. There is nothing I can do specifically to access this state. It turns on when I start writing or sharing my information.

I used to resist it. It was like an echo in my head, and it felt unusual. You lose the sense of time and space and feel disoriented. The head feels heavy, like in a helmet. This is how I usually feel now. I don't have any outside thoughts. I am always here and now.

Every artsy, creative person experiences this state. It may disappear if you watch the news and shut yourself down with substances. When you connect to the frequency of society, this forcefield of energy disappears along with inspiration and awareness.

Some people never experience it because they are always on the rough frequency of the mind. *The Little Prince* story describes that kind of people as people of numbers. They evaluate everything by numbers and attach a monetary value to everything. They never encounter the state of being out of a calculative and judging mind. Some hear about it and use substances and medicinal drugs to alter their mind artificially. They convince themselves that they feel it when they go to some trendy retreats and take psychedelic substances. It is not natural and might destabilize the psyche. This is not the right path to awareness. People who do it are materialistic, closed, and sinful. It is crucial to stay on an organic and holistic approach to development. You can disconnect from the frequency of the mind by using relaxing techniques and practices, calming the mind, and turning the heart on. You can simply calm down, play chess for a month, feel your rhythm, and turn on your heart instead of attending trendy, over-popularized retreats and courses offered by sinful, self-proclaimed coaches who vulgarized spirituality and turned it into a money-making mechanism.

Question:

"Alexandr, I can't control my attention. I try to avoid scrolling Instagram; however, I occasionally see some trashy news on my friends' pages that steal my attention. What should I do? I block people, but some disturbing news pops up and distracts me. I don't want to give my attention to it. How can I be stronger? When I stay in countries where Instagram is blocked, I feel it is a blessing. But when it is accessible, I tend to check it twice more often than I want."

Many of my books talk about social media and its impact on people. You should start by analyzing what you would do with the time you spend scrolling the content. Think about it this way: if you used all that time for yourself, who would you be? This is where you must start from. How would your life be different if you didn't spend time online? What would you achieve? If you dedicate your time and energy to yourself instead of checking social media, how would the quality of your life improve?

The answer is you would be a different person. What makes you different now from the rest of the herd, slowly moving towards the abyss? Nothing. What makes people identical are their identical actions. There is no space for individuality and awareness when everyone does the same thing. It is a paradox. I spoke about it long ago when it was an unfashionable topic.

Fashion is an effect of a herd of morons. If a hundred chickens wear something, the rest will also wear it. This is how fashion is created and steered. Fashion is not only a prerogative of the clothing industry. There are trends in fashion, lifestyle, travel destinations, everything. You might think you chose an occupation based on your personal preference. However, it is also dictated by trends and fashion. Individuality is a rarity. People who are authentic and unique are not visible on social media. Their lives are wholesome and abundant, and they have no desire and time to demonstrate their lifestyle to others.

I don't understand what is so good about social media, and frankly, it indicates the level of awareness. The fact that you are interested in news and stories on social media and find it essential to demonstrate the details of your personal life makes you a primitive person.

I don't understand the logic of doing something on social media. Why do I have to show something, and to whom? Who are those people? What is the purpose behind it? It is the same thing that monkeys do in the zoo. They put a finger up their buts and then smell it. When you see monkeys do it, you feel disgusted. But this is how I see people's behavior nowadays. It is strange and disgusting. A global transformation is happening. There are pandemics and wars, people are scared, and many are dying. And what I see is that people continue to post food and their tan bodies. What is happening? How is it possible? What kind of nonsense is that? People continue to post naked photos to provoke and get attention. People don't care. They have no soul. Do you like looking at all of that? Then, it is an indicator.

You ask me, "How can I get rid of it?" Let's start from a different angle. So you are who you are. We just met. You described to me your problem. I can immediately conclude that you are very dependent on Instagram, and we have nothing in common. I am not saying it to make you feel bad. I want you to understand that it is a catastrophe, and you must get out of it. This is my way of convincing you. Think about it – this is your personal indicator.

I am working on my scientific research and articles. I am writing books, and they are distributed globally. I work with artists and actors and study languages. I am entirely engaged in it. I have thousands of discoveries and inventions. Besides that, I am building my farm. Despite any provocations, I am trying to keep my lifestyle as healthy as possible.

And you are a victim of Instagram. This is how I call it. You watch who knows what, listen to random songs, read and "like" random posts. This is you. This is your soul. Think about it. This is the level of your values. This is your focus of attention, your frequency, your world. They are your gods. My gods are people of science and art, and yours are impostors who are trying to steal your attention online. They use all sorts of algorithms to get visibility. This is your world. You chose it. Start with sobcring your mind and strengthening your internal power. You can resist the temptations, starting with the following reflections I will show you.

Analyze the circle of your friends and acquaintances. People around you characterize you and your lifestyle. Your future spouse will be from the same group if you are single. What do you read? What do you watch? This is your reality. You are pushing away another reality that I describe in my books. You will never be able to connect with highly educated people or deep, meaningful information. This is what you need to think about. If you want something different, you must act and think differently. Concentrate your entire mental capacity and resist the temptation of social media. If you say you don't have the power to resist it, start by reflecting on it.

You have apps on your phone, and you check them automatically. Delete them. What's the problem? If you want your life to be different, delete Instagram. It is simple. This is your precious life that you are burning. Society was different ten or fifteen years ago when I was writing about it. Now, it is just a waste of life. What is happening now on social media is shameful and immoral. Spend time with family, work out, read, and walk outside. Do anything to replace mindless browsing. You spend all your time there.

I don't feel for people who are unconsciously dependent on social media and novelty trends. I am on the other side. I am from a different cast and upbringing. There might be some rock musician who writes music while everyone forgets about him. He is not on social media, and no one remembers him. He is much closer to me than you, and I would love to talk to him. You chose your idols. Some bloggers declared themselves the greatest and gave themselves unlimited rights. How convenient – everyone calls himself as they want. One impostor calls himself a coach; another is a self-proclaimed spiritual guru or a pseudobillionaire. They declared themselves gods of knowledge, and you bow to them. Do you not understand? They called themselves whatever they wanted. Before the pandemic, they were just low-lives, unknown and miserable. They greedily transformed themselves to deceive people to make money off them.

I am real. People are asking me why I am not making videos based on the materials of my books. I know it would be different than what deceitful bloggers do. But I can't. My soul is hurting when people talk to me about it. I understand that readers will forget about me if I do not start making videos, but it is alright with me. Let them forget. But I know that I am clean before God. I am truthful to myself and not letting myself down. I don't want to become a blogger. This is how I think. My soul is happy and alive. So you are skiing about Instagram… Delete it. What is the problem? You can't? It is a dependency. Is it your choice? Delete messengers and create new ones where you have your parents and your best childhood friend. Don't "follow" anyone. It will be difficult at first. If you feel anxious and irritated without social media, think about how deeply it affected you. If you didn't care, then you would be independent. If you feel annoyed and can't delete the apps, then it is a sign of dependency and unconsciousness. If you are reading this treatise, then you haven't forgotten me, and your spark is still in your heart. I am like an old generation. Old, ancient, rusty robot. And you didn't forget me. There are so many shiny objects, glitter, and tinsel around, and people are ready to tell you sweet lies and give you hugs and kisses, but you are still here. It means that something inside of you is alive.

If something else happens in the world, then that will be it. If I organize a presentation of my book in half a year, I feel like no one will be there. I see the stats. The numbers are dropping. Where are we heading?

I won't do anything. But if I shut my soul for a month, turned off my virtues, spit on God, and sold my soul to the devil, I would be all over the media immediately. Everyone would be dying to talk to me and get an interview with me. I have all the tools and means for it. But I chose another path. I always chose another path. All my friends and relatives told me I was crazy, but I told them I preferred to be Nobody. I will not sell my soul. I don't care if people don't remember me, but I know my soul. And my soul never failed me. I have a feeling everything will turn upside down soon.

Question:

"Hi Alexandr, I often meet elderly people with sharp attention. Their minds are still vibrant and flexible even in old age, even if they don't read a lot and their bodies are quite weak. Can you please explain it?"

Because they have hearts, these people are conscious, first of all. It means that their lifestyle is active, and their attention is not frozen at one point, unlike many other retirees. It may be related to their previous professional activity. Most likely, it was a job with a dynamic movement of attention. It is also possible that they know foreign languages. Any switches between rhythms are favorable for people. It helps to prevent the development of dementia and early aging. First and foremost, it is necessary to stay alert, not always relaxed. Those who let themselves go into a permanently relaxed mode become vegetables. It is happening now with young people a lot. My grandparents are way more alert than thirty-year-old adults. Many people are going out of their minds in their own way. When you talk about conscious older adults, they are not tied to some comfort zone. They are probably traveling; they like crosswords and scanwords. Therefore, they are not rusty and aware and live by their hearts. It means they have good virtues. This is essential because they are connected to nature. These people can converse at eighty and understand everything the same as me.

I am fascinated by my Grandfather, whose mind is as young as mine. I only know a few who can reason as sharp as my Grandpa. Many of my employees and friends in their thirties behave like they are a hundred fifty. They are absent-minded and delusional. It happened during the past few years. Well, my Grandfather was always a superhuman. But what happened to my friends and employees was a disaster. They are really out of their minds. They don't understand or remember anything. Their thoughts and speech are not attuned. Such a disaster.

It is a very close subject to me. There were people who I cannot name who reached out to me asking to research this phenomenon. What are the causes of mental disorders and dementia, and how to prevent them? I spent a lot of time researching the origins and causes of mental disorders. It is an important topic because I have observed people deteriorating rapidly during the past few years. It was a part of my personal story, and I will share it. The pandemic and multiple military conflicts created mass turmoil worldwide. Disturbing and aggravating news was streaming from all sources. The level of aggression in people was overwhelming. I could feel the vibration of stress, anxiety, anger, and fear from everyone. I could not be around people and could not read their letters. At some point, it was best for me to disconnect from all channels. I felt the noise and intoxication from people so much that I felt that I could die. People were transmitting mass distress. When I started researching it, I found the reasons. Now, I feel more aware than I felt when I was born. It was a long and laborious journey to figure out all the "BUT" that surrounded me. What was that evil influence that distracted me? I was studying relentlessly to understand. Fascinating, but you don't need money for it. I searched for tools and remedies to resist the hysteria that gripped the world.

When you make a dish and follow the recipe, you monitor the proportions of the ingredients you use. The result will be different depending on the quantities. If you increase the amount of one component and decrease another, you will receive different outcomes. Therefore, the dosage is essential. I concluded that it is not WHAT influences us, but HOW. In what quantities and in what dosage? Remember the example of alcohol and cigarettes? It is not the ingredients that are bad for you but the fact that both are elements of a particular frequency. When you drink and smoke every day, you are connected to that frequency every day. You are in your comfort zone when you are in the same daily rhythm. The mind becomes weaker and degrades. Controlling how long we are exposed to a complex of elements of one frequency is crucial. Each rhythm has an arrangement of components like music, movies, clothes, and people. I understood that the key is not in the quality of the music, movies, and movies we surround ourselves with but for how long.

One of the topics I will continue working on is the "Zero" frequency. I also called it the "corridor," "spiritual," or "nameless" rhythm. In addition, I will further research the impact of the frequencies on a person. I proved before that connecting a person to a particular frequency is possible if you remove all elements of his current mode from his life and surround him with the components of a different world. If you remove all elements from the frequency number Five from your life and surround yourself with the elements of the frequency of number Ten, you will connect to the frequency number Ten. It was a groundbreaking research. I was able to explain it to people. This is how the world works. Then, I came to the conclusion that the sequence of order is essential. The elements might be the same, but diverse arrangements impact the outcome. I have gradually worked on this subject for over ten years. One of the experiments I demonstrated was that if you fold a piece of paper in a certain progression, you can watch a miracle. But later, I had a scientific explanation for it. It is related to algorithms. I saw it clearly through the algorithm of the artificial intelligence that is used in social media. The key is in the sequins of actions. For example, I told my assistant to write a letter in three sentences, and she changed the order, assuming it didn't matter. But it is essential indeed. The addressee will react differently because the tone of the phrase will change based on the order of the sentences. I have had this feeling since I was very young. Another example is that there are many bananas on display. When you are on one rhythm, you will see one banana, and when you are on a different rhythm, you will see another.

There is another observation I had a long time ago when I was getting ready to go for a walk as a kid. If you draw a route on a map according to which you need to go straight, then turn right, then go straight again and make three circles… then, bam! – you will connect to another frequency. The sequence of actions makes a significant impact on the events. The same applies to the numbers. It is a secret and sacred information, but for me, it is just science. I think many scientists would appreciate the explanation that I found. It is a new topic for me that I will be working on soon. There were people who used to laugh at me, asking, "Alexandr, is there an end to the stream of your information? Where do you get it from? When will it end? How do you do it? Where does it come from, and why does it never end?" There are two themes that I have to work on, and I barely have time. But I will manage it because everything comes in the right sequence, and I keep things in order. I am doing one assignment till September and will start a new task at the end of September.

Question:

"How do you break a vicious circle when constantly thinking about changing your life? I want to start exercising and learn new skills to start a new profession, but I don't have the motivation to do anything."

A person I know had the same problem. This is a common situation for many nowadays. It is problem number one. People don't know what they want to do – play guitar or study a new language. They often think about it but don't make any moves. It happens because you can't focus. The attention is distracted because it is connected to society through social media and news.

If I go on YouTube, check Instagram, and start messaging people on WhatsApp or Telegram, I will immediately feel the same. I would feel the same every day. A day will pass, and you don't do anything except for the most essential. It feels like it is challenging to concentrate, and your productivity is extremely low. However, it is an illusion. In my conscious world, I can work out, immerse myself in my creative work, and then shoot a video. People who have known me for a while have always wondered how I manage many tasks. The point is that my attention is entirely free. There are no interferences. Interferences are everything that creates noise in your head and influences your mood. You feel like you want to do something, but not today. It is as if you don't have any energy, and something heavy is pressuring you down.

Many people on my team went through the same situation. It may sound rough, but I fired many people from my team. Why did I fire them instead of helping? Because I am not a teacher. Everything is in the books I wrote and accessible to anyone. It is every person's personal choice and decision to take life under control. I am not here to babysit and nurture them. I am not their mom or dad. I give a chance to everybody. You feel scattered and distracted due to the noise of social media. It is a problem for the entire society. There are exceptions, but those people escape social media's influence or have a unique lifestyle like me. Social media is robbing you of your happiness, relationships, career, and everything.

You say that you can't switch, but at least you are thinking about it. You are in your comfort zone! Reduce cigarette breaks. Stop wasting time on endless messaging about nonsense. You don't need to spend that much time messaging with your friends. They will wait. Enough is enough. Stop being codependent. Spend time alone with your phone turned off. Feel yourself. You will notice how amazing it feels to disconnect from society and dive inside yourself. Stare at the ceiling for five hours. Feel how you are disconnecting from the influence of the noise. I practiced it myself to check how it works. It is a connection to what is holding your attention, including society.

I was helping a friend to break a vicious cycle. It was very hard for him at the beginning. He was repeatedly checking messengers and social media. His attention was connected to all that junk. It was his rhythm, his comfort zone. He didn't know what to do with himself when he blocked all sources. It was an unhealthy dependency. It looked like a condition. It is not normal. You will notice a difference if you remove all dependencies and spend a couple of days without your phone. Help your mother cook dinner, do some push-ups, and realize you have nothing digital except for a book. You will rediscover yourself. It will not be easy for the first few days, but internal peace and happiness will increase daily. No one will tell you about it because it has taken over most people nowadays.

Question:

"Is it effective to go camping for a few days without the phone? Can I use hiking as a technique to refocus attention and regain inspiration?"

Camping and hiking are beneficial. But everything goes back to the status quo. That is the problem. People don't know how to build the boundaries. People need to understand the harmful effects of social media. Many people will not be able to switch within two days of camping because they have been stuck in their comfort zone for the past ten years. If a person goes on a camping trip, he might not be present there with his mind. His body is hiking, but his mind is connected to the rhythm of society. Some won't wake up even if they see a bear. Some people have more control and will be able to recharge and reset during the expedition. They will feel rejuvenated at first, which will benefit their life for some time. Ideally, one must hike, if that suits him, weekly. Find an activity you enjoy and use that time to disconnect and reset. Go out of town, take a walk in nature. The transition dynamics between rhythms will balance your psyche and bring harmony to your mind.

It is excellent if you have family and relatives. It is fantastic if you have a hobby and alternate your attention between various worlds. The more worlds you can create and travel between the better. It is great to have separate rituals and outfits for particular frequencies.

I emphasize the importance of living between different rhythms. People often ask me where they should live, in the city or the country. It is better to alternate and change rhythms. Travel and explore as much as you can. An urge for consistency and a comfort zone signifies early aging. Travel restrictions during the pandemic greatly impacted people's mental health. People who were used to traveling a lot and changing locations went insane. I felt it as well and, therefore, did a lot of local travel. People were wondering why I was constantly changing places. Because I need it. Global traveling was restricted, and my mind needed a change of scenery and climate. Regular changes in climate rhythms improve physical and mental health. You live longer and healthier, and your awareness grows. You need to travel the matrix, the labyrinth of North-South-West-East. It is a different topic, though. We won't touch it now.

So, a change of picture is vital. If a person takes a trip once, he will feel little difference. He would still be connected to a customary frequency of his everyday life and dive into his comfort zone as soon as he returned.

You need to consider everything I wrote earlier. A camping or hiking trip will work as one of the elements. One-time excursions will not change much. He would return to his rhythm right away when he came back or even stay there during the entire trip.

I will give an example of people's behavior when they lack attention. I like to demonstrate it in actual cases. Some time ago, I announced a presentation of my book online, and people signed up. One lady was new, attending my presentation for the first time. She made a payment and sent three letters right after, asking where the information was. She wrote to my assistant that all she saw online were two audio recordings and sent us several screenshots of the online broadcast channel. We told her that the presentation format is mostly Q&A and that we will post questions as they come and respond to them in order. She was still impatient and continued to disturb my assistant and me. She was asking if the two recordings were the whole presentation. What should we do with this person? This is one of the reasons that my assistant will have limited access to me. Even if you go to the news and announce something on your forehead, I will never find out. I am limiting access to me because I value my attention. This situation demonstrates a lot for you to take notes of what attention is. If I were a weak person who is steered by emotions and instincts, I would get upset if I received this message. I would switch to a negative rhythm and feel disturbed. All negative feelings are negative vibrations and a part of a particular world. So, If I were weak, I would feel differently and would continue writing this book on a different rhythm and with different energy. It would influence my writing. I recall people asking me before, “Alexandr, how do you not only achieve a vigorous, clear, and concentrated state of mind but also keep it when everything attacks and provokes you?” It is essential to understand that if I weren’t so strong spiritually and didn’t have a balanced lifestyle, I would react as an ordinary person. However, I am permanently in a state of happiness and bliss and don’t feel anything besides warmth in my heart. I am in a creative flow right now and write my books in the flow. I look at this letter from the outside of the situation. If I had unhealthy habits and would always scroll through social media, messaging, and discussing rumors and news, I would react like a naked wire. It would be an uncontrolled reaction. I would feel upset. Most people react this way. Nothing can shake you when you reset regularly and take breaks between the transitions of the frequencies. This is essential in our unstable times. What would happen to me if I were connected to society and my mind was spinning? I would feel panic and fear if I saw some terrifying news. All these emotions (which are not mine) would take over, and I would act unconsciously. When you have internal harmony, and your attention is disconnected from everything, you see everything from the outside. It is your choice whether to connect to something or not and what to concentrate on.

As for that lady, I greatly respect her because she has hope. That reader was new. She didn’t know about me and probably found me online recently. She was unfamiliar with the event format, and it is excellent that she signed up and reached out. I am very grateful to her. She started worrying because she had no idea how the presentation usually works. However, her emotional stability needed improvement. If she was that upset by such a minor cause, what would happen if she got into serious trouble? Her mental and physical health will be in jeopardy. But why does she behave this way? Indeed, it is not her fault. There are many reasons why she reacted this way. Some of them I described above. I noticed that people are almost ready to kill you if something seems to them. This example is a case of an early beginning of something like that. It happens on a large scale as well. People seem to feel something and react very viciously. Thankfully, she didn't start threatening me, even though I wish all the best to her and have nothing against her. Do you see where we are going with this? It is one of the questions I planned to discuss in this treatise.

Patience. She was lacking patience. I noticed that people lack patience, and they get in trouble because of it. We have to take note that patience is essential. Don't jump to conclusions, especially in a negative form. When something triggers you, don't react immediately out of impulse. Reset, switch the rhythm, and evaluate the situation from another angle. You must be in a neutral state of mind to assess the situation objectively. When a person from an unstable society wants to attend my presentation, he sees everything negatively through the prism of the negative emotions that he brought in. You know well that my books have no negativity.

People have been acting negatively against me since my childhood, as if I am evil. It is their own irritation. They are constantly offended and perceive everything in a negative way. They are ready to destroy and rip apart because they are angry. What does it have to do with me? Now you understand why I don't want to be in society. I don't want to read any letters. I don't want to know about anybody. If I am studying bugs, I want to be in the world of bugs, and it is beautiful. If I am writing books about something deep and philosophical, it is awesome. I recommend you do the same. You witness now that I still have one foot in your world. I am reading your letters and connecting with you. Soon, I will remove this foot from your world and disappear. I will say my goodbyes. If people perceive me as an evil person and think that my work is no good, why do I need to communicate with people? What do I need it for? The reader provokes my assistant, and then my assistant writes to me, and the whole chicken coop is stirred up. If I engaged in it and let it distract me, I would be the same as all imbalanced people you see in society. Take care of your piece of mind. That girl, I am sure, is a normal person. It is not her fault that she felt this way. I was always worried when I saw people acting this way. It is especially sad when you know someone who was normal before. This is what my books are about. Hopefully, this story will help her and teach her not to take everything so anxiously.

I always think positively about people. When a person promised to bring me something I purchased and didn't show up, I would think that something might have happened. I don't get upset, and I instead worry about him. I would still think well of that person. My crew would say, "Sasha, you got fooled again." It is customary for society to lynch people immediately when they screw up. If you are five minutes late, people think all kinds of crap about you. What if you are sick or have an injury? People don't think this way. They assume only bad stuff. Do you know why? Because the mind is negative. The mind is always assuming and overthinking and always in the negative format. People who are free from negative assumptions are living not by the mind but by the heart and good virtues. This is how it works.

I hope that girl appreciates my act of goodwill. I would simply refund and block her before. Now, I am giving her a chance. Let her understand. Hopefully, she will realize that she rushed a little bit too early and will take note of that. This treatise will give her information to think about. It is good for her. Maybe she will become super aware and super balanced and will write a book in thirty years. Who knows?

PS. The girl apologized later and said that she couldn't control herself.

I am reading a letter now, and it is huge. I will not publish it entirely, and I will explain why. This is my personal approach as an author. I am a peculiar author and have my quirks. For ten years in a row, I told my readers to ask questions clearly and one by one. It is related to attention again. Some people write long letters where they mix various topics into one message. They start by thanking, telling personal stories, and then jumping into questions. This kind of communication does not show high awareness and focused attention. Long letters with mixed topics have the vibrations of abstraction and noise. It is too excessive and not good feng shui. I can't read these kinds of letters because they may distract me. The message must be short, clear, and to the point. When you go over and over some topics, repeat, then ask something… I don't read things like this. If you want to grasp my attention with this approach, I won't give it to you. I stay in a particular state of mind when answering questions, broadcasting, and writing books. If I read your letter, my vibrations will lower, and I will become more shallow and dull. I don't need it. Thank you very much.

Question:

"I believe that gadgets, movies, and shows with special effects are part of progress. If it is so and the result harms us, does it mean the progress went wrong? Or maybe we are not handling the progress correctly if we are glued to our phones and sunk in social media?"

There are many versions of answers to this question. I don't know which one is the right one. One of them is that whenever something new is invented, people need to learn how to apply it correctly. For example, humans created a sharp tool that helped them cut trees and hunt animals. Then, a man might use it to hurt another man. There have yet to be any regulations on how to use it. Same with the guns. Later, humans understood that there needs to be a law on firearms. The law regulates the license process and determines who is allowed to operate it. Only particular people can use guns.

The same is happening with the internet. People invented it, but what's next? A while ago, some startup people convinced me that people would develop flying cars. I disagreed, which made them angry. Why did I disagree with them? Because I was a little older and wiser. They didn't consider the fact that society was not ready for it yet. People are barely paying attention when they drive cars on the roads, and there are so many accidents every day. People need to be ready to use flying vehicles. It would create a huge commotion and danger. There is so much crime and immoral behavior still in the world. Would you want people to use flying cars to spy or break into people's houses? Imagine a vehicle falling on people. I tried explaining it to the startup people, but they didn't hear me. They are still in their foggy dreams, without money and flying cars. I told many startup people who thought they could intervene in God's plans. I told them, "It is your ego. Don't forget God has a plan. Nature has a plan. Everything comes at the right time and in perfect order. Who do you think you are?"

What happened with the internet? In the beginning, people explored the internet cautiously. It was difficult for people at first. It was uncommon to make videos of oneself and post them. I observed the cyclicity and saw how things evolved. I started making videos in 2010 when it was very uncommon. People were afraid to post videos of themselves online. Nowadays, everyone is doing it. The same people who were shy about it before find it normal. When I offered people to take videos of them before, they were afraid. And see what is happening now. They were afraid back then, and it is a norm now. They make and post more videos than me now. Well, it is a tendency of a herd of morons. People are adapting. They didn't know how to use this instrument at first. When they figured that the internet was a tool, many sinful and greedy people started taking advantage of it. The internet world will go to some extreme and be restricted somehow soon. It is happening now. Ten years ago, people could post anything without consequences, but it is different now. People get prosecuted for distributing false information. The situation will keep changing if the meteorite doesn't fall on Earth. People will adapt to social media accordingly. The adaptation is evolving gradually, as with photography, videography, gadgets, and connections between people.

There is also a factor of the internet erasing the boundaries between the countries. People used to live in their own countries and had very little information about other countries. Now, everything is mixed up and trivialized through social media. Cultures and religions are mixed up, and true values are depreciated. Is it progress? If there will be no cultures, no religions, and no traditions, is it progress?

Something should happen in the world to rebuild the status quo. I don't know. Or maybe I know but don't want to tell. Currently, we see the internet as evil, but it may change. Anything may happen. For now, the tendency is detrimental. Shameless people are taking over social media and preaching sinful and vulgar messages to naive crowds. Maybe it will continue this way. Maybe sinful and shameless impostors who make easy money and pour themselves whatever they want will go further. They will be acting in the movies, and it is already happening. They will become musicians, and next, they will go into politics. Everything is leading this way now. If it happens, I will escape to my country house and research bugs. I will not be a part of it. I will be like an old generation of our grandparents who grew up in different music and movies. I will think about the '90s and 2000s and live the rest of my life thinking about the past and resenting the new.

The new generation is growing on these messages, which has become normal. Face tattoos and explicit sex images will be normal for them. They will do dumb stunts and make videos for money, and it will be normal for them.

They will vulgarize religions and distort everything more and more. People will be walking around naked. Maybe this will be a reality. This is scary.

Something dramatic should probably happen in the world for people to wake up. This is a second version of the events. It is often a topic of many conspiracy theories, and many movies about the end of the world exist. Maybe it is just an illusion of comfort. Do I believe in it or not? Do I think something should happen in the world and change for the better? When I see how low we fell. Religions are devalued, and society makes spirituality trendy and false. I want to believe that a higher power will intervene and save people from falling into an abyss. Maybe it is a design of the Universe to have a period of hell on Earth at this time as retribution for people like me. The only escape is to create your world, surround yourself with good music, appreciate nature, and read books *like Little Prince*. You can live happily in your world and not participate in the hysteria and agony.

When I emphasize a strong accent on something in my books and give information, it doesn't mean that I think about it every day, and it disturbs me. Not at all. I can connect to it, write and publish three chapters about and then return to my fairytale planet.

Question:

"Can you please share more information about the relation between music and attention? If possible, maybe share some tracks that help you focus and increase productivity in the rhythm of 500 and stay in the rhythm of the home when you are home. Thank you."

I can't share music tracks.

I will tell you a long and conflicted story about it. As I mentioned earlier, building boundaries between the rhythms is crucial. If you have a family, it is a separate world and a separate soundtrack.

Yes, work is work, family is family, and hobbies are hobbies. But there is something else. What closes a person and makes his mentality weak is absence of new experiences. It is a comfort zone. You need to do something else when you are ready to leave your comfort zone and create new worlds.

For example, you have your favorite cafe, and you take the same route to go there. It is your comfort zone. You are doing it automatically, without thinking about it. It is your familiar route and familiar place. You order the same salad every time. Every time I see it, I ask people:

- Why do you live like a zombie?
- Sasha, can you not, please? I order the salad that I like.
- You don't know what you like. You order it not because you like it or not. You order it because you are a zombie. It is autopilot. Do you know how many various foods there are in the world? Do you know that there are foods you will never try because you are limited in your rhythm? Try something else.

If you want to sober yourself, prohibit all customary things you do. Indeed, stay mindful, don't go to extremes, and stay within the laws and regulations. Just replace everything you usually do with the new one. For example, you always eat oatmeal. Order something else. Choose a different type of tea or lemonade. Replace everything you used to completely new. Don't go to the same stores you used to go to. Imagine that they disappear because it is your comfort zone and your weakness. People slow down with age because they surround themselves with too many fixed elements. Their attention is attached to a particular cluster of components filling their lives. They are not looking for new experiences, and their mind becomes idle. You should return yourself to a state of mind when you are learning new things.

Do you know what I did? I erased all contacts. I had celebrities, politicians, entrepreneurs, military commanders, and wizards. I didn't save a single one. This is power. When you are afraid to erase a photo, when you are holding on to some items, places, or people – it is weakness and cowardice. This is not a life of faith.

Conservative people always use the same routine. They use the same roads to visit the same mechanic they have used for ages. There are so many places where they fix cars. Why not go to a new place? Why do you go to the same place over and over? Stop doing things on autopilot. If people push you to do something they did for ages – refuse. Tell them, "Let's find something new." It is vital. Imagine you need a doctor. People immediately give you the contacts of doctors they used before. Tell them, "Stop! Let's find a new doctor consciously. There are so many doctors." Let new things in. When people are attached to old habits and objects, it creates stagnation.

Start with changing your habitual routine. Visit new places and explore your city from different angles. Again, I am reminding you to stay within the boundaries of the law. Don't do some crazy stunts and tricks. Keep your mind cool and under control. The world is so vast, but people lock themselves in their tiny, stale space with no fresh air. People who live like this are very conservative. They are boring and stuffy. They always use navigation and are not ready to open something new.

Imagine there are so many streets, boulevards, and places where you have never been before. They are right here in front of your nose. There are so many musical genres, and you are holding on to something particular. It is awful. How long have you had that avatar for? You have had it for seven years since that time when I told you to change it in one of my books. It is still the same.

On the one hand, it is excellent that you don't pay attention to these things, it might be an excuse. On the other hand, it is awareness and attention. If you want your attention to be free and if you want to avoid mental disorders and dementia, fall in love with newness and changes.

Change your wardrobe, give away or sell your old clothes, and buy all new ones. Move your furniture, or do a complete remodel. Changes are great. Those who resent changes deteriorate, age, and degrade.

Talking about music… I will not give it. It is one of the things I write about in my books and fight with. All people in society and the mind have this weakness. It is a desire to snatch and put into the pocket. It is possessiveness. You saved my presentation, photo, shared images, or a music track. You are stealing and shaming. Or you saw a girl buy something and ran to that store. You see someone eat something, and you run there. This is bad, and it is a sin.

If you want to feel how your energy multiplies, delete everything you collected from my lists that you saved for years. It will give you attention. It will make you conscious. If you have my music playlists – delete them. I gave you all the movie collections – delete them all. Delete all audio recordings, photos, everything. Your desire to find out who I am hanging out with… I don't have any friends. You're fooling yourself with your desires and actions.

Desire to understand me is a mistake as well. I am my books. Don't try to get to know me. You will never know. It is useless because all you see is the cover. When people want to know about my personal life, I post some photos of me with my friends so people leave me alone. You don't even understand how much I control everything. Some people think they know where I live. They don't know that I always have two locations. One place that I let people see is a showroom, and the real one is unknown to all. You never saw anyone who was close to me.

It is ridiculous when some people think that they understand me. The desire of your hungry mind to understand everything is devaluation. It is one of the problems as well. People lose interest in everything. You don't need to understand. You heard a song, and you like it, so listen to it. Don't download the entire album; don't research who the musician is. Stop consuming everything with your beastly mind.

Choose using your feelings. The desire to consume with the mind devalues everything. People thought they understood me by my social media profile. I posted photos, and they lost interest because they decided that I was an ordinary person. Just Sasha, who writes some books. People are following themselves. I am the same writer as I have always been. I see the world differently. I know how it works. I know all secrets and mysteries, and my knowledge keeps growing. But I see the more I progress, the more society degrades. I am the only jewelry maker who can evaluate his own work. No one can really understand the value of my books and my works.

The desire to consume is evil. I want you to search for music yourself. There is nothing complicated. Don't you know what kinds of music should be on the frequency of a family and home? If not, it is sad. What kind of music should be in the background of your work depends on your work. It should be some active tempo.

I like how you guys feel now. I opened the curtain a little, and many felt a boost of energy or tingle in their head. Do you feel it?

How do I manage to do it? Actually, it is just a correct lifestyle. Be kind to people. When people are unfair towards you, don't respond. Be a martyr. That is how you will become spiritually aware.

Question:

"Hello, Alexandr. I just returned from a trip that was so enjoyable that my perspective has completely changed. I feel like I expanded from the inside. It is attention. Does it mean that my attention capacity grew? And how can we expand it even more?"

It is excellent that you can disconnect from your usual routine during your trip. A new experience helped to reset your lifestyle. The key is completely disconnecting from the customary rhythm and connecting to a new one. The switch between the modes is more important than the trip's destination. The transition reinforces awareness. You can also use the clues I gave before.

You switch by traveling between the worlds. You connect to a spiritual frequency when reading books, playing music, drawing, or visiting your relatives in the countryside. When you feel that rhythm, you notice the energy of your attention amplifies, and your awareness grows. You might think the reason is the particular frequency, but the key is in the switch itself. During the transition, you enter the frequency of "Zero." "Zero" is a magical frequency of a corridor, a space with no name. When you are in that rhythm, you are in complete solitude. Your thoughts are high and philosophical. You are fully relaxed and calm. Some meditate, some people pray, and some write diaries. It is a great time to do some creative projects.

Creativity also helps to disconnect from the outside world and focus on yourself. This is how to turn the attention back inside. I talk about natural creativity when you are alone and fully engaged in the process. I am not talking about trendy paint classes and gatherings like people do these days. I mean real creativity, and you paint without some fancy tools using what you have. You paint for hours and days, may forget to eat, and don't even think about your phone. This is real creativity, and sadly, many forget about it.

Turns out fake people also do creative projects but can't do it right. They are failing even in this aspect. They are trying to look creative, but they have no idea how creative and artsy people live and how they create…

You asked me about attention. I answered you. I have more discoveries about it, and I will talk more about it in my future books. To give you a glance at it, here it is.

You have your energy, which is your attention, and you are trying to consolidate it. Let's take a computer as an example. You have several open windows on the screen. Multiple apps and software run simultaneously, and the computer starts glitching and freezing. People experience the same burnout. The solution is to close all windows and focus on just one. Be here and now and concentrate your intent on one subject. Focus on one window, and nothing will freeze and glitch because you freed your attention and directed it to one task. This is attention control, and you need to train yourself to operate it. You focus on one task, then disconnect and turn your attention to another. Your attention is your energy. Please learn how to regain your energy. The more you practice and exercise controlling your attention, the more you grow. You can grow so much that you can use the power of your attention and the entire Universe. You can connect to the cosmic energy and multiply your capacity a hundred, even a million times. I use this flow of energy and attention for my work and to make discoveries. Your efficiency becomes super-powerful, and you can achieve anything. It is important to remember that your lifestyle must be holistic to access and hold a high level of awareness. Nurture good qualities in your character. Stay kind and open-hearted like a child. Don't fight back even when someone mistreats you. Stay naive and light as a child; the power will be in you. It is not easy to achieve it, but you must keep reaching. But it is hard. It is very, very hard.

Question:

"I notice that if my work affairs are in order, something happens at home and vice versa. Why does it keep happening?"

The fundamentals of life are based on attention. Imagine this. A man comes home from work, but his thoughts are still at the office. His wife and kids unconsciously behave in every way possible to attract his attention. It is an animal instinct, and it is natural for people. But without control, it leads to conflicts and provokes confrontations. The wife and kids behave this way unintentionally. They feel that the husband and the father are not present. He is home physically, but his mind is absent. If this situation occurs often, it will undoubtedly damage the relationships.

Another example. Imagine, I would go on a date. A girl would feel I am not here, and my mind and thoughts are elsewhere. Then we will go to the movies, and that's it. No continuation. I disappeared because I was somewhere in my thoughts. Therefore, there was no connection. People love human connection. They love showings of care. "How are you?" "Did you get home safe?" "Hugs and kisses." "Good morning." "Good night."

When you don't do it, the connection doesn't happen. Do you need the connection – it is a different topic.

It may also happen at work. You come to the office on Monday and join the meeting. Your boss and your colleagues are there. Everyone is active and energized except for you. If you are absent-minded, people will start picking on you.

Your boss may scold you, and your peers will pick on you. They are doing it unintentionally.

Why does the system work like this automatically? I know why. I just look at the algorithms, and I know them all. Your boss is reacting this way because your attention is absent. And what he is paying you for is your attention, not your physical presence at work. Nowadays, people don't have enough attention, and they get laid off and fired because of that.

Most people can't control it. Many events have happened during these past few years. Horrifying news shook people, and uncertainty horrified them. Just Covid had a significant impact on people's psyche.

Attention control is the cause and effect of everything. Accidents happen when a person is distracted. There is no mystery or misfortune. If a person is focused and organized, nothing out of the ordinary happens to him. If something fell on your head or you pinched a finger, it means that you were distracted. It is simple logic. You won't accidentally pinch your finger when you are fully present, and your attention is focused. Your attention was absent, and the accident brought it back.

There is another aspect as well. Our world system is set in a way that requires your attention. Nature wants your undivided attention. There are two opposite forces – the society that steals your attention through the internet and nature that we belong to and must stay connected to. Nature wants you to be present and wholesome and be here and now. When we disconnect from nature, we get into situations and accidents that wake us and bring us back.

When your heart is shut and lost in society, you don't hear the call of nature. Society also has conflicts because there is warfare for people's attention. Various channels speculate on people's attention. Those connected to nature are not lost. They have an inner spark. They have a personal connection with nature. Nature communicates with people through circumstances. When a person loses his relationship with nature, it creates events to wake him up. Accidents serve as reminders to reset and bring back awareness.

Many tend to relax when things are going well. You have to stay energized, focused and organized. Most people dream about stability. They want to buy a house and live there forever. They want to get married and settle. When you relax, the system will bring you circumstances to stir you up. If not today, then in a year. If not in a year, something terrible will happen after five years. It is better to have immediate but small slaps rather than huge but later. It will come to you anyway. If you want to avoid problems, stay active. Let's say you were poor, didn't have much, your mindset was weak, and your attention level was

500. Suddenly, you advance to the next level and have a house, a car, money, and a romantic relationship. It means that your attention and your level of vibrations have to operate at 1000. You have to grind even more in terms of the transition dynamics. But what happens usually? A person gets a new job, marries, buys a house and a car, and his efficiency performance drops from 500 to 200. Then, the system, which is nature, takes everything back from that person to wake him up and raise his efficiency. All of that is connected to attention. When I hire a person, I see if he has attention. While his attention is focused – he is present. I don't need it when a person is constantly on his phone, or his mind is absent. He will get fired because he is a victim of social media and has a constant noise in his head. He might be dreaming about great things, but he is forty and nobody. A lot of people went downhill during these ten years. Those who are still listening to me through my books are still alive and not lost. God and nature want you to be alert and give you a slap when you get distracted. If my attention is in the family, and I must grow, then all problems will be happening in the family. People tend to stay primarily on one frequency. I was talking about the concept of frequencies. However, people don't live like this. Some are entirely focused on the family and relationship and slowly degrade there. Another is only concentrated at work and pushes the rest aside. Then he gets kicked on the head there because it is his world of habitat, and his attention is there. The system is educating people in their primary habitats. When you are stuck on a particular rhythm, all adventures will happen in that mode. Most of the time, I write books; part of my work process is reading letters and answering people. If I stop reading letters and stop writing and start producing furniture, I will experience adventures there. People will stop attacking and criticizing me for my books, but the heat will be happening in another field of my activity. If my attention is in the furniture business, my character will be challenged there. Maybe one of the guys who makes furniture parts will attack me with a chair or will try to steal money. Something will happen to maintain balance and ensure growth. This is a path of development we all go through.

Question:

"I have a friend who is very different from me. I observe our differences and notice that she does not influence me. My mindset stays the same after we spend time together. I also saw that certain communications affect me at work, and I

try to fix the impact and adjust myself. Do these interactions affect me even though I am fully aware when they happen?"

Good question. First, you need to discover the impacts you may not notice, see, or know. You need to take note of that. What's the point of writing about things that are obvious to everyone? I write about things that you have no idea about. How do you check if there is an influence or not? Only by checking it in practice. Every person impacts our lives willingly or unwillingly. It is a chemical reaction. Some results are positive, some negative. You can experiment and disconnect from someone for half a year and see if your life has changed. Some people may have a good influence on you and support your good virtues. You may not notice it, but maybe a person close to you brings goodness in you and keeps your spark lit. If you stop seeing that person, you might shift in the opposite direction.

I observed people who I worked with or were friends with. When someone is close to me and connected to my world, he experiences joy and lightness. His best virtues arose, and his life situation changed for the better. When I left for another country (and I travel a lot), we disconnected, he shut down, and the quality of his life dropped tremendously. He would start drinking, take drugs, or act somehow immorally. There were plenty of cases like that. Why? Because your surroundings matter a lot. Instead of listening to classical music, you listen to some trash, drink beer with people from your past, or something else. One thing after another, and a person is gone. The influence is decisive in people's relationships. Maybe some of you think you are so strong and resilient that nothing can impact you. Everything affects you. It is inevitable. I am a "street scientist". I am not a trendy hotshot and can't flash many diplomas. I am honest before God and nature. I spend way more time researching the world's essence, structure, and people and classifying everything around us. People are one united organism in society, and everyone is connected. A person may feel or not realize the impact of the community, but it exists. No one is entirely free from the influence. You can't be solely independent of anyone if he lives by his mind. I know how the matrix system works and how the points of connection interact with you. Some people are above you and below you. Each person is in the structure of the matrix, and he is an active part of it. There are cells, lines, and points. I see it mathematically and geometrically. There are also exceptions.

Another thing I know is how your mind works and how your sins are orchestrated. Many of you will cling to this theory and think that it is about you. No, it is not. There are people outside of the system who are fully connected to nature. They have some divine qualities. Their unique qualities make them irresistible to the pressure of society. When you are one with nature, society cannot affect you. But these are exceptions, and these cases are described in many books. You don't see that many people like that in our time.

This is all. I am glad you decided to read my story despite the temptations. There are so many shiny and fun things around, and here you are, reading my book. I appreciate it very much and am very grateful to you.

I see the world is set. There are two types of people – people of the sins and people of the heart. Serpent Tempter controls the first group, and the God of Light rules the other. As it is shown in the movie *The Matrix*, there are agents of higher forces who can possess people and destroy them. Demons can steer people to harm others. There is perpetual combat between darkness and light. I see how the system works. Since many people have dark souls these days, the demon can possess anyone. A person like that can attack me. That's why I stay away from people. The danger is everywhere. There is crazy warfare going on in the world. Imagine how interesting it is!

Some people jump into preliminary solutions about me and say I went to an extreme. Who are those people, and what do they know about me?

It is incredible when you have your own world, and only you decide what to delete and what to dismiss. You don't depend on anyone. I am not on social media. This is absolute freedom.

I am my books and my creative work. I must continue writing. This is my duty before God. Everything else is minor. If there is some focus of attention on me on social media, it is ok. When I have new chapters or new books, my team will publish them.

Those who are not "here and with me" but on the other side may think they know and understand me. They post angry comments on my social media and think they have a dialog with me. It is amusing.

I love you all. Please keep your spirits high and keep going. We live in a very unusual time. Take my word – everything will be ok.

I am comparing and researching and giving you examples. Imagine me in your place. This guy, Alexandr Korol. He is not a writer, but maybe a musician. If I saw him deflate spiritually, I would be sad. I would think highly of that person, and he would be a source of inspiration. And all of a sudden, I see him losing heart. I would be devastated that the world is doomed, and it is the end.

As you see, I didn't lose my heart. I am all fired up.

Please stay inspired and keep your spirits high. Everything will be good.

Good will overcome evil, and goodness and truth will win as it has always been.